The Statesman

The Statesman

Reflections on a Life Guided by Civility, Strategic Leadership, and the Lessons of History

Ambassador David Abshire

Edited by James Kitfield

ROWMAN & LITTLEFIELD
Lanham • Boulder • New York • London

Published by Rowman & Littlefield
A wholly owned subsidiary of The Rowman & Littlefield Publishing Group, Inc.
4501 Forbes Boulevard, Suite 200, Lanham, Maryland 20706
www.rowman.com

Unit A, Whitacre Mews, 26–34 Stannary Street, London SE11 4AB

British Library Cataloguing in Publication Information Available

Library of Congress Cataloging-in-Publication Data

HB ISBN 978-1-5381-0921-2
PB ISBN 978-1-5381-0922-9

♾ ™ The paper used in this publication meets the minimum requirements of American
National Standard for Information Sciences—Permanence of Paper for Printed Library
Materials, ANSI/NISO Z39.48-1992.

Printed in the United States of America

"History doesn't repeat itself, but it often rhymes."

—An aphorism attributed to Mark Twain

To my beautiful wife, Carolyn;
my five children, Lupton, Anna, Mary Lee, Phyllis, and Caroline;
and my eleven grandchildren, Patten, Wilson,
Cartter, Anastasia, Malia, William, Phillip, Hannah, Addy,
David, and Kathleen.

Contents

Acknowledgments

On behalf of the Center for the Study of the Presidency & Congress (CSPC), I would like to thank the following for their contributions to *The Statesman*, the memoirs of Ambassador David M. Abshire.

First and foremost, I would like to express my deepest gratitude to Carolyn Abshire and the entire Abshire family for their tireless efforts to ensure that Dr. Abshire's most important memories and life lessons were accurately depicted in these pages.

Beyond the family, these memoirs reveal the essence of Dr. Abshire's life and leadership and the impact they had on those who worked with him. Because of this impact, the memoir was a labor of love for all of those involved in this project:

James Kitfield, the editor of these memoirs, deserves special thanks for his strong leadership and countless hours dedicated to this project. The amazing relationship that Dr. Abshire and "Jim" had clearly comes alive in these pages, and I am extremely proud of the product James has produced. Collin Odell deserves recognition for his many years of service to Dr. Abshire and the painstaking work he dedicated to the cultivation of these memoirs.

This project would not have been possible without the vision of my predecessor, and protégé of Dr. Abshire's, Max Angerholzer. Max's close friendship with Dr. Abshire and devotion to CSPC will not soon be forgotten. I also want to thank the CSPC trustees whom we often refer to as the core of the "Abshire mafia"—Wayne Berman, Jay Collins, Dan Lubin, and Pam Scholl—for their advice and support throughout this process. Additionally, I want to thank Robert Day and Ambassador Francis Rooney, both close friends of Dr. Abshire's, for their support and guidance on this project and their years of leadership at CSPC. Another close friend, the acclaimed journalist and author Evan Thomas, also deserves thanks for capturing the essence of David Abshire the man in his thoughtful foreword to these memoirs.

I would like to thank the entire CSPC Board of Trustees for their ongoing dedication to the center and its programs. Much appreciation goes to those at Rowman & Littlefield for their hard work and encouragement, most especially Jon Sisk and Kate Powers. Finally, I want to thank Elizabeth Perch and Dan Mahaffee for their efforts on this project and their leadership at CSPC, and Hurst Renner, Sara Spancake, Madeline Vale, Jordana Schmierer, and Joshua Huminski, whose support was invaluable.

Glenn Nye
President & CEO
Center for the Study of the Presidency & Congress

Foreword

David Abshire had good manners. He was raised in Chattanooga, Tennessee, to be genteel, and trained at West Point to hold himself correctly. He valued civility above all virtues (with the possible exception of courage, which he showed as a combat infantry officer in Korea). But what distinguished Dave, what made him memorable in a city of distinguished men and women, was that he was a generous man.

He had the kind of patient confidence in the face of adversity that only comes from a truly decent and benevolent nature. He understood how to care for men in foxholes, and in a grander sense, for his country. He held people, but especially himself, to a high standard. But he was understanding and forgiving of human foible, as long as intentions were honorable. It is not surprising that both Richard Nixon and Ronald Reagan called on David Abshire when their presidencies were in crisis. It is also unsurprising that Dave said no to Nixon and yes to Reagan. He knew that Reagan was worthy of his trust.

Many of us have experienced the Abshire treatment: the good cheer; the easy, chortling laugh; and the iron grip of persuasion that is very hard to resist. Abshire put it to good use through a long and valuable career of service.

He tells that story here. From army days, to working with lawmakers for the State Department, to international diplomacy, to his time as counselor to presidents, Dave was a fixture in the effort to make America a superpower with a higher purpose. (His interactions with Henry Kissinger alone make the book a memorable read.) It is natural that Dave created a seminal think tank for international affairs. He was the embodiment of high strategy and practical (which is to say political) application by men and women of good will. Dave's story mirrors America's golden age of global responsibility. There were defeats and mistakes, yes, but the nation and its leaders learned from them and tried to exert American will as a force for the better.

Toward the end of his life, Dave worried that Americans and their leaders were turning away from the hope and promise of America's role in the world. He might have been more anxious had he lived to see the Trump presidency.

It is fair to say that Dave would have been disappointed by rude tweets, "America First," and a decision-making style apparently driven more by impulse than measured thought. But it is equally true that Dave would not have lost heart. He probably would have wanted the chance to talk to President Trump—to try to reason with him, to help him find his way, to share his own faith in civility, in America's global responsibility, in compromise and grand strategy.

Dave was at heart an optimist. He lived through the deaths of comrades in battle and the failure of policy and politics on small and large stages, but he remained determined and hopeful. Dave always said we should learn from history. We can learn from *his* history. After reading this book, I think you will understand how much we miss him.

Evan Thomas

Author of *Ike's Bluff: President Eisenhower's Secret Battle to Save the World* (2012) and *Being Nixon: A Man Divided* (2015)

1

Dark Days and Enduring Lessons

On Strategic Leadership, Trust, and Reform

My life has spanned the Great Depression, World War II, and the rocky aftermath of the Cold War. I saw our nation emerge from the Second World War as the most powerful in the world. I fought in the Korean War. I served in government during the Vietnam War, which divided the nation. I watched as our nation came together in response to the horror of the September 11, 2001, terrorist attacks and then came apart over the war in Iraq. As an "elder statesman," I offered counsel to our nation's leaders in the aftermath of both those tumultuous events. The United States of America that today has risen to the heights of global power was forged in fire and hardship, each step in that long ascent a conscious decision to persevere and prevail.

I am a historian at heart and by training. Throughout this book, I will try to share real lessons I have found useful, explaining the places where I learned them and the ways I have applied them, and the results I have been fortunate to achieve. I grew up reading about the heroic statesmanship of leaders like George Washington, John Adams, Thomas Jefferson, James Madison, Henry Clay, Abraham Lincoln, Rutherford Hayes, and Theodore Roosevelt. These men and their stories inspired me to attend and graduate from the United States Military Academy at West Point, and to earn a doctorate in history from Georgetown University. They instilled in me a lifelong love of narrative history and steered me toward a career in public service.

For much of my career I led the Center for Strategic and International Studies (CSIS), the think tank I cofounded in 1962 with the great strategist Admiral Arleigh Burke. I persuaded Admiral Burke to join me in founding the center by arguing that the political partisanship and the compartmental-ization of the executive and legislative branches that we both recognized were the enemy of effective strategy. For decades during the Cold War and after-ward, CSIS has brought together individuals from both sides of the political aisle to debate the important issues that bear on national strategy and govern-ment reform. The center has always served as a convener, reaching out to the best and the brightest from numerous fields of expertise and bringing them together with officials from the executive and legislative branches. At the Center for the Study of the Presidency & Congress (CSPC), where I served as president for the first decade of the twenty-first century, we have continued with that same tradition.

In a long career leading think tanks and working in both the executive and legislative branches of government, I have wrestled with many of the issues that have come to define America, both our prosperity at home and our out-sized role in the world. I have had the privilege to work with several of our nation's great modern leaders, men and women who have fostered trust through civility and demonstrated strategic vision, and who knew how to think anew when necessary. I have also seen leaders squander trust and lack civility. I was personally approached for help in saving the presidencies of both Richard Nixon and Ronald Reagan at the lowest point in their White House tenures, during the Watergate and Iran-Contra scandals, respectively. I declined the former and accepted the latter request for help based on the deceptively simple element of trust, and how much faith I had in each presi-dent's sincerity and character.

As I write this at the end of my career, our country has lost its sense of strategic direction and common purpose. Our politics have entered a period of hyperpartisanship and gridlock. Overseas we are transitioning from a uni-polar world of uncontested American power to a multipolar world where we face challenges to our interests and security from multiple directions. Allies question our once trusted leadership. Dangers gather on every front. Put sim-ply, our country is in deep trouble.

We have come to this impasse in large part because of a great deterioration of civility over the past decade and a half. It is ironic that George W. Bush in his inaugural address emphasized civility. Bush said, "Civility is not a tactic or a sentiment. It is the determined choice of trust over cynicism, of commu-nity over chaos. And this commitment, if we keep it, is a way to shared accomplishment."[1] Guided by that lodestar, George W. Bush's initial response to the attacks on 9/11 was a brilliant call for justice, resolve, inclu-siveness, and tolerance. Then he surrendered this high ground by launching an invasion of Iraq that divided the country and our allies.

More recently, the House of Representatives has been the epicenter of political divisiveness and ineptitude. This toxic environment does not allow the relationship between Speaker of the House John Boehner (R-Ohio) and President Barack Obama to be anything close to constructive. Contrast it with the relationship between former Speaker Thomas "Tip" O'Neill (D-Mass.) and President Ronald Reagan, who used to engage in tough political bargaining during the week and then regularly meet for drinks on the weekend to swap Irish jokes. O'Neill and Reagan might not have been close friends, but they respected one another and the offices and responsibilities that each upheld. Meeting socially set an example for their staffs and colleagues that served the nation well.

Today, too many in Congress have forgotten this kind of leadership. Yet this was the approach that created the Constitution that so many uncivil modern leaders, to include many of those in the so-called Tea Party, claim to revere. The Tea Party chose an appropriate name, honoring those who in a fit of anger threw tea into Boston Harbor rather than paying tax on it. That involuntary taxation was one of many grievances against the British that produced the Declaration of Independence. The spirit of the original tea party was embedded in the Articles of Confederation, a triumph of idealism over even minimal functionality. The Articles were so ill-suited to the needs of our new nation that under them the United States was nearly bankrupt and ungovernable, and all but at war with itself. These were the circumstances that prompted leading citizens across the thirteen states to start the dialogue that culminated in the Constitution.

The Constitutional Convention in Philadelphia was an exercise in bargaining and compromise by men from states large and small, free and slave, rich and poor, farming and trading. To deal with those profound differences, the Framers had to negotiate and compromise. To allow future leaders to improve the imperfect bargain they made, correct errors of judgment or assumption, and reshape the government to meet evolving needs and changing circumstances, they built into the Constitution enormous flexibility. A core element of the Constitution is the power of amendment, suggesting the perpetual need for reform. Reform is both a core Constitutional value and a central theme throughout American history, an instinct for self-improvement and belief in the possibility of an ever more perfect union that served as the inspiration for many of our proudest accomplishments as a nation.

The final success of the Constitutional Convention was secured only by the determination of leaders like Benjamin Franklin, who stated, "On the whole, sir, I cannot help expressing a wish that every member of the convention who may still have objections to it, would, with me, on this occasion, doubt a little of his own infallibility, and, to make manifest our unanimity, put his name on the instrument." So was created the "miracle of Philadelphia," a story of compromise to its core. Indeed, practically the only matter on which the Framers would not compromise once they committed themselves to a union of democratic states was the very idea of the United States of America. As the Founders exited Independence Hall following their secret deliberations, a fellow citizen asked Benjamin Franklin what form of government they had settled upon. Franklin's answer, and the warning it implies, echoes down through the ages. "A republic, if you can keep it."

If members of today's Tea Party had been present at the birth of the nation, I fear the Constitution they claim to love so much would never have been possible. At times they seem more animated by the spirit of the Articles of Confederation that failed us so dismally before Philadelphia. Meanwhile, the lack of civility that political partisans so frequently embrace today has in turn produced a profound deficit of trust. And if civility is the springboard for trust, then trust is the springboard for compromise and cooperation, the essential ingredients of democratic governance. Yet too many politicians today seem utterly opposed to any of the compromises required for our Constitutional system of republican federalism to function at all. They do not seem to understand the political consensus required for our leaders to take the country to higher ground. It must be their way or no way. So on top of a deficit of civility and trust, we also confront a leadership deficit.

Chris Howard and I wrote to CSPC supporters the following:

> What makes the modern Tea Partiers different from prior generations of post-Constitutional anti-Federalists is the way they understand their patriotic duty. For 220 years, anti-Federalists worked to restrain the federal government through constructive engagement, bound by their oath of office to support the functionality of Constitutional governance even when they opposed the results. Modern anti-Federalists seem to view their oath as being only to Constitutional principles, not to Constitutional government. This allows them, some would say even obligates them, to "shut it down" and "prove" the folly of the Constitution's strong central government by forcing dysfunction upon it.

We as a people are now living with the bitter fruits of that dysfunction. We can see it in the political gridlock that led to the downgrading of the United States' credit rating for the first time in history. It's evident in the routine budgetary impasses that diminish the strength of an already stressed U.S. military even as dangers gather, and in domestic infrastructure that was once the envy of the world but is now crumbling into disrepair and obsolescence. It's there for all the world to see in a political discourse of embarrassing crudeness and banality. We are in danger of becoming a nation so absorbed by our divisions and bitter internal squabbles that we no longer attempt great deeds nor dare lead free peoples.

Can American exceptionalism be preserved, and trust and civility returned to our nation's capital? I believe that is not only possible but absolutely necessary. If I were to advise the next generation, I would suggest they acquaint themselves with the wisdom and habits of our best leaders. Their examples would tell us to reinvigorate a politics of lively, robust debate within a framework of respect and civil behavior. Only by our shifting the national discussion from the emotional to the intellectual, from personal motives to shared objectives, can trust take root again and grow strong enough to enable our system of compromise to function as it was designed.

Over my lifetime I have come to recognize certain attributes that contribute to effective leadership. I have leaned on them personally, witnessed them in others, and read about them in the history books. These attributes prominently include the ability to establish trust through civility, an instinct for perpetual self-improvement and reform, and a strategic mindset. Throughout this book, I will repeatedly return to these themes and illustrate how they create habits of thought and behavior that have distinguished our greatest leaders.

Throughout my career, for instance, I have personally witnessed trust achieved through civility. By *civility* I do not mean simply following rules of etiquette. Nor does civility require that you agree with someone else or sacrifice strongly held beliefs or opinions. Rather, true civility starts with the practice of respectful listening. From that underappreciated talent understanding can be gained, which in turn serves as the basis for honest dialogue that builds trust. Such honest and respectful exchanges foster creativity in developing solutions to common challenges, the ultimate goal in the art of self-governance.

George Washington is a wonderful example of a leader who thought strategically and acted with civility. As a boy, he transcribed and learned "110 Rules of Civility & Decent Behavior in Company and Conversation." Because he lived by those rules as a grown man, Washington naturally engendered loyalty and trust in others. Washington also learned from his setbacks, exhibiting the determination and drive for self-improvement that are evident in so many of our great leaders. As a young man, for instance, Washington was a Virginia militia officer serving in the British Army. During an expedition into French-controlled territory in southwestern Pennsylvania, he established Fort Necessity in an open, exposed area, confident that the coming battle would be fought in nearby Great Meadows. A surprise attack by the French and their Indian allies, in the midst of a heavy rainstorm that flooded his low-lying redoubt, forced Washington into an ignominious surrender. He was written up in the *Times of London* as a disgrace to His Majesty's service. And yet George Washington persevered, fighting heroically in other battles, and later answering three calls to serve a young country that was just rising on shaky legs, thus becoming the father of our country.

George Washington's example points to another key attribute of the American character that is evident in our best leaders: determination. At opportune moments throughout our history, our leaders have shown uncommon perseverance, even in spite of past failures, and even in the face of gathering dangers. Great leaders are forged as much by their defeats as by their victories. More often than not, these extraordinary individuals have fallen, and failed, and fallen again, only to get back up even more determined to push on and succeed. That is the essence of truly heroic leadership.

George Washington is the archetype of a leader with strategic vision who acted with civility. Even as a young man he instinctively grasped the wisdom of my favorite maxim, passed down to me by President Dwight Eisenhower's speechwriter and congressional liaison, Bryce Harlow: "Trust is the coin of the realm." If we accept the truth of that maxim, then the logical question arises: Trust to do what? If the body politic cannot agree on at least foundational notions of what defines us as a nation, and what we stand for, then trust in politics will serve little purpose. The genius of the Framers was that they understood that fact, and thus laid out in the Constitution the core principles on which all could agree. Our best leaders have built on that foundation, using strategic vision to advance the national cause and guide us through dangerous times.

Let me explain what I mean by *strategy* and *strategic vision*. When writing about a *strategic mindset*, I am referencing habits of conceptualization that bring order to the complex interactions between governments and people, the better to get the big, global issues right. That kind of strategic leadership requires marshaling the best and brightest individuals, regardless of political leanings, to examine issues from all angles, and thus developing the kinds of comprehensive approaches that are the essence of grand strategy.

Of course, strategies in wartime, when the lifeblood of the nation is at stake, are about marshaling troops and resources to defeat an enemy. The perfect military strategy was defined by Sun Tzu, who described it as winning against a foe without having to fight, as we did in the Cold War (more on that later). But a true *grand strategy* takes into account all elements of the nation's well-being and health—cultural, socioeconomic, technological, military, and geopolitical. It harnesses all elements of national power to a strategic blueprint for progress.

I mention strategic vision and a thirst for progress in tandem because they are integral to the character of many of our best leaders, and to the nation as a whole. In sizing up America in the 1830s, Alexis de Tocqueville noted, "The great privilege of America does not consist in being more enlightened than other nations, but in being able to repair the faults they may commit."[2] That's why I have always believed that reform is critical to the enduring success of nations. Reform was the central theme of the Progressive Era, and again after World War II with the Congressional Reform Act of 1946, and with the 1947 Hoover Commission convened by President Harry Truman to recommend changes to improve the efficiency of the federal government. I was part of the Commission on the Organization of the Government for the Conduct of Foreign Policy in the mid-1970s, and the desire to look anew at the old ways of doing things has played a central role in my lifelong work leading think tanks.

Franklin D. Roosevelt showed uncanny strategic vision and a burning desire to reform the old ways both in his New Deal programs to pull a staggering nation out of the Great Depression and with his strategic pivot to prepare the nation to fight and win World War II. Roosevelt was a lifelong Democrat who was ferociously partisan in his early time in office. And yet as need dictated, Roosevelt underwent a remarkable transformation. He became a master of civility, reaching out and working with Republicans as the war clouds gathered, eventually recruiting even isolationists into a unified front to achieve victory. He knew how to think anew, reform and organize the nation, and bring in those with the most talent, regardless of party or personal affinity, to face the great challenges of his time.

Dwight Eisenhower similarly exhibited the leadership traits I most value and espouse: civility, strategic vision, and a progressive drive. With his experience leading the largest military invasion in history, Eisenhower was exceptionally well-suited to the challenges of his time as president. He recognized the great scope and danger of the Soviet threat, and launched Project Solarium to determine the best strategy for confronting it. He developed a "long-haul" strategy for underwriting military power with sustainable economic growth. More than any president since James Monroe, Eisenhower established parameters for using and husbanding U.S. military power, resisting immense pressure to intervene on behalf of the French at Dien Bien Phu in Vietnam, a restraint that his successor Lyndon Johnson would later abandon, to his everlasting regret. In contrast to his carefully cultivated image as an amiable old duffer, Dwight Eisenhower was the consummate grand strategist.

When he was elected president, Ronald Reagan was known as a fierce Cold Warrior, a strong conservative, and an unapologetic partisan. Not a back-alley fighter, perhaps, but certainly not a master of civility in political leadership, either. However, on a personal level, the man himself embodied the principle of civility. His applications of the principle of civility were natural and easy for him, not because he was an actor by profession, but because at his core he was a gentle and profoundly decent man.

As the reader will learn, and I personally witnessed, Ronald Reagan knew what he believed, and why he believed it, and he had the courage of his convictions. This shone through, and it helped him not only reach across the political aisle but also bridge the gaps of culture, style, and intellect with British prime minister Margaret Thatcher, who became his best friend among his fellow world leaders and with whom he stayed very close after they both left office. Ultimately, Reagan's innate civility and trustworthiness were even able to bridge the chasm of forty years of hostility and Cold War distrust that yawned between him and Soviet premier Mikhail Gorbachev. By practicing what I call the *martial art of civility*, these two leaders succeeded in changing the world.

In reaching back to our best leaders for inspiration and instruction, I don't ask that we blind ourselves to their faults. Faults are a natural part of the human condition, and every leader, certainly every hero of mine, had them. What I have strived for is the intellectual maturity and curiosity to learn worthwhile lessons from these extraordinary individuals, both good and bad.

Mark Twain is thought to have said, "History doesn't repeat itself, but it often rhymes." I believe in history's rhymes. I believe it is the highest achievement of a public servant, and of a leader, to avoid the bad rhymes of history and to seek to replicate the good ones. I believe that doing this requires both knowledge and inspiration. As a society, we need to reacquaint ourselves with the stories of heroic leaders from our collective past. We also need to pay attention to what is happening around us. The worthy citizen is engaged in society, not standing on the sidelines in repose, but aware, constantly learning and applying those lessons to the betterment of all, taking part in the events that will shape their own slice of history. This was a key lesson of my childhood.

2

Beginnings

A Student of History

My boyhood narrative played out in Chattanooga, Tennessee. As I was growing up, my physical development was uneven and different from that of many of my contemporaries, and in retrospect there were benefits gained even from my shortcomings. Indeed, I grew too tall too fast, growth spurts that left me vulnerable to infections. I thus spent much of my childhood at home, even bedridden for some periods. Yet these hours were spent reading about great leaders in strategy and politics. I was lucky to have had access to a very large home library, which my father began assembling during his days as a doctoral candidate at Princeton University.

If the historic leaders in my books seemed larger than life, my physical surroundings were also storybook beautiful and equally historic. I grew up, with my parents and two brothers, living in my Grandmother Patten's home. It was a beautiful mansion with a half-dozen elegant columns out front, set on a large hill in Chattanooga. My grandmother's husband named the estate Minnekahda. Perhaps the best features of the property were the magnificent views. Stretching across the front end of the mansion was the Civil War battlefield Missionary Ridge abutting Lookout Mountain. From the other end of the house, one could see the Tennessee River rounding the famous moccasin bend through Chattanooga Valley. I do not believe there was a finer view anywhere in the South.

My father's side of the family, the Abshires of Roanoke, Virginia, had been relatively poor. My mother's side of the family, the Pattens, established themselves in Chattanooga following the Civil War and became a large, prominent, and very wealthy family. Unfortunately, our branch of the Patten family had been a partial owner of one of the banks that Franklin Roosevelt closed during the "Bank Holiday" in 1933. In those times, the preferred stockholders were personally responsible for creating cash reserves and liquidity during a crisis. Because of the run on banks, our family's wealth was greatly diminished during the Great Depression. Despite this hardship, my brothers and I were still able to enjoy growing up in the lovely Minnekahda.

My devotion to history resulted from many influences, but foremost among them was my father, Jim Abshire. My father graduated from Roanoke College with a full graduate scholarship to Princeton University. During his time at Princeton, the university's president, Woodrow Wilson, was in a vicious fight with the graduate school dean, Andrew West, over the quasi-independence of the graduate school. My father's enduring dislike of Wilson, and the League of Nations he would later propose as president, ultimately stemmed from this fight. Needless to say, Jim Abshire subsequently became a strong Wendell Willkie supporter, and then a Taft Republican.

In his early days, my father used the money from his teaching to support his widowed mother. Fortunately, his teaching experience at Princeton ultimately led to a position as the head of the history department at the University of Chattanooga. There he met my mother. Although my father eventually went into business, there remained hundreds of history books around the house from his days as a college professor. Through these books, I was introduced to ancient military history, the Civil War, and the First World War. They also offered a look back into my own Patten family history.

My great-grandfather George Washington Patten and his brother Zeboim "Zeb" Cartter Patten were the first of their family to settle in Chattanooga. They were also among the more than a quarter million volunteers from Illinois who answered President Lincoln's call, in 1862, to join the Union's fight against southern secession. George was the first to join, but was followed soon after by Zeb. George Patten wrote back to his mother from the battlefield:

> I have been a soldier and carry a gun. I am proud of it, and I carry a gun in the hardest campaign. We marched through [Kentucky], and marched on a dusty limestone road with only mud to drink and not water. We have inexperienced officers that made us march in file from morning to night, who allowed us no privileges, which experienced officers would have done to make it easier for us, but I am proud and thankful that I suffered as I did. It was a lesson for me. It taught me how to be a soldier and an officer . . . I hope mother that you are not among those who thinks

a soldier is such a miserable being. Mother, take it from one year to another, they are the jolliest and happiest set of beings I ever saw.

The Patten brothers were reunited in Tennessee at the Battle of Chickamauga, one of the bloodiest battles in the Civil War. Zeb was a corporal in the color guard and as a result of his exposed position was injured in his foot during the battle. Still, he was lucky to be among the 9,756 wounded rather than the 1,657 killed. He was taken to the battlefield hospital, crying out in pain. The doctor, who was busy tending to cases more serious than his, responded, "Keep your mouth shut Zeb, I'll be over to cut off your foot as soon as possible!" Following that declaration, Zeb Cartter Patten kept his mouth shut, kept his foot, and recovered from his wound in Chattanooga.

Bloody Chickamauga was the warm-up for one of the strangest battles in human history, the Battle of Missionary Ridge. On Missionary Ridge, Captain George Patten, and hundreds like him, decided to take the ridge without receiving General Grant's command to do so. However, Grant forgot to put such details in his magnificent memoirs.

The plan called for Union forces to advance and capture the enemy's entrenchments at the base of Missionary Ridge, and to hold them. However, when the Union troops took the rifle pits at the base of the ridge, they had little protection from the rebel fire coming from the heights above. As a colonel later noted, the area was in danger of becoming "a hideous slaughter pen." The Federals, thus trapped, found that the only way out was an assault straight up the ridge. When General Grant saw the assault, he was furious. He had not given the order. He turned to his subordinate General Thomas to ask who had ordered such a charge; someone was going to pay for this.

As it turned out, the assault up Missionary Ridge was one of the most magnificent charges in the American annals of war, with flags flying and bugles sounding. While far apart on the line, Captain George Washington Patten and young Sergeant Arthur MacArthur both participated in this charge. By some act of fate, they both reached the top of the ridge relatively unscathed. Sergeant McArthur later received the Medal of Honor, the nation's highest award for valor. Captain Patten was promoted to major.

In part, the success of the Union attack was due to the fact that Confederate general Braxton Bragg had clumsily placed his weapons on the topographical crest of the ridge rather than the military crest, where fields of fire could cover the approaches below. That single oversight created blind spots that the Union soldiers exploited. As the advancing Federals moved toward the ridge crest, there was no way for the Confederates to bring their cannons and other heavy weapons to bear to stop the assault. Thus, the Union forces overwhelmed the Confederates and ended the siege of Chattanooga. Ironically, despite the fact that the assault was carried out against his orders, General Grant was promoted to commander of all Union forces when news of the great victory at Missionary Ridge reached President Lincoln.

After the war, Chattanooga became a politically remarkable town. The blue and gray mixed and overcame their wartime prejudices and antagonisms. It was perhaps the most progressive town in the South in that way. The younger Patten brother, Zeb, stayed in Chattanooga and started a publishing company called Patten and Payne. In 1877, he met the twenty-year-old Adolph Ochs, a Jewish immigrant who had recently come to the country by way of Knoxville. Ochs wanted to purchase Zeb Cartter Patten's *Chattanooga Times* newspaper. Zeb Patten offered Ochs a very good deal. Ochs only paid $250 for a controlling interest in the newspaper. Eventually he profited so much from the deal that by 1896 he was able to purchase the bankrupt *New York Times*. Ochs was on his way to creating the greatest newspaper in the world.

In 1879, Zeb Cartter Patten established the Chattanooga Medicine Company (now known as Chattem) in a simple two-story brick building located on Market Street, then just an unpaved muddy road in downtown Chattanooga. He persuaded his older brother George to return to Chattanooga from Illinois to join him in its operations.

The company's two signature products were Thedford's Black-Draught and Wine of Cardui. Black-Draught was a senna-based laxative patent medicine, which was originally created by the Dr. A. Q. Simmons Liver Medicine Company but was later purchased by the Chattanooga Medicine Company. To boost its sales, the medicine company began an aggressive advertising campaign, which included almanacs, wall calendars, flyers, and even churchgoers' songbooks. These efforts along with the use of widely distributed testimonials from satisfied customers led to strong sales. So much so, in fact, that in 1882, they decided to increase their product line.

The Patten brothers next acquired Dr. McElree's Wine of Cardui for women's monthly ailments, which was based on the sedative and antispasmodic properties of *Cnicus benedictus*. Botanical *Cnicus benedictus* had been used for hundreds of years in central Europe. Those who tried the plant leaves reported positive results, and after the Chattanooga Medicine Company bought the rights to Wine of Cardui, the product became a huge success. It quickly rivaled the northern product Lydia Pinkham's Vegetable Compound for "female complaints." Soon these products were sold all over the South and in Latin America.

Zeb Cartter Patten's daughter Elizabeth was a true beauty. She married handsome John Thomas Lupton of Virginia. Through the marriage, he joined the medicine company, first as its legal counsel and eventually as its vice president and treasurer. Unlike the Pattens, who never went to college, John T. Lupton had a law degree from the University of Virginia in an age when few had even bachelor's degrees.

Later, with a remarkable vision and knack for entrepreneurship, Lupton became one of three national leaders of Coca-Cola bottling. To obtain the money for the purchase of the Coca-Cola shares, he sold his interest in Chattanooga Medicine Company to my grandfather. Perhaps I can be forgiven for wishing that it had been the other way around!

The background of Lupton and Coca-Cola is fascinating and a story worth telling in its own right. Two Chattanoogans, Benjamin Thomas and Joseph Whitehead, had been in the Spanish-American War and had witnessed attempts to bottle water and other drinks. They explored similar bottling techniques with the over-the-counter drink Coca-Cola. Up until that time, Coca-Cola had been sold only at soda fountains, and the head of the company, Asa Candler, had no interest in bottling it.

In the meeting with Thomas and Whitehead, Candler remarked, "Gentlemen, we have neither the money, nor brains, nor time to embark in the bottling business."[1] The two Chattanoogans, however, were not easily deterred. Knowing of Candler's great love of baseball, they returned to Atlanta to argue that Candler could have his bottled Coca-Cola at every baseball stadium in the country. Remarkably, this time Candler agreed, though he warned them, "If you boys fail in this undertaking, don't come back to cry on my shoulder because I have very little confidence in this bottling business."[2]

Under the terms of their deal, Candler supplied the Coca-Cola syrup and Thomas and Whitehead were given the exclusive bottling rights for the Southeast, Southwest, and Midwest. This contract has been dubbed one of the most valuable contracts in the history of American business. In addition, this unique distribution system still characterizes the entire soft-drink industry to this day. Thomas and Whitehead opened their first bottling plant in Chattanooga in 1899. However, disagreements led to a split in their partnership and bottling rights.

In 1900, Whitehead turned to John T. Lupton for financial assistance. Lupton in turn went to his first cousin by marriage, my grandfather John A. Patten (son of George Washington Patten). John Patten offered to sell his holdings in the Chattanooga Medicine Company to acquire the needed capital. With that financial injection, Lupton and Whitehead established the Dixie Coca-Cola Bottling Company plant in Atlanta. Unable to keep up with demand, they developed a franchise system, which led to the creation of approximately one thousand independent bottlers by 1920. Lupton was on his way to becoming a multimillionaire. In 1986, Lupton's grandson Jack sold the family's bottling operation back to Coca-Cola for $1.4 billion.

The first Coca-Cola bottling franchise was the Johnston Coca-Cola Bottling Company of Chattanooga, which purchased the rights in 1901. The grandson of the founder, Summerfield K. Johnston Jr., would inherit the company and turn it into the largest independent bottler of Coca-Cola in the world. In 1991, he sold Johnston Coca-Cola to Coke's own bottler Coca-Cola Enterprises, creating the largest individual Coca-Cola bottler, and would serve as the CEO of Coca-Cola Enterprises for the next ten years. In 2010, Coca-Cola Enterprises sold its domestic operations to the Coca-Cola Company for $15 billion. I am proud to say that Summerfield, or "Skey" as he is called, is a lifelong friend and a distant cousin, as he and I are proud to both be direct descendants of David M. Key. I have always been in awe of Skey's business acumen and shared love of life.

Back in the early twentieth century, John A. Patten was also a leading Methodist in the country, holding the highest lay position. Ironically, in 1916 an article in the *American Medical Journal* all but accused my Methodist, teetotaler grandfather of fraud. The article charged that the Chattanooga Medicine Company, in which he was a dominant shareholder at the time, was built on deceit. Its product, Wine of Cardui, was characterized as a vicious fraud, owing any medicinal effects solely to its alcohol content.

The fallout caused my grandfather Patten to resign from the many high offices he held in the Methodist Episcopal Church. An indignant John A. Patten rented a train and, with a horde of lawyers and righteous wrath, went to Chicago to sue the American Medical Association for $200,000 in damages.

Tragically, during an adjournment of the court, my grandfather was seized with acute intestinal pain. He was rushed to the hospital. An ulcer had formed in his intestines, which required immediate surgery. Whether it was from faultily administered anesthesia or from a rupture of the ulcer following the surgery, he did not survive, passing away at only forty-seven years of age. While he was a bit overweight, he had appeared otherwise healthy. The drinking Episcopalian members of the family argued that his weight problems were actually a result of his abstinence from alcohol, which they claimed he compensated for with an overindulgence in sweets.

The news of my grandfather's death came as a great shock, not only to his wife and family but to all of Chattanooga. *The National* magazine wrote, "this man's unselfish and unobtrusive generosity had become known . . . all classes and colors and creeds joined to pay reverent tribute to his memory." Upon his death, schools closed and a proclamation by the mayor of Chattanooga shut stores during the funeral hour. The church was overflowing. Thousands who could not fit in the church patiently lined the streets to watch the funeral procession pass by. John Patten was widely known as a major philanthropist, and he had become a leading citizen of Chattanooga, which bore respectful witness to his passing.

By the time of his death, my grandfather had already begun an ambitious transformation of Minnekahda. He razed the hilltop on which the mansion stood, built a road system, and constructed two caretaker houses and a ten-room servants' home and garage. The family lived there while waiting for construction on the main house to begin.

With the passing of John Patten, my grandmother, the Methodist, decided not to proceed with his more lavish plans for the mansion. She expanded the existing ten-room building to fifty-two rooms, but without a pool and a gymnasium. My grandfather had also drawn up plans for an elaborate farm with room for sheep, cows, and pigs. Grandmother, less interested in farming, instead transferred parcels of property to her children as they married. During the Roaring Twenties, three of his six children built mansions on the property, including the most elaborate mansion, which her son Manker had decorated by Tiffany and Company of New York.

My grandfather had six children. I knew them all well, as they regularly convened with their families at Minnekahda for lunch on Sundays. My mother's older sister Charlotte married an athletic coach who was a great inspiration to me. Her husband, Alex Guerry Sr., was a natural-born fund-raiser. He became the head of Baylor Preparatory School and did much to advance its development. During the Depression, Guerry went on to lead and protect the University of Chattanooga. The son of an Episcopal bishop, he was persuaded to head the University of the South in Sewanee, Tennessee, during World War II. Alex Guerry managed to keep the elite Episcopal University of the South alive during difficult times. In fact, it thrived as a result of generous gifts from the DuPont and Ball families.

Guerry often gave talks on his experiences leading a machine-gun platoon in World War I. As a teenager already deeply interested in history, I was mesmerized by his recollections. Initially in his World War I campaign, Guerry and his men were in the trenches, on the defensive. Later, in the Meuse-Argonne campaigns, they were on the offensive with victory in sight. Guerry would elaborate on the sharp contrast in mind-sets between being hunkered down in the trenches, consumed with self-preservation, and being on the attack, forging ahead in search of victory. It was a lesson in the power of seizing the initiative that I never forgot.

Dr. Guerry told me that I could always do better in whatever endeavor I chose. For him it was never enough just to do well; one had to win. That attitude undoubtedly explains why Guerry was a father of champions. His son Zan, in fact, is in the Intercollegiate Tennis Association Collegiate Tennis Hall of Fame, and at the time of this writing was head of Chattem. In 2010, Chattem was acquired by Sanofi, the French pharmaceutical giant, for $1.9 million. The next generations of Guerrys also included Alex Guerry Jr., who ended World War II as a highly decorated lieutenant colonel and fighter pilot in the Pacific theater. His exploits were written up in *Reader's Digest.*

As for Alex Guerry Sr., I remember when the noted reporter Jonathan Daniels came to visit the University of the South and then Chattanooga. Daniels would later go on to become Franklin Roosevelt's press secretary. Upon his departure, Guerry boasted that Daniels thought the University of the South was the "Oxford of America." However, in Daniels's subsequent book, *A Southerner Discovers the South*, he tagged Sewanee instead as a sleepy place. With regard to the family he wrote, "the big folks in Chattanooga are made up of the generous Pattens and the stingy Luptons." My mother, always the peacemaker, reassured me of the Luptons' generosity and public spirit.

My own father thought Guerry was a bit of an ass because he was so preachy. But there was something in Guerry's coaching style and infectious spirit that was able to kindle a fire in the hearts of young, impressionable men. His sons obviously felt it, and so did I. He inspired me.

3

Student, Soldier, Cadet

Early Lessons in Strategy

After my own parents married, they moved to Greenwich Village in New York, where they lived for three years while my father worked for the Henry Holt publishing company. Even though he was offered a position as an officer of the company, he was persuaded by the two Patten brothers to return to Chattanooga as the number two at the Chattanooga Stamping and Enameling Company. He later became its head and led it through the Great Depression.

Having started his career in academia, my father excelled in every subject and was good at teaching. He consumed books, often using the index as an impromptu study guide to test his retention of the material. I think my father and I bonded most over our mutual love of books. The collection of books he and my grandfather assembled at Minnekahda was certainly my salvation growing up, especially when I was laid up from either a sports injury or illness.

While I resented my poor heath at the time, I actually have it to thank for the vast knowledge of military history that I acquired early in life. In those days I received an allowance; to further encourage my study of history, my father agreed to pay for half of any book I wanted to purchase on the topic. The study of military history took on special significance for me as the country headed into its most consequential war.

My readings triggered a fascination with the nature of great strategic leadership. In the 1930s, there was a big disagreement in the country between isolationists and interventionists. My father was definitely in the isolationist camp, and already I sensed that I leaned toward intervention. Due to the rise of Hitler in Germany and the Japanese attack on Pearl Harbor, the interventionists were decidedly the winners of that argument. As I followed the news from the war front both in print and over the radio, the heroic leaders in the Atlantic and Pacific enthralled me.

The more I read, the more I began to think about the nature of leadership in all its dimensions. I read about the full gamut of military leaders, from Alexander the Great to Napoleon to the great field generals of the Civil War. I absorbed Clausewitz's *On War* and Napoleon's *Maxims*.

Of course, Clausewitz was widely read in the United States, and he was required reading in military circles. Clausewitz believed that war was politics by other means. He reinforced my appreciation for Napoleon's maxim "The moral is to the physical as three is to one." In other words, the human factors are three times more important than the sheer numbers and size of an army. This stood in contrast to the French geometric strategies of Antoine-Henri Jomini, whose text was taught at West Point.

Edward Mead Earle and his collaborators, Gordon Alexander Craig and Felix Gilbert, produced the book *Makers of Modern Strategy: Military Thought from Machiavelli to Hitler*. As a teenager, I devoured this book. Professor Earle received funding from the Carnegie Corporation of New York to produce this magnificent compendium on the best strategic thought. What is most important about *Makers of Modern Strategy* is its emphasis on nonmilitary factors in the formulation of strategy, be they economic, psychological, technological, moral, or political. Meade correctly noted, "Diplomacy and strategy, political commitments and military are inseparable; unless this is recognized foreign policy will be bankrupt." Writing in 1943, Professor Meade noted, "Alfred Thayer Mahan is our only military theorist that can be considered as a grand strategist."

Admiral Alfred Thayer Mahan, America's first grand strategist, had an enormous impact at the turn of the last century. In the early 1940s, I delved into Mahan's two books, especially *The Influence of Sea Power upon History, 1660–1783*, which he wrote while head of the Naval War College. This publication garnered him acclaim around the world, but especially in the United States, Great Britain, Germany, and Japan. He wrote of the critical importance of sea power in building global influence. He introduced core concepts such as deterrence, sufficiency, and globalism. Mahan would lead a revolution in U.S. strategy and help transform the nation into a world power. The United States would not have been able to join the fighting and influence the outcome of World War I, for instance, if we had not had a strong naval capability. It was U.S. naval power that made it possible to move the American Expeditionary Force to Europe in time to win a war that was clearly being lost.

Years later, on January 29, 2010, I delivered a lecture to the U.S. Naval

Academy's Class of 2012 on the impact Mahan had on the development of
U.S. strategy during the Admiral George W. Anderson Jr., USN (Ret.) and
Mary Lee Anderson Leadership Speaker Series. The lecture was later published with a written introduction by then Chairman of the Joint Chiefs Admiral Mike Mullen. He noted the important impact of Mahan's writings
worldwide, which "helped end American isolationism and revolutionized
American thinking regarding the projection of power." He went on to add,
"We are at a similar inflection point today in a new and exciting strategic
environment."[1]

I knew my ancient history as well. Given my Methodist grandmother's frequent Bible readings, it would have been difficult for any of us to escape
without a strong familiarity with the stories of the Bible. I was especially
intrigued with the military lessons in the fight between David and Goliath.
The great Goliath was clearly more powerful, but he was weighted down with
body armor, a heavy shield, and other armament. Young David had only his
sling, but he knew that to be successful all he needed was one accurate shot
to Goliath's temple.

I also learned how Robert E. Lee won his battles with an agile strategy,
and of Stonewall Jackson's motto: "mystify, mislead, and surprise."

When I later read about World War II's impregnable Maginot Line in my
early teens, it reminded me of the supposedly impregnable armor of Goliath.
As NATO ambassador decades later, I would drive down a two-lane road
through the supposedly impregnable Ardennes forest, where it was assumed
that the dense foliage made for its own fortification. And yet, in May 1940,
Germany's light vehicles shot down that road, supported by dive-bombers,
and charged all the way to the English Channel. France collapsed in only
twelve days. By education and experience, I have never been confident in so-
called impenetrable defenses.

As a youth I also consumed the books of B. H. Liddell Hart on the strategy
of the indirect approach. He wrote in reaction to the frontal attacks by massive armies in battles such as Verdun or the Somme in World War I. I studied
the differences between Sir Douglas Haig, who commanded on the western
front in that war, and Winston Churchill, who was First Lord of the Admiralty
at the time. Churchill saw the fallacy of attacking the strongest armies on the
enemy's strongest front. Blessed with a brilliant strategic mind, Churchill
examined alternative ways, through a tactical innovation, to break through
the barbed wire and out of the trenches in Flanders. From this line of thinking
came the original concept of the tank. However, it was not until 1917 that the
first tanks were developed enough to make a maiden effort in the Battle of
Cambrai.

The Battle of the Somme, with the British and French assault on the ridge of the Somme River Valley beginning on July 1, 1916, epitomized Haig's strategy. The battle finally came to an inconclusive close in the third week of November 1916, with the British having lost some 420,000 men and the French approximately 200,000, while estimates of German casualties ranged from 437,000 to 680,000. Despite the horrible carnage on both sides, there was never a breakthrough, with the Allied front line advancing by about six miles on a front of roughly twenty miles. German defenses remained as strong as ever. In truth, because of Haig's strategic folly of attacking the strongest armies on the enemy's strongest front, the British and French forces lost the Battle of the Somme before it even began.

A. J. P. Taylor noted, "The Battle of the Somme was an unredeemed defeat. The enthusiastic volunteers were enthusiastic no longer. They had lost faith in their cause, their leaders, in anything, except loyalty to their fellow comrades. The war ceased to have a purpose. It went on for its own sake, as contest of endurance."[2] On the other hand, Liddell Hart's indirect approach emphasized drawing the opponent into a trap, such as with Battle of Cannae in the Punic Wars.

Reading about the early Greeks, I learned that they were the first to develop and codify strategy and the art of war in the West. Even before the military genius of Alexander the Great, the Greeks knew the necessity of trapping and upsetting the equilibrium of their enemy, the Persians. When the Athenians overextended themselves with the expedition to Syracuse, it was Thucydides who recorded it as a military blunder. We have seen time and again how an overextension can mark the first step in a decline of a great power. In the Civil War, Lincoln's cabinet wanted to go to war against the British for interference on the high seas. Lincoln, the great strategist, said, "One war at a time."

As I approached my senior year in high school, a professor at the University of Chattanooga wrote a letter of recommendation for me. It stated, "David Abshire has an intellectual curiosity far beyond his years." Certainly I had intellectual curiosity as to what made bad and good generals and admirals. During my senior year, my parents and aunt had a fascinating visitor at Minnekahda. Frank Thomas, the famed head football coach of Alabama, visited and took a liking to my work in military history. He announced that I should go to West Point. This had been a longtime desire of mine, and he started the wheels moving, which led me to take the train to Washington, D.C., to visit Senator Kenneth McKellar from Tennessee, a powerful leader in the Democratic Senate.

In Washington, I stayed at the Harrington Hotel, and on the morning of

June 6, 1944, I turned on the radio and heard the news that we were invading Europe. With me was a lobbyist for the Chattanooga Medicine Company called "Uncle" Jimmy Huff. He was everyone's "Uncle Jimmy," and wore spats and a top hat to Capitol Hill. Uncle Jimmy accompanied me for the morning visit with Senator McKellar, this being my first trip to Washington.

As we got into the car, I spied a couple of covered crates of Jack Daniel's in the back seat. When we arrived at the senator's office, McKellar greeted us, and Jimmy said he'd "brought the hooch!" Things were done a little differently back then. The senator was very cordial, proclaiming that I should absolutely go to West Point. Unfortunately, he did not currently have an appointment to West Point available, just one for Annapolis. He suggested that I take the one for Annapolis with the hope that he might get one for West Point down the road, at which point I could make the shift.

My first lesson on the politics of Washington took place behind closed doors when McKellar started to talk about the danger to the nation of "a takeover." I thought he was speaking about Adolf Hitler. As he continued to gesticulate toward the other end of Pennsylvania Avenue, it finally occurred to me that this powerful Democratic leader was talking about the Democratic president of the United States, Franklin Roosevelt. As head of the Senate Appropriations Committee, Senator McKellar disagreed with Roosevelt's Tennessee Valley Authority, and especially with the little compensation given to his home state landowners when the TVA took over their land. McKellar withheld funds until the landowners were given fair market value. It was a good introduction to Washington power politics for me.

Meanwhile, I had my own moment of glory with my Uncle Alex Guerry. In early December 1944, the invasion of Europe was going well. Our forces under General Eisenhower were pressing forward in Belgium, Luxembourg, and Germany. There was much optimism regarding a possible early end to the war in Europe. As was the tradition every Sunday, all of my cousins gathered at Minnekahda. That particular Sunday, I engaged in a spirited argument with Dr. Guerry. I forecasted that the Germans would be successful in a major counterattack. At that point, Uncle Alex reflected on his experiences in World War I. He said that with modern tactical airpower, it would not be possible for such a counterattack to take place. After all of my reading of military history books, I argued that the Germans would adopt a strategy of surprise.

Of course, surprise is exactly what happened when the Germans counterattacked in the offensive that became known as the Battle of the Bulge. On a subsequent Sunday, my cousin Lieutenant Colonel Alex Guerry, himself recently back from the Pacific theater, remembered the exchange. "Did Dad ever tell you he was wrong?" asked Alex. I simply laughed.

After I waited and waited, the West Point appointment never came through, so I proceeded with the Annapolis appointment. As it turned out, however, I flunked the eye exam for the Annapolis physical, which required 20/20 vision as opposed to West Point's less demanding 20/30 requirement. So, the following year I was back in Washington still hoping for a West Point appointment.

In the meantime, I traveled to Atlanta and reported to the U.S. Army induction center as an enlisted man. Having recently learned the touch system of typing, I was quickly spotted for my typing ability and drafted into doing temporary work at the reception center. The war had ended, but the draft was going forward, even as thousands of soldiers were getting discharged. After a couple of weeks, the corporal I was helping announced that he was getting discharged as well and that I should move over to his desk. In a few more weeks, the captain came over to my desk and congratulated me on a promotion to corporal. A few months later, the captain came to me again, saying, "Congratulations!" I responded with curiosity, "What for?" His response: "You're a sergeant!" The quick promotions convinced my family that I was a military genius after all, but I had only my typing skills to thank for them.

My sudden rise actually became quite a source of consternation and some embarrassment for me. Here I was contemplating entering West Point as an infantry sergeant, and I had never even fired a rifle. I requested to the captain that I be allowed to ship out with the next group of soldiers heading to Fort McClellan for basic training.

"Abshire, you've got the best goddamn job in the whole goddamn Army. This does not make sense," he retorted. I patiently explained that it would be very awkward if I were to attend West Point having never fired a weapon. The captain snarled, "OK, it's up to you."

When I arrived in Fort McClellan with my recruits, I received exactly the kind of reception I feared at West Point. The sergeant couldn't comprehend my lack of training.

"You have never fired an M1 rifle?" he asked incredulously. "You are a disgrace to the goddamn Army of the United States! I am going to keep my eye on you. Make one goddamn mistake and you'll end up Private Abshire!"

My mechanical aptitude had never been high, but luckily I passed the rigors of basic training. I was very happy to have had that training when I later arrived at Beast Barracks at West Point, having finally received my appointment from Senator McKellar.

I must add that I was always rather uneven in my abilities. This was evident in my course work at West Point, where I was at the top of my class in military history and about at the bottom in engineering and math. I was so poor in math and science, in fact, that I was forced to repeat my first year after failing advanced algebra. This turned out to be a blessing in disguise. I thoroughly enjoyed my repeated year and became much more active socially. While I may have been weaker in math, I received a commendation for the work on strategy I completed for the head of the department of social science.

Some of my West Point classmates would go on to very impressive careers. One was future astronaut Buzz Aldrin, who after graduation went on to the Air Force and then to NASA, later becoming only the second person to walk on the moon. Another, E. C. "Shy" Meyer, became a four-star general and the chief of staff of the Army, and was instrumental in rebuilding the service after its post-Vietnam decline. Fellow classmate Joe Clemons later became famous for his actions at Pork Chop Hill in the Korean War, as I will recount later. Two of my roommates also remained close friends throughout the years, Phil Gwynn and Gerry Hendrix. Gwynn later married my cousin, Sarah Key Patten, who lived at Ashland Farms in Chattanooga. Following our graduation from West Point in the spring of 1951, I was delighted to serve as best man in Hendrix's wedding. He went on to serve in the Air Force and eventually retired as a two-star major general. Little did we know at the time of our graduation that we would soon be putting our West Point military training to the test.

4

Crucible of Leadership

The Korean War

In June of 1950, the West Point Class of 1951, my class, had a month off before reporting to our summer duty to train new plebes at Camp Buckner, north of West Point. At that time there were opportunities for West Point students to hitch rides on Army troop transports heading for Europe. Naturally, a handful of us merrily set out for Europe along with some recent graduates.

On June 25, we received jarring news on the ship as it steamed toward Europe. The ship ticker tape reported that the North Koreans had invaded South Korea. News poured in over the next week. As a West Pointer, it was clear to me that we were witnessing one of the most disastrous collapses in American military history. We all knew that there were four U.S. divisions assigned to Japan. None of them were ready to fight. The 24th Division was on the Japanese island closest to Korea. My colleagues and I could never have imagined just how disgracefully unprepared for combat it was.

We soon heard news that the 24th Division was deploying to South Korea to join in a protective defense perimeter around the port city of Pusan. Next came the news that a so-called Task Force Smith had been created to venture north. Then we received the devastating news that the task force had been annihilated. Seven communist divisions were leading the overwhelming enemy attack.

With the fighting intensifying, many of the Class of 1950 graduates would receive new orders to immediately deploy to South Korea to bolster the collapsing defenses around Pusan. They possessed no special training. We also read of the high casualty rates, especially as a result of chaotic night fighting. As all of this devastating news was pouring into our ship via the wire service ticker tape, the United Nations Security Council passed a resolution urging member states to provide assistance. General Douglas MacArthur, already in command of U.S. forces in Japan, would take on this new United Nations command.

Given that American military history had long been my favorite pastime, I began running a military history seminar on board our troopship. We recalled that prior to World War I, no one believed the alliance commitments of the day could possibly lead to the Great War. Once again we reviewed the miscalculations behind the assumption that the Japanese, while clearly threatening Dutch and British possessions in Asia, would certainly never attack the United States at Pearl Harbor. None of the seminars on military history I conducted aboard a troop transport heading for Europe brought comfort to the participants.

With Korea there was little doubt that we Americans had badly miscalculated once again. Months earlier, in January 1950, Secretary of State Dean Acheson had given a major speech at the Council on Foreign Relations about our Pacific defense perimeter. While he included Japan, Acheson made no mention of Korea. Acheson's speech had, in effect, given North Korea the notion that it could invade South Korea without risking U.S. involvement.

Given the recent experience of World War II, I expected to be sent directly into combat in Korea, even though I still had a year to go at West Point before graduation. Because of mounting criticism of the high casualty rate among the Class of 1950, however, the decision was made for the Class of 1951 to first have a tour of duty in the United States before being thrust into a combat zone. This meant I would get to graduate as expected the following spring. But all cadets vacationing, such as myself, were told to "get the hell out of Europe immediately" for transshipment back to the United States.

Along with many officials in the Truman administration, my good friend and classmate Saul Jacobs and I decided that Europe might soon be at war again repelling a general communist aggression, and perhaps much of it would end up destroyed. So we decided to have a last look and see Europe for ourselves, making sure that we could not find available space on the military transports until the end of the month.

Our tour took us to Paris and an extended stay in the City of Lights, and to some of the great cities in Germany, before we finally booked passage on a troopship in Hamburg. Through a mutual friend I even scored a date with the charming daughter of Lieutenant General Clarence Huebner, a commander of U.S. forces in Europe. We had a great lunch, and Miss Huebner seemed eager to meet again.

General Huebner announced at the time that he had ordered Major General

Maxwell Taylor, who commanded in Berlin, to report to Heidelberg that afternoon. Authorities at the time did not question *whether* the Soviet Union would take advantage of the Korean conflict and open up a second front by invading Europe, but only *when* the Soviet Union would attack.

Only in the Crazy Horse Saloon in Paris did we find a truly relaxed group. The French proprietor and bartenders said, "It is very simple. This time when the Germans come, we just don't fight; we'll just shift from champagne to their favorite beer. It would be business as usual. No more fighting!"

By this time on the Korean War front, the North Korean forces had managed to rapidly push through to Pusan to form a defense perimeter. The communists' string of victories ended in September 1950 with General Mac-Arthur's Inchon landing, a risky amphibious assault that was one of the most brilliant operations in American military history. A surprise attack far from the Pusan perimeter that the U.N. and South Koreans were desperately defending, the massive operation included more than 260 naval vessels and some 75,000 troops. It led to the recapture of the South Korean capital of Seoul two weeks later, and severed the supply lines of North Korean forces in the south.

Unfortunately, the Inchon landing was followed up by the decision to launch an offensive by U.N. forces north to the Yalu River. This triggered the Chinese Communists to join the battle in a vicious counterattack. Thus, the strategic victory of the Inchon landing was matched with the strategic blunder of pushing to the Yalu River and bringing the Chinese into the fighting.

Following graduation in 1951, I received orders to report as an instructor to the Officer Candidate School (OCS) at Fort Benning, Georgia. My platoon was the cream of the crop, including a mix of officer candidates from Harvard and Princeton. I was quite impressed. I hope they were, too, since I believed we were potentially the best platoon at OCS. I certainly set out to make us the best.

Toward the end of this tour of duty, I experimented a bit. I introduced into my company a system whereby all candidates were confidentially graded by their peers, in all areas of performance, highlighting their strengths and weaknesses. This system was also applied to instructors, including myself. Even my cadet platoon members graded me. All submissions were in sealed envelopes to preserve confidentiality. The process was similar to what is mentioned in Thomas Ricks's book *The Generals* under the concept of "360 degree evaluations," in which superiors, peers, and subordinates all assess the strengths and weaknesses of military leaders.[1] My evaluation system was used throughout the school in subsequent classes, and I received my first letter of commendation for introducing the initiative. The letter of commendation read:

The system you initiated will give candidates an opportunity to see themselves as their fellow candidates see them, thereby providing a means of self-improvement. The effect of the system you developed should be two-fold: a higher caliber of graduates, and an increased percentage of graduates. It is by your determination, ingenuity, and hard work that this system was instigated. Your alertness to possible improvements, initiative in seeking new means of improving the Officer Candidate Program, and attention to duty are highly commendable.

As with so many others in my West Point class, I set out for Korea in the spring of 1952. I reported for duty on the West Coast and boarded a troopship. After more than a year of bloody combat, both sides had begun truce talks that raised hopes that the war would soon be over. However, the fighting and dying continued unabated. The eastern U.N. lines were anchored on the Sea of Japan midway between the Korean towns of Kosong and Kansong. From there the front moved south to the "Punchbowl," a large circular valley surrounded by rough mountains. From there the line headed west to the so-called Iron Triangle, which was the strategic communications hub surrounding Pyongyang, Kumhwa, and Ch'orwon. The front then dropped south to the Imjin Valley. Amazingly, 554,000 U.N. soldiers eventually manned this line, of whom 250,000 were Americans.

Soon after my arrival in Korea, I found myself a platoon leader in the 25th Infantry Division, which was being held in reserve in the area of the Punchbowl. The location had seen hard fighting earlier in the war but was by then rather quiet. Our battalion was in the reserve position in case of a breakthrough in the line.

In taking command of my platoon in Company A, of the 14th Regiment, 25th Division, I became particularly impressed with my incredible platoon sergeant, John Morris. There will never be another like him. He simply loved to fight. Morris had already been awarded the Silver Star for valor from earlier fighting, and rather than be sent home, he had volunteered for further combat. Much to my surprise, I later learned that, apart from being able to write the names of the platoon members, he was illiterate.

On my second day in command of the platoon, Morris broke me in as his new lieutenant. That's when I first learned that Sergeant Morris loved to have fun, especially when it was at my expense. We were to climb the mountain at the south rim of the Punchbowl. This was where we would deploy in a blocking position in the event of an enemy breakthrough in the defense line down in the valley. With his eyes narrowing, Sergeant Morris said, "Lieutenant, we are supposed to climb that peak today. I know you West Pointers like to be first. I will be right behind you in this training exercise."

Being very out of shape from the long ship voyage, I was worried. We started the climb. I thought it would be terrible if I could not make it, and I was determined not to show any weakness. Doggedly, I continued pushing myself up the mountain. By the time we almost reached the top, I felt faint.

I might have fallen over, but Sergeant Morris spoke up, "Lieutenant, don't you think you should call a break?" I shouted, "Break!" I didn't dare sit down. My legs were so rubbery that I could never have gotten back up. So I walked around a little bit and happened to overhear one of my men complaining: "What the hell is this West Pointer trying to show us? If Morris had not suggested a break, the son of a bitch would have taken us all the way to the top without a break." Morris had a special way of concealing his smile. This was my first experience with Morris's sense of merriment, but far from the last.

Some weeks later, we were on the line in the Mundung-Ni Valley. In a letter on September 8, 1952, I wrote to my parents:

> Well, we have moved. No longer in the Punchbowl. One morning early we suddenly packed up and motored over the mountain's familiar peaks—familiar from climbing them. We went west just beyond Heartbreak Ridge to the Mundung-Ni Valley. We're on the mountains to the left of the valley. It's really a setting of some scenic beauty: high mountains with many rushing creeks and green valleys. Our company's sector is an exceptionally strong one.
>
> I don't intend for one minute to glorify war, a saying that has produced more good than bad. But I will say that my job is a deeply satisfying one. My platoon has an extended front to defend, which is strongly held by our 90 men. Imagine that, a platoon of 90! We have the attached firepower, which gives us more firepower than a company in the last war.
>
> This has presented a problem in organization and administration. For our platoon was not meant to be that large. But we have overcome those drawbacks, and things run smoothly and the men work well together. It is just like J. T. Lupton always said about business, "It's a personnel problem: getting people to know and understand their jobs, and realize the importance of those jobs."

Mundung-Ni Valley was strategic because the Chinese and the North Korean forces met there on the battle line. The generals decided the time had come to probe this nexus. I was told that my company had been selected for the probe. The war-torn Heartbreak Ridge was on our right. At that time no contact had been made with the enemy for months.

My first patrol dropped down that valley in the middle of the night. We moved around vacant trenches. Then suddenly, through the darkness, the valley lit up all around us from rifle and machine-gun fire. My first concern was to avoid the bullets whistling barely over my head, coming not from the enemy but rather from the corporal just behind me with his Browning automatic rifle! Fortunately, I was able to reposition him before becoming a victim of his friendly fire. As we rapidly returned fire, the whole valley was alit for fifteen minutes or so. I called out to my men, "Everyone okay? Stay steady!"

An amazed battalion commander was on the telephone line. He couldn't believe my unit was still intact. He said, "I think you have accomplished your mission. You have done your probe. We now know that there is real resistance in the valley. Pull back!" We did so with relief.

A week later, another patrol was sent probing into that valley. The lieutenant was shot up and lost a leg, and three others were badly wounded. We had been lucky. Through luck I had immediately gained the reputation as a tested and outstanding patrol leader. Going forward, I would lead a patrol once or twice a week.

I also began taking my platoon on regular night patrols. At about this time, my father sent me a magnificent pearl-handled knife with a holster, which Sergeant Morris admired tremendously. He would often kid about it. The protocol was for the lieutenant and the platoon sergeant to never go on the same patrols. So, when I was going out, he would always say, "Lieutenant, you have got nothing to worry about. If you get into trouble, I am going to come out and rescue your knife. It will be safe!" When I later received command of my own company, and Sergeant Morris and I finally parted ways, the knife would be my gift to him.

As the months wore on, I realized I was riding to fame on Sergeant Morris's shoulders. He built the best bunkers on the entire Army front. When the colonels and generals would come to inspect, the reputation of our platoon as top-notch was clearly established. I did not write my parents about Sergeant Morris's lack of religious faith but I did describe his practical abilities. I wrote, "Three days ago, he commented

> that our platoon command post was inadequate, and that he wanted to build another one. So I gave the word and construction started. This natural-born engineer then began construction on the best command post I had seen in Korea, quite a bit better than the regimental commanders' post, much to my chagrin. This was downright embarrassing."

As the weeks passed, Sergeant Morris began to egg me on a bit. We looked across the valley to a Chinese outpost. The top of the small mountain was rimmed with trenches. When Morris learned of my interest in military history, he announced that he wanted to enhance my military experience. We began to work together on a battle plan for a dawn attack on an entrenched enemy outpost. For one month, each morning just before dawn, a recoilless rifle platoon temporarily attached to my platoon would fire directly on those trenches for fifteen minutes. With the daily shellings the Chinese forces would become accustomed to taking cover in the trenches with their heads down. On the day of the planned attack, the recoilless rifle platoon would once again fire into the enemy trenches, but this time the plan was to surprise them. We would climb the steep side of the hill to the top of the trenches during the shelling and, when the shelling stopped, storm the trenches and capture the outpost.

Because of concerns about likely casualties, we had to go through corps headquarters to gain approval for the plan. The predawn attack was approved, and we began shelling the outpost daily for an entire month. When the morning came for the actual attack, I led my men to a point just below the steep rise toward the enemy trenches, where we waited. With the first sign of daybreak, I ordered the direct fire that would force the Chinese to stay crouched in their trenches, unaware of our ascent.

The first recoilless round was fired on time, but to my utter astonishment, it didn't land anywhere near the Chinese trenches. Instead, the round landed on top of my platoon. I assumed it must have just been a single misfire, but I was wrong. The next rounds of fire continued to pour down on us, the shrapnel whizzing through the air amongst my men.

To make a very bad situation much worse, the Chinese seized the moment, climbing on top of their trenches, and, with a clear view of our exposed position below, they began to throw satchels of dynamite in our direction. Our first man was wounded, soon followed by others. Morris called out to me, "Let's charge the trenches!" I shot back, "We are not here to slaughter our own platoon. We don't have a chance. Something has gone terribly wrong!"

With several of my men already wounded, I ordered the platoon to pull back. On the way back, I received a radio message that the battalion commander had already relieved the recoilless rifle platoon commander. For some inexplicable reason, that morning he had shifted from using direct fire, the way we had practiced it for an entire month, to indirect fire. That required calculating the horizontal plane and elevation angles instead of relying on a direct line of sight between the weapon and the target, and clearly his calculations were way off. What came over him, we will never know. We were damn fortunate that we got out with a few casualties, but no loss of life.

Even amid all of this chaos, Sergeant Morris managed to distinguish himself. He began firing at some of the grenades being tossed down at us from the Chinese trenches, and actually managed to hit a few, and that may have saved my life. That earned him a cartoon in the *Stars and Stripes* newspaper with the caption, "A modern Sergeant York."

After four months, I had come into my own as a platoon leader. Despite the setback of our daring raid run amok, our platoon was riding high with successful patrols. A widely respected general, Major General Samuel T. Williams, with the nickname of "Hangin' Sam," took over our division. He earned that nickname by relieving so many company commanders.

Over the course of a few months, we had the good fortune of relieving the 1st Marine Division multiple times, after they had faced heavy fighting and managed to quiet down the sector. Falsely or not, we attributed this phenomenon to General Williams's aggressive leadership of our division. We figured the enemy feared him.

I first met General Williams when my company occupied a blocking position on "old Bloody Ridge," not far from the eastern front of the Punchbowl. He visited my company just as an incoming round arrived. Fortunately, no one was injured, but it was an inauspicious welcome. My next contact with the general was in January, in the Kumhwa section, when Hangin' Sam arrived with three other generals in tow. He wanted to show them our company's dug-in position, holding it up as a model. He showed them our bunkers, trenches, machine-gun emplacements, and observation posts. We put on quite a show for the visiting generals. Hangin' Sam was pleased. He patted me on the back and told me the whole thing was "pretty goddamn good."

We had begun picking up stories about General Williams's WWII exploits, and the heroic actions during the invasion of Normandy that earned him the Soldier's Medal. He was assistant division commander of the 90th Infantry Division when he landed on Utah Beach on the day after D-Day. When his transport ship struck a mine, he supervised the evacuation of the wounded soldiers onto rescue crafts despite not knowing how to swim. He bravely risked his life going below deck, through the smoke and darkness, to verify that everyone had gotten out. He was the last to leave the ship before it sank, without the loss of a single life.

In Korea, whenever a fellow general took needless casualties while accomplishing little or nothing, Hangin' Sam would send word back to the division commander, with a typically blunt message: "If you goddamn people who stay in the rear would get out of your foxholes, you'd see the real situation." Yes, that's how General Williams addressed the big boys. I always felt that he was the most colorful, most respected, and toughest leader among the division commanders in Korea.

About this time I suffered a terrible loss when I learned that one of my friends, Dick McCullough, had been killed in action. He died as a result of his extraordinary acts of heroism near Ch'orwon in mid-July. Among my classmates, none was more interesting than Dick McCullough, who had drawn remarkable cartoon books on life at West Point. With his talent, he could have easily been a highly paid professional.

I later learned the story of how McCullough lost his life. In a bitter firefight, one of his soldiers lost his helmet and carbine. Dick replaced them with his own and then fearlessly continued to lead the attack. As the troops approached their hilltop objective, they faltered under a shower of enemy grenades. Dick bravely managed to toss many of the grenades that had not exploded back into the emplacement. He was wounded during this fighting, but successfully led a withdrawal and set up new defensive positions. He moved about the perimeter, encouraging the men, distributing ammunition, and directing the operation, but he sustained more wounds in the process. Even in this wounded state, he organized and spearheaded a counterattack toward the crest of the hill. He lost his life leading the charge. Dick McCullough would later receive the Distinguished Service Cross for extreme gallantry, the second-highest award for valor after only the Medal of Honor. In a letter to my parents after Dick's death, I wrote, "If the value of life is measured in things done rather than years lived, Dick's life has been fuller than most who reach their seventies and eighties."

In wartime, loss of life is an occupational hazard, and, tragically, so it was with my time in Korea. In my company I had a young lieutenant and platoon leader from the Chicago area called "Swede" Roskam, who remained a friend throughout my life. His son Peter Roskam serves in Congress. Swede was the opposite of Sergeant Morris, being a very devout, Bible-reading Christian. His faith was tested not long after his arrival in my company, when Swede received the devastating news that his close friend Dick Wasson, part of his Bible study group, had been killed in combat. Wasson was a born leader without guile, and his early death seemed an affront to justice. Swede Roskam was about to go out on his first patrol when we received this devastating news. In spite of the losses, our work continued. About this time I wrote my parents:

> I am on the line in front with my new command. I've gotten rid of the old dead wood in certain jobs and put in younger and more capable people. We've gotten a lot of the bad habits broken and morale and pride are beginning to show when the men sense that now they are doing better than the other companies on the same things. But I can't sit back and be satisfied until this company, like the platoon in C Company, has a reputation of being head and shoulders above their contemporaries. Hard work? Yes!

One day I was called in to meet with the regimental commander. Much to my amazement, he informed me that I was to take over C Company of the 14th Infantry. While this promotion would typically come with the rank of captain or major, I would remain a lieutenant. It was a challenging experience assuming command of a company in combat. It was made doubly challenging by the fact that the company had to be reorganized from top to bottom. The regimental commander told me that I was being sent there for that expressed purpose. The company had suffered heavy casualties on Heartbreak Ridge and didn't seem able to snap out of it.

When I arrived to take command, my new company was deployed to the front, and the weather had turned very cold. There had been a recent ice storm, and the trenches on the steep mountainside were frozen over and slippery. I was cold and my boots lacked good traction. I was slipping all over the place.

It seemed ironic. I had finally fulfilled my dream of becoming a company commander, and yet I was so miserable. I took comfort in an extraordinary book from World War II that I had brought with me. *Company Commander* was written by war veteran Charles MacDonald, who described war in its most unglamorous terms. In the opening page of his classic, he wrote:

> The characters of this story are not pretty characters. They are not even heroic, if lack of fear is requisite for heroism. They are cold, dirty, rough, frightened miserable characters: GIs, Johnny Doughboys, dog faces, foot sloggers, poor bloody infantrymen, or as they like to call themselves combat infantrymen, but they win wars. This is a personal story, an authentic story. And to make a story about war authentic you must see a war—not a hasty taste of war but the dead.[2]

In any event, I had long aspired to be a company commander in combat. For better or for worse, I had my aspiration fulfilled in Korea. It recalled the old adage that you should be careful what you wish for.

Nevertheless, wartime is a unique if unforgiving crucible for forging leaders and leadership qualities. I believe that there is no greater challenge, nor greater opportunity for personal development, than commanding an infantry company for an extended period in combat. At higher levels of command such as a battalion or regiment, commanders have to make their presence felt only episodically. A company commander has to be present and accounted for at all times.

I did have the sense, however, to know when to command, when to hover, and when to lay back. For example, I understood that there was no more important person in the company than the mess sergeant. Cooking was one area where my personal ability to affect morale was limited. So, when I obtained an outstanding mess sergeant, I was smart enough to make him feel like a king, ensuring that no one was allowed to touch him. I made sure he had the required elbow room to do things as he saw fit.

I learned another important lesson in leadership when I went on rest and recuperation leave to Japan. I worried that my deputy in charge of the company in my absence did not know how to listen. Sometimes he would just slam the phone down when irritated, and he had a tendency to shut people out. Sure enough, while I was away, some real troubles developed. When I returned, the colonel took me aside to say, "David, you have been a great company commander, but the real test is what happens when you are not there." That was another lesson in leadership. I neglected to give my deputy the appropriate training, and thus his failure was on me.

An exciting interlude occurred in this period with a visit from the renowned commentator Edward R. Murrow in January 1953. When I heard that Murrow might pay us a visit on his trip to the battlefront, I ordered the entire company to spruce up. We had a talkative and gossipy sergeant temporarily assigned to us, who was often called "Sergeant Blowhard." I made it very clear to the staff that in sprucing up for the Murrow visit, this sergeant was to be out of the picture. When I was alerted that Murrow had arrived, I rushed out of my command post only to find that the talkative blowhard sergeant was already bending Murrow's ear. Fortunately for me, I really hit it off with Murrow, and he came back the next day. Unfortunately, he actually enjoyed the company of Sergeant Blowhard and asked that he accompany us as well. Murrow and I would form a friendship that carried on long after the war, but I never could figure out what he saw in Sergeant Blowhard.

In another instance, the regimental commander called me in to inform me that my company had been selected to serve as the honor company in the corps. For the next two months we would serve back at corps headquarters as the honor guard. I soon learned that the previous honor company command-ers had been relieved of their command, and a congressional investigation had been launched looking into a rash of accidental injuries. General Wil-liams was furious, and he sent word, squeezed in between a lot of cussing, that he knew no accidental injuries would occur during Abshire's tenure as commander of the honor company.

As for accidental injuries and wounds, I had a long-standing policy that whenever a patrol came back from duty, both the squad and platoon leaders would double-check the breeches of their weapons to ensure that they were not loaded, and then record this action in writing. We kept a foolproof log that I initiated for this singular purpose. I was confident we would have no problems with accidental wounds.

We also had a platoon of the company that would be in the rear of the corps for extra protection. I had no lieutenant in command of the platoon at that point, but I did have an outstanding sergeant who had volunteered to stay on, effectively extending his time in Korea. We were in good hands, or so I thought. Seven days after we had settled in, the orderly handed me the phone and said the sergeant in command of my platoon's rear area needed to speak to me urgently. When I took the phone, he said, "Lieutenant, one of our men was shot." I was in denial. "That's not possible. We have that sheet proving that everything was double-checked."

"I know, sir, but we've had a man shot," the sergeant said. My orderly interrupted, "General Williams's aide wants to speak with you." I picked up the phone expecting the worst, already trying to convince myself that I really did not want to have a military career anyway. I was informed that the general's helicopter would escort me to division headquarters. I was on my way to see Hangin' Sam, certain I would be his next victim.

I entered into the general's tent and threw a salute. He got to the point. "Goddamn it!" he said. "When we selected you, I was assured there would be no more problems. Now we are disgraced. There is already a congressional investigation underway!" He was all ablaze, throwing out a long contrail of expletives. As I tried to offer not an excuse but an explanation, I said, "Sir, this sergeant is outstanding. I believe he has two Silver Stars."

Williams cut in quickly, "Abshire, you said, 'this sergeant'? Don't you mean 'this private'? I'm sure you have already busted him." I did not have anything to lose now. I shot back, "I did not, and I do not have any intention of busting him. I will not break Sergeant Johnson. If you give the order to do so, I will carry out your direct order to demote him, but I will not do it on my own, only on your command. His past performance has been too outstanding."

General Williams appeared livid. He put his two hands on his pearl-handled pistols as if he were getting ready to shoot me. Then, to my surprise, he shouted, "Get back onto my goddamn helicopter and get back to your goddamn command before someone else is shot! I'm flying to corps headquarters. Somehow I'm going to have to explain why we are not going to break Sergeant Johnson."

Life can be strange at times, and never stranger than during wartime. This incident actually brought General Williams and myself much closer, and we even became good friends.

Following my time in the honor guard, we were back in the action. Beginning at the end of May, my L Company came under a furious assault by the Chinese Communists with their attacks on Outposts Vegas, Carlson, Elko, and later Berlin. After heavy suppressive fire, the enemy struck these outposts in battalion strength on the night of May 28. The attack was repelled and broke off, but only to be renewed in the early morning hours of the 29th. Elements of my regiment, the 14th Infantry, were thrown into battle to reinforce the Turkish forces holding these outposts. Heavy fighting continued during daylight hours, with the enemy renewing new attacks on Carlson and Elko. The 14th Infantry's counterattack on May 30 regained and secured

Elko, where we relieved a Turkish brigade. Nevertheless, the communist forces were eventually able to capture and consolidate at great cost Outposts Carlson, Vegas, and Elko.

On the night of July 7, 1953, in the vicinity of Sonch-on Dong, elements of the 21st Marine Division began to relieve some of the Army's 25th Division. The operation was about half complete when the enemy suddenly fired concentrated heavy artillery and mortars in the midst of a replacement-in-force operation, causing much confusion among the troops.

Despite the heavy enemy shelling, I had to leave my company command post. All communications were cut with the second platoon, delaying departure until further orders. In all of the commotion, either the second platoon convoy lost me or I had lost it. In any event, this was not my finest hour. I had no choice but to turn back around and head into the fire in search of the lost platoon. Luckily, when things were at their worst, my jeep driver and I bumped into the lost platoon, and we led them to safety.

Ironically, for what seemed like my biggest failure in the war, I was recommended for the Silver Star. I eventually received the Bronze Star Medal with V for Valor for going through a field of fire and a near-death experience of my own making. The resulting citation for valor noted my "saving many lives and much equipment" but omitted the part about me somehow losing a marching unit. The former makes better reading than the latter. South Korean president Syngman Rhee honored the 25th Division by bestowing the presidential unit citation, which cited us for "gallant and courageously defending the Munson-Changdan sector and these outposts, and the 14th Infantry relief of the Turkish brigade with high acclaim."

I could not recount my Korean War experience without a tribute to my classmate Joe Clemons. My exploits pale by comparison. He somehow avoided death and elevated himself into the annals of wartime fame at Pork Chop Hill in the spring of 1953. Pork Chop Hill became an apt symbol of a war in which much was lost and relatively little gained. S. L. A. Marshall wrote a book on the battle, which then became a film starring Gregory Peck. The hill was one of several exposed outposts in front of the main line of resistance, each defended by a single company or platoon positioned in sandbagged bunkers that were connected with trenches.

After veteran Chinese forces captured the outpost on Pork Chop Hill in a surprise attack, Company K, commanded by Lieutenant Joe Clemons, and Company L, 31st Infantry, were ordered to counterattack. Their attack began at four thirty a.m. on April 17. By dawn they reached the main trenches on top of the hill but suffered almost 50 percent casualties, and half of Company L's troops had not been able to leave the trenches of an adjacent outpost, Hill 200. Joe Clemons, in tactical command of the assault, requested reinforcements. Company G, commanded by Walt Russell, was immediately sent forward. All three companies were subjected to almost continuous shelling by artillery as they cleared bunkers and dug in again. The fighting went on for five days before General Maxwell Taylor finally drove up to the division commander, Major General Art Trudeau, and told him retaking the hill was not worth any more American lives. In trying to retake the outpost, Joe Clemons had gone up Pork Chop Hill with 135 men. He came back down with only 14.

The companies of the 31st Infantry were down to a combined 25 survivors. In *The Coldest Winter*, noted author David Halberstam concludes that Pork Chop Hill was "almost a symbol of the emptiness of the last stages of the war, so much to be invested for so little gain." Pork Chop Hill was also a symbol of the inefficacy of attrition warfare, with the shelling during the battle exceeding that of Verdun and Kwajalein. After the war, the very modest Clemons retired from the Army and deservedly enjoyed life in Hawaii.

When Dwight D. Eisenhower entered the White House in 1953, he brought a new toughness to the U.S. approach to national security, one that sometimes included threats of escalation unless adversaries backed down. After all, this was the general who had successfully conducted D-Day, the greatest military action in the history of the world, and his threats were taken seriously.

But Eisenhower's leadership was about much more than intimidation, as I would note in my war letters. I was from a Taft Republican family from East Tennessee, one that was especially close to Congressman Carroll Reece, who had been the chair of the 1946 Republican Party. In a letter home, I wrote:

> Eisenhower has shown a kind of genius in the campaign. Last July, the Republican Party was split right down the middle. Spite and hatred popped up again and again and again at the convention. Yet, Eisenhower united, smoothed over, and consolidated. He didn't do it just as a flabby politician, or a yes man. Though he got the idea from Lodge and Dewey, and made them pull in the direction of mine and Taft's, and MacArthur's.

I went on to predict that in view of his actions from July to November of 1953, "He is going to make one of the greatest presidents, for I believe that he is going to be the great commander of many fine minds that will go to Washington."

Even as representatives from the United States, Korea, and China negotiated an armistice in 1953, the Chinese mounted brutal limited offensives to gain leverage and show their continued resolve. Some of the most intense fighting during the entire war ensued before the truce finally came in June 1953.

That was the big picture, but my company commander's picture was more granular. My company was moved to the extreme left of the front line. Just in front of my position, the Imjin River broadened in a wide sweep. The Chinese attacked viciously and often, and we were pulled out in preparation for counterattacks to regain the lost ground.

Having already endured intense fighting, B Company of the 14th Infantry was badly beaten up in the first counterattack. C Company, now commanded by Swede Roskam, who started out in my L Company, was also put on alert.[3]

As a Marine colonel briefed me on the plan for the counterattack, he pointed toward two war-torn hills devoid of any trees. "There lies our objective. We have already lost seven marine platoons trying to capture it." I asked, "Sir, how did you maneuver these seven platoons?" He responded, "In the Marines, we go straight up the hill. That is the way we fight. This is not the Army, and I know that you never fought in the Pacific in World War II. So, you haven't had the experience of going straight up the hill."

After this staggering briefing, I wrote my parents what I thought would be my last letter. I told them that I had had a fine life. In an attempt to raise the spirits of my men, I told them they had never had a finer hour. In my hearts of hearts, having studied many brilliant campaigns, I realized my operation at dawn hardly qualified as even sane. The battle plan was reminiscent of Tennyson's "The Charge of the Light Brigade": "Theirs not to reason why, theirs but to do and die . . ." After the meeting, I dared to "sack out" for an hour until midnight. I slept fitfully. The corporal gently shook me awake and said that the attacker would be delayed for another day. I was relieved. It was delayed each day for ten days straight until it was finally called off.

Little did I know that the attack was called off because of the armistice negotiations in Panmunjom. On June 5, 1953, the communist forces had finally agreed with the U.N. proposals. It was not until July 9, 1953, that South Korean president Rhee agreed to not obstruct the armistice, though he still refused to sign it. In the three weeks following the general agreement on June 5, the United Nations forces suffered some 17,000 battle casualties and more than 3,300 fatalities. As it turned out, I was one of the lucky ones.

Why the delay? Rhee was angry that he was to only rule "half a country," and he sought to undermine the talks as a way to preserve his position and influence after the war. In violation of the current deal on repatriations of prisoners of war between the communist forces and the U.N., for instance, Rhee ordered a mass release of North Korean prisoners of war. It took considerable hand-holding by Assistant Secretary of State Walter Robertson before Rhee finally relented to the terms of the armistice. A secret plan, code-named "Everready," was in place to take Rhee into custody if he did not ultimately agree to the armistice, at which point the vice president of South Korea would have taken his position.[4]

As Halberstam noted in *The Coldest Winter*, "Korea was a place where almost every key decision on both sides turned on a miscalculation." He argued, "In the single greatest American miscalculation of the war, Mac-Arthur decided to go all the way to the Yalu because he was sure the Chinese would not come in, and so made his troops infinitely more vulnerable."[5]

I had long studied the differences between wars of attrition and wars of agility and maneuver, having the greatest distain for the former and the greatest admiration for the latter. As I read about such strategies as a teenager back at home in Minnekahda, I never imagined that one day my own life would, in fact, hang precariously in the balance between those very different approaches to war. And yet it did in Korea.

I will end this chapter with a letter I received some fifty years later. It represents the most redeeming aspect of my time in Korea and my experience as a combat commander in a time of war.

Sir,

Fifty years ago we stood together as the guns in Korea fell silent. A long time ago but how swift time passes. I can't express my gratitude to you for saving my life and whether you believe it or not is irrelevant. I was privileged to take out much more than I brought to Korea. The impact of you and your men focused my life, for which I will be grateful forever.

Thank you
I will never forget

Love,
One of your lieutenants
Charles W. Parrott, Jr. M.D.

5

A Master in Strategy

Georgetown, Eisenhower, and Project Solarium

With the implementation of the Korean Armistice, I decided to further my global education. I did this by agreeing to help escort an Allied troop transport back to the United States from Korea. Along the way we delivered Korean, Turkish, Greek, and Belgian troops back to their home ports. With the stress of the war behind us, our playful sides had a chance to emerge.

I remember a homemade trivia game we played with Allied officers over the course of a few weeks. The game was actually rigged, both by the Dutch officer who played the game's host, posing the trivia questions, and, I must confess, by myself. All of the questions and answers came from one book, which I had studied well in advance. Game after game, I looked smarter and smarter. The others were dumbfounded by my seemingly impeccable knowledge of all things. Eventually, as we docked, the Dutch officer and I shared our secret with the other players. Fortunately, they laughed as much as we did.

I mention this anecdote because it is a bit ironic. The role I played in this "fool 'em once, fool 'em twice" exercise was exactly the opposite of the way I was in real life, both back then and throughout my life. In the game I played the role of the slick guy with all of the answers, regardless of the subject, who needed help from no one. Yet in my real life, any success I achieved resulted from my ability to recognize the areas where I fell short and then reach out to others who possessed the needed expertise to bridge the gap. The anecdote about the rigged game is also ironic because ultimately I believe that much of my success in real life stemmed from my reputation for

41

sincerity. As I look back at my career, it was sincerity in my devotion to the matter at hand, coupled with my persistence, which repeatedly were the key elements in my successes.

Two of the most important milestones in my life illustrate the point about the value of sincerity and persistence. It took no less than three proposals before my wife Carolyn accepted my hand in marriage. Coincidentally, it also took three pitches before the former chief of naval operations, Admiral Arleigh Burke, accepted my proposal to create what would become the Center for Strategic and International Studies (CSIS). But I'm getting ahead of myself.

When I left Korea, I just missed, by one month, a battlefield promotion to the rank of captain. Such promotions were typical for company commanders with similar records as mine, especially after I had led a company in combat for nine months. When I learned that promotion would be delayed for a year or so, I first began to consider leaving the Army and creating a new life in Washington, D.C. Furthermore, the new Eisenhower administration was discussing cutting back the Army. At that time it was all but unthinkable to imagine that the United States would get involved in yet another ground war in Asia in little more than a decade, let alone in a place few of us knew much about called Vietnam.

Because I had so immersed myself in the study of strategy growing up, it felt fortuitous that I was beginning my new career in Washington with one of the greatest strategic thinkers of modern times leading our nation. President Dwight D. Eisenhower's strategic leadership was inspirational to me personally, and it came at a critical moment when the nation was still setting the course that would culminate in the "American Century."

When I arrived in Washington, Eisenhower had recently won a crushing victory over Democrat Adlai Stevenson. There was much excitement surrounding the administration of this new president, the former five-star general who commanded the largest invasion in history during World War II. Certainly Eisenhower confronted a daunting inbox the moment he entered the Oval Office: end the war in Korea, secure Western Europe, stabilize and strengthen a U.S. economy burdened by wartime spending, and devise a grand strategy that would keep the nation secure.

While in Korea, I had used all of my sources back in Washington to follow the sweeping new initiatives proposed by President Eisenhower to meet these complex challenges. Given my background in strategy, I was particularly interested in an initiative the Eisenhower administration was calling Project Solarium.

The purpose of Project Solarium was to examine different policy options in response to the Soviet Union's post–World War II expansion. The goal was to bring strategic coherence and sustainability to that critical effort.

The Truman administration had put in place a number of outstanding programs and initiatives, including the Marshall Plan for rebuilding Europe and the creation of NATO. But it had done a poor job tying them all together and integrating them into a functional grand strategy. The Eisenhower administration launched Project Solarium to answer that challenge. In true Eisenhower consensus-building fashion, the exercise included not only his own national security team but also experts in the field from across the government and the private sector.

Project Solarium was structured around three competing teams working in parallel. Each team comprised high-level experts collaborating to develop a specific, comprehensive strategy for defending the United States and meeting the challenge of Soviet expansionism. Team A was assigned the containment policy option, which sought to limit Soviet expansion and minimize the potential for armed conflict. Team B had a similar mandate, though it was encouraged to take a harder line toward the Soviets, relying less on allies and more on nuclear options. Team C examined the "rollback" option aimed at reversing Soviet expansion.

Project Solarium took its name from the White House Solarium, where the initial organizational meetings on the initiative were held. As the project advanced, it took on the more prosaic title of "The First National War College Round Table Seminar," chartered to consider "American Foreign Policy, 1953–1961." Most of the work over the course of the three-month initiative was done at Fort McNair, at what is now the National Defense University.

Each task force met separately and submitted individual reports on their findings to the National Security Council and the president. After three months, the teams met together with President Eisenhower to discuss possible areas of consensus and overlap in their results, but they were too dug into their respective positions to see many such opportunities. Gifted with strategic insight, Eisenhower saw them clearly.

The president outlined a hybrid of the two containment options that eventually became his administration's "New Look" strategy. George Kennan, the Team A leader and former State Department director of policy planning who first proposed the "containment" strategy, later wrote in his diary that Eisenhower displayed "mastery of subject matter, truthfulness, and penetration."[1]

New Look became America's new grand strategy. It was comprehensive, internally coherent, and sustainable by design. The fundamental approach was an aggressive containment policy that coordinated and focused efforts across multiple government disciplines, including diplomacy, defense, and intelligence. The strategy emphasized budget and management discipline and

encouraged new approaches to old problems. Many of the subsequent investments dovetailed neatly with a domestic agenda that aimed at creating a
stronger, sounder national economy that could sustain an aggressive containment policy over the long term. The New Look strategy also depended
heavily on international alliances, nuclear deterrence, and aggressive covert
activity.

The New Look strategy diverged significantly from that of the Truman
administration. Paul Nitze, who had been Truman's director of policy planning at the State Department, believed that we were approaching a point of
maximum danger, beyond which the Soviets would achieve military superiority over the United States and its allies, leaving them open to Soviet intimidation and aggression. In contrast, the new Eisenhower doctrine that emerged
from the Project Solarium discussions and other studies was quite different.
Instead of preparing for a single, looming showdown, it looked at the long
haul, preparing for what could be years or even decades of a cold war. In that
type of scenario, the state of the economy would play a critical role. Eisenhower took the view that the health of the economy and all of the engines of
production and research and development were essential to matching the
Soviets over the long term. While many elements of New Look were
revised and adjusted by succeeding presidents (not least the commitment to
balanced budgets), this was the fundamental strategy of aggressive Soviet
containment coupled with sustainable economic development and growth
that—thirty-five years later, and twenty years after Eisenhower's death—
won the Cold War.

Among Eisenhower's first steps in implementing his new grand strategy was
to overhaul the National Security Council. The NSC was established by the
National Security Act of 1947, largely as a device to moderate some of the
conflicting bureaucratic interests that were created by the act. It was ostensibly a tool to help the president manage foreign relations and national defense,
but President Harry Truman had viewed it as an imposition of congressional
authority on his national security turf, and thus rarely convened it until the
initiation of the Korean War forced his hand.

Eisenhower, by contrast, met weekly with the NSC, and it served to keep
lines of communication open between various members of the cabinet and
the institutions they represented, and the White House national security team.
Eisenhower appreciated the importance of harmony and regularity, particularly in quelling bureaucratic infighting, but he also saw the NSC as an under-
utilized resource. He thus created the position now known as *national
security advisor* for business executive Robert Cutler, who had been on Secretary of War Henry Stimson's staff during World War II. Cutler reorganized

the national security staff and its processes, creating the Planning Board to develop and vet policy options for dealing with national security issues proactively. Independent of the rest of the NSC staff, which was largely reactive and focused on policy execution, the Planning Board provided the NSC with a full range of policy alternatives, highlighting departmental points of disagreement—or so-called policy splits. This provided Eisenhower and his NSC staff with the means to deliberate, and make decisions objectively, independent of the back-room trade-offs between rival bureaucracies that too often produced "a fait accompli to be accepted or rejected,"[2] as author John P. Burke noted in his book *Honest Broker? The National Security Advisor and Presidential Decision Making.*

I believe that maintaining unity of effort and freedom of action are critical components of successful strategy. Eisenhower was able to successfully balance those elements of strategy as he faced the Indochina crisis of 1954. Despite the American tradition of anticolonialism, the United States had been supporting France's defense of its Southeast Asian colonies since 1946. The policy was initiated to secure France's role at the center of a stable, peaceful, and prosperous postwar Western Europe. Its continuation was justified on containment grounds once Ho Chi Minh, the leader of the independence movement, secured Soviet backing and declared himself and his movement as communist. By 1954, the U.S. was paying 75 percent of the cost of France's war in Vietnam, but the French were still losing. That spring, when Viet Minh guerrillas besieged a large contingent of Foreign Legion troops in an isolated northeastern valley called Dien Bien Phu, the French asked for U.S. air strikes and further direct engagement. The strident French requests created a serious challenge for Eisenhower, who needed to manage the demands and expectations of an array of disparate allies whose interests often conflicted. He did not want the communists to win, but neither could he have the United States intervene directly in defense of colonialism. In the aftermath of a Korean War that claimed the lives of more than 35,000 U.S. troops, he also wanted to avoid another Asian land war.

To justify his preference not to rescue the French, Eisenhower put a number of conditions on a U.S. intervention. While the conditions were specific to the situation, Eisenhower's use of objective criteria to depoliticize the question of intervention was not. It was another example of his use of civil discussion and political debate as potent tools to protect his policy initiatives and presidential prerogatives. He is the only president to have articulated our criteria for military engagement so clearly. In the end, the administration declined to intervene in Vietnam, and the French suffered a historic defeat at Dien Bien Phu, ending their colonial presence in Indochina.

Eisenhower further strengthened his New Look grand strategy with investments in the national security sector, diplomatic and intelligence initiatives, and the U.S. economy as a whole. He appointed a presidential science advisor and established the Advanced Research Project Agency in the Defense Department, now called the Defense Advanced Research Project Agency, or DARPA. He also created the U.S. Information Agency to bolster official diplomatic efforts and increased funding through the Central Intelligence Agency for the nominally independent Radio Free Europe and Radio Liberty. He created the President's Foreign Intelligence Advisory Board and filled it with scientific and intellectual heavyweights, including Bill Baker, the president of Bell Labs, and Edwin Land, perhaps the world's foremost expert in the science of optics.

Most famously, Eisenhower launched the National Interstate and Defense Highway System, now referred to as the Interstate Highway System, to modernize America's transportation infrastructure and support economic growth and investment for generations to come. The creation of the highway system was indicative of Eisenhower's leadership style and strategic frame of mind.

As a young Army Tank Corps officer back in 1919, Eisenhower was an observer on a cross-country expedition from New York to San Francisco undertaken by the U.S. Army Motor Truck Corps. American roads were so bad at that time that the trip took two months to complete, at an average speed of less than six miles per hour. In response, Congress funded a system of paved, two-lane federal highways.

With the Federal Highway Act of 1956, Eisenhower sought to replace that system with a network of multilane, limited-access, divided motorways. The highway system was patterned on the German autobahn, which he had seen while leading the Allies to victory over Germany. Eisenhower's plan called for 41,000 miles of divided highways at a potential cost of $101 billion. To maintain a balanced budget, Eisenhower proposed a self-financing option under which a national gasoline excise tax would cover 90 percent of the project's costs and the individual states would provide the remaining 10 percent. As Geoffrey Perret notes in his contribution to *Triumphs and Tragedies of the Modern Presidency*, Eisenhower won the support of Democrats in Congress and governors from both parties through an "approach [that] was non-partisan yet persistent . . . he had a clear idea of where he wanted to go and was flexible about how he got there, and he did not seek to capitalize, either personally or as the leader of his party, on this legislative success."[3]

The civility of America's Founders, and its greatest political heroes, guided Eisenhower's modus operandi, both as General of the Army and president of the United States. He reached out to all sides with respect. He listened in order to gain understanding, and in so doing he fostered trust. He firmly believed that "trust is the coin of the realm." Eisenhower always sought out support and engaged Congress to win its backing for his policy initiatives. For him, achievement was the arbiter of success, not credit. As a result, for a generation after he left the White House, President Eisenhower's reputation lagged far behind his actual accomplishments. But those accomplishments stand as proof that even in the modern era, civility remains an essential tool of political power.

During these exciting times, I arrived back in the United States, serving first as a general's aide and then teaching at the prestigious Infantry School at Fort Benning, Georgia, where I groomed officers for the future. I also began to write frequent articles for the *Infantry Journal* and other publications. Topics I covered ranged from night operation patrols to the tactical use of nuclear weapons.

As a West Point graduate, I then made the tough decision to resign from the Army to begin graduate work in history at Georgetown University. Looking back, I am very glad that two classmates of mine made a different decision at the end of their obligatory five years of service. Cadet E. C. "Shy" Meyer was a close colleague at the Infantry School. He too had been at the point of resigning, which would have been a tragedy. Instead, Shy Meyer remained in the Army and went on to become one of our greatest Army chiefs of staff, doing much to rebuild the army after Vietnam. Another classmate and lifelong friend who did not leave service was Buzz Aldrin, who as an astronaut would become only the second human being to walk on the moon. In more recent years, Aldrin joked to me that at his advancing age they could send him on a trip to the moon, without having to worry about the return trip.

In addition to the funds I received from the GI Bill, I managed to bring in some income from my writing, including from a regular column for the *Infantry Magazine*. For the *Naval Institute Proceedings*, I did an analysis of the dramatic events of the Battle of Navarino in the Greek War of Independence, where the British Lord Codrington sent the Ottoman fleet to the bottom of the sea without clear orders to do so. I also started a column in the *Chattanooga Times*. A big breakthrough occurred when noted author and columnist on military affairs Hanson Baldwin asked me to write several book reviews for *The New York Times*. Thus, I began to assemble a pretty big scrapbook of my writings, which would help enormously in later job interviews.

In 1955, I began my doctorate program at Georgetown University, studying full-time under revered scholar Father Joseph Durkin. I was truly smitten with everything about Georgetown University, beginning with its remarkable founder, John Carroll, who came from an aristocratic Maryland family. Today a magnificent statue of him greets visitors at the entrance of Georgetown University.

In 1776, the Continental Congress asked Carroll, his cousin Charles Carroll, Samuel Chase, and Benjamin Franklin to travel to Quebec to persuade the French Canadians to join the revolution. Although the group was unsuccessful, it introduced Carroll to the government of the new republic. After the Quebec bishop Jean-Olivier Briand excommunicated him for his political activities, Carroll accompanied the ailing Franklin back to Philadelphia.

Among my most treasured achievements are the Ph.D., John Carroll Award, and honorary doctorate that I received from this great university, where I also taught as an adjunct professor. During my time at Georgetown, I became a great admirer of the Jesuit order and grew especially close to Father Durkin. With his guidance and help, I was able to fast-track my doctorate without first completing a master's course. He also helped convince me to write my doctoral dissertation on Senator David Key.

Key was thrust into the spotlight after the 1876 presidential election between Rutherford B. Hayes and Samuel J. Tilden, which proved to be one of the most contentious and controversial in our nation's history to that date. Tilden had won the popular vote, and, after a first count, Tilden appeared to have won 184 electoral votes to Hayes's 165. However, 20 electoral votes were in dispute in four states. The compromise that eventually put Hayes into the White House called for the removal of all federal troops from the South, the construction of a railroad linking southern states to the transcontinental railroad, and legislation to help industrialize the South. It also called for the appointment of a southern Democrat to Hayes's cabinet.

Key, a former Confederate colonel, had vigorously campaigned against Tilden, yet intermediaries approached Key to join the cabinet of former Union general Rutherford B. Hayes. Against much outrage in the southern wing of the Democratic Party, this "turncoat" Key made the move in the secret dealings and was given the powerful cabinet position of postmaster general. He controlled more than 27,000 post offices and the mail-service subsidies for state coaches, railroads, and steamships. Since the days when Andrew Jackson instituted the spoils system, the postmaster general had been called the "cabinet politician," for he controlled the most gigantic patronage organization in the nation. In an attempt to quell the partisanship, Key tempered patronage with an effective merit system.

Key, with the backing of President Hayes, set out to promote reconciliation, as Lincoln would have had it. The former Confederate colonel David Key and the former Union general Rutherford B. Hayes toured the North and the South to promote reconciliation and to seek to erase the color line. In

1878, there were rumblings that Democratic control of the House and the Senate in the next Congress would result in an attempt to oust Hayes and inaugurate Tilden. Key turned on his own party in his "Letter to the South," which was featured in newspapers around the nation. No Congress, present or future, wrote Key, had the power to subvert President Hayes's title, once "settled irrevocable by the Forty-fourth Congress in the act creating the electoral commission under which he was legally inaugurated." The postmaster general asserted that "the Forty-sixth Congress will have no more right to ignore him and to recognize the defeated candidate, Mr. Tilden, than Mr. Hayes would have to send a file of soldiers to the House of Representatives" to unseat some congressman that he might think fraudulently elected. In the final analysis, his actions helped preserve the Union.

I was able to take advantage of a Chattanooga family connection, which provided me with valuable original source material for my dissertation on Senator Key. My great-aunt Sara, the second wife of Cartter Patten, was David Key's daughter.[4] As a young girl, she had filled scrapbooks with family correspondence. This vast body of material became the basis for my dissertation of Senator David Key, the reconciler.

Among the grand mansions in Chattanooga, few are better preserved in their original form than Ashland Farms, which is nestled at the foot of Lookout Mountain. There I sat with my great-aunt Sara Key Patten. As she reminisced on her father's career, I sorted through boxes, some of which had remained unopened for decades. This treasure trove of information became the basis for both my dissertation and the book I later wrote, *The South Rejects a Prophet: The Life of Senator D. M. Key, 1824–1900*, which was published by Praeger in 1967.

This was a glorious period of intellectual exploration for me. As an adjunct to my work at Georgetown, I began to write whenever possible. During this time, I lived in a small apartment in the State House building on Massachusetts Avenue, just off of Dupont Circle. I generally walked to evening classes at Georgetown across the bridge spanning Rock Creek Park. My apartment overlooked the Cosmos Club, housed in a very elaborate former home of a wealthy Washington family. The club was established in 1878, and membership was awarded on achievements in the fields of literature, science, and the humanities. At the time, I never imagined that one day I would be an elected member of the Cosmos Club.

In spite of its small size, I managed to entertain friends and relatives in my apartment at the State House. One of my friends, Charlotte Black was also my second cousin. She worked directly for the CIA's legendary Kermit Roosevelt, grandson of Theodore Roosevelt. She and her Georgetown housemates were part of a highly entertaining social circle of CIA employees. To my eternal gratitude, Charlotte Black was able to gain admittance to this group for an old infantryman like David Abshire.

One evening Charlotte brought a beautiful young lady over to the apartment named Carolyn Sample, who had dancing eyes and was full of fun. Like Charlotte, she too worked for the CIA. I took an instant liking to Carolyn but feared, with her family's strong naval heritage, that my Army background might work against me. Nevertheless, life is filled with the unexpected, and so I began my courtship of this beautiful young woman from Pensacola. I was unaware at the time, as a West Pointer who had been so grounded in the great land battles of history, that I was about to be swept out to sea by the Navy. Carolyn's father, Bill Sample, had been the youngest rear admiral in the Pacific theater during World War II. He made it through the war with just a single wound, but in October of 1945 his aircraft went missing after it failed to return from a familiarization flight near Wakayama, Japan. Soon after take-off the plane had communicated with a nearby ship, and there was nothing to indicate any problems at that time. Nevertheless, that would prove to be the last time the crew was heard from. In 1948, Admiral Sample's remains were discovered, along with those of the seven other members of the flight crew, in the aircraft's wreckage. The cause of the wreck is unknown, although in his last letter home, he wrote that daily flight patrols of the Wakayama area would continue "if the typhoon permits." One can only speculate about the possibility that the plane encountered inclement weather left over from the typhoon.

Carolyn's mother, Mary Lee Lamar Sample, eventually remarried another naval officer, Captain George W. Anderson. Anderson was a widower with three young children. He was a surefooted type, good-looking, and was selected to serve on Eisenhower's staff working on the formation of NATO. By the time I had started courting his stepdaughter, Anderson had risen through the ranks to admiral in command the United States Sixth Fleet. Clearly Anderson was going places. President Eisenhower thought so highly of him that he noted in his autobiography that he almost appointed Anderson as White House chief of staff.

As Carolyn and I moved into our next year of courtship, there was a great deal of speculation regarding whether Admiral Anderson would become the next chief of naval operations (CNO), replacing Admiral Arleigh Burke. Those would certainly not be easy shoes to fill. Burke had already served three terms as CNO, and was a legend going back to his naval victories at the Solomon Islands during World War II.

One of Carolyn's closest family friends was Rear Admiral Albert Cushing "Putty" Read. Read was the first man to make a transatlantic flight. In 1919, he flew his famous NC4 over the Atlantic with stops in Newfoundland, the

Azores, and Lisbon, before finally arriving in Plymouth, England. He subsequently received the Congressional Gold Medal. Putty's opinion of me carried a great deal of weight. The Reads were quite wealthy; one of their homes was right on the shore of Virginia Beach. Carolyn and I were invited to come down.

Putty was a man of few words, and I was unsure of what he thought of me as a suitor. The Reads took us to the beautiful Princess Anne Country Club. Putty kept quiet throughout, but that was not unusual. At one point I did overhear Mrs. Read say to Putty, "Why didn't she keep waiting for the right Annapolis man?" At the end of dinner, however, to my shock and surprise, Putty opened his mouth for the first time. "Take our cottage for the honeymoon," he said. To be clear, Carolyn and I were not even yet engaged, but at that point I felt I had it made. As it turned out, I was right, though, as I mentioned earlier, it did take three proposals before Carolyn finally agreed to accept my hand in marriage.

My wedding to Carolyn Sample took place in 1957 at Saint Alban's Church and was followed by a reception at the Chevy Chase Club. Some say there were one hundred admirals present. My bride still jokes that I married her just in time for her to type my dissertation. She even wrote a little poem about it:

> For David,
> There was a young girl from our nation,
> Who typed a Ph.D. dissertation,
> Said she I'm not fit
> For Ibid. and op. cit.
> And I'm sic, sic, sic of this oration.
> Love,
> Carolyn

When pressed, Carolyn would admit that she actually found my dissertation fascinating. I began racing to complete it and find a publisher. I had the advantage that, increasingly at that time, American Ph.D. candidates were allowed to ignore the English tradition that tended to push doctoral applicants to write on very specialized topics, which no publisher would want to print. The dramatic story of David Key, a violent secessionist who became a great unifier, begged for a wider audience, and it received one when Praeger eventually published *The South Rejects a Prophet.*

It is hard to convey the debt I owe to Congressman Carroll Reece for his support at this pivotal time in my life. At the time, he served as the chair of the Republican National Committee. Reece was an intellectual and a war hero. As a soldier in World War I, he had singlehandedly cleaned out a machine-gun nest. Being well-heeled financially, he decided to run for Congress from East Tennessee, with his district office headquartered in Johnson City. He shrewdly formed a quiet alliance with the Democratic Crump machine in West Tennessee and became a political force in the Republican Party throughout the country. The Reeces became very close to the Taft family and even raised the money for the Taft memorial on Capitol Hill. Carroll Reece became something of a mentor for me, a mentorship helped by his closeness to my Uncle Lupton Patten. I shared a special bond with Lupton, who was my mother's youngest brother.

Congressman Reece obtained a research office for Carolyn in the Library of Congress, and, as I was also looking for a job, Reece offered to call the House Republican Campaign Committee on my behalf. In preparation, I collected clippings of all of my published articles and taped them into a photo album. Reece cut through the red tape. He phoned the head staffer of the campaign committee and said, "Young Abshire here has this very impressive book of his writings. You ought to hire him." I went to see the head of the campaign committee, and he said, "We will hire you at nine." I did not know whether he meant $9 an hour or $900 a year. Much to my surprise, it turned out to be $9,000 a year, which was good money indeed at the time. In this first position, I was put on the "truth squad," which wrote speeches for the House floor to refute political attacks and untruths.

There was an attempt in 1958 to overthrow Republican congressman Charlie Halleck as House minority leader. The attempt failed, but the close call made the older generation of Republicans suddenly willing to empower the House Republican Policy Committee. The Congressional Reorganizational Act of 1945 had allowed for a government-funded policy committee, but up until that time the House had let the idea languish. John Rhodes, Gerald Ford, Mel Laird, and Al Quie were all key in getting the committee up and running.

That's how I came to be installed as the staff director of the House Republican Policy Committee. Bryce Harlow was also instrumental in my recruitment. In my work on the committee, I came to know Harlow well. I would have breakfasts with him at the White House often, and we would work together years later on Republican Party platforms. Early in his career, Harlow had been a staff director of the Armed Services Committee on Capitol Hill. He had a golden tongue with the spoken word and a writer's flair for the written word.

I often joked that the anti-intellectual House Republican Party selected me to be staff director because I was the only one around at the time with a Ph.D. More seriously, I believed there was a need for greater depth in the Republican discourse of the time.

One of my first tasks was to escort three young, outstanding Republican "comers" on a trip to Midwest college campuses. John Byrnes, the titular head of the House Policy Committee, assigned me the task of writing, critiquing, and coordinating their speeches on the various college campuses. We started in Minnesota and ended in Wichita, Kansas. The speeches went extremely well. Al Quie was a natural-born speaker and was very popular with the young students. Mel Laird would eventually become an eloquent speaker, but at this time he needed some coaching. To conclude, Mel did a magnificent job, however, in presenting one of my speeches called "Creative Conservatism," which I had originally presented during a lecture at the College of William & Mary. Milton Friedman was in the audience that day and shook his head left and right in a sign of disapproval. When the speech was over, Mel asked if Friedman suffered from St. Vitus's dance, a medical disorder characterized by involuntary jerking movements. Milton Friedman didn't believe in creative conservativism, but rather adhered to the idea that one should never tamper with the free market, period.

The next initiative, which I created on my own, was entitled American Strategy and Strength. The goal was to produce a major national report aimed at sustaining and continuing the Eisenhower defense policies. With the blessing of Congressman John Byrnes, chairman of the Republican Policy Committee, I sought out Gerald Ford to see if he would lead this initiative. Ford had been a truly outstanding member of the House Appropriations Committee on defense and was better positioned to lead the initiative than Mel Laird or any other Republican due to his superior grasp of defense issues. Ford agreed to lead my initiative.

The introduction to the *American Strategy and Strength* report read:

> Early in 1960, it seemed to certain Members of Congress that the then current debates over the so-called missile gap reflected a lack of real depth and appreciation—both of our national strategy and strength, and of how to build upon our present strategy and strength constructively for the decade just entered.
>
> It was shortly after this that the chairman of the Republican Policy Committee of the U.S. House of Representatives appointed a task force of Members to study the total strategy and strength of this Nation in relation to its conflict with the Sino-Soviet bloc.[5]

American Strategy and Strength was produced with the input of more than a dozen scholars and experts, with the top scholar being Dean William Yandell Elliott of Harvard University, who had groomed both Henry Kissinger and Zbigniew "Zbig" Brzezinski. The task force ultimately produced twenty-one separate papers, and the report summary was released on June 20, 1960.

The run-up to the 1960 presidential election produced numerous political attacks on Eisenhower's long-haul strategy. These attacks were based on the erroneous claims of a growing "missile gap" between the United States and the Soviet Union, in the Soviets' favor. Unfortunately for Eisenhower, the truth was classified. In a widely syndicated article in 1959, Joseph Alsop even went so far as to falsely describe "classified intelligence" as placing the Soviet missile count as high as 1,500 by 1963. In reality, the gap was actually in the favor of the United States. The Soviet Union really only possessed four ICBMs. However, this information had been obtained through secret U-2 flights over the Soviet Union, and Eisenhower believed that if these flights were revealed, U.S.-Soviet tensions would spike.

Nixon was so impressed with the task force and its chairman that he contemplated tapping Gerald Ford as his vice presidential candidate for the 1960 election. Unfortunately, Ford lost out after he appeared on *Meet the Press* and revealed a tendency to pause at the wrong time, which made it seem like Ford did not know the subject matter.

I'll end this chapter on a little-known historical moment that I was privileged to witness. At the 1960 Republican convention, I was in charge of the Republican national security platform, which defended Eisenhower's long-haul strategy. Given the attacks made by Republican governor Nelson Rockefeller on that strategy, Nixon acquiesced and demanded that the national security platform be changed. This infuriated President Eisenhower. He had his representative call the command center for the convention at the Blackstone Hotel in Chicago to relay a cryptic yet important message to Nixon. I happened to be standing near the phone at the time and overheard Eisenhower's message: "It's obvious Dick does not need my support in the campaign."

Sure enough, Vice President Nixon did not get President Eisenhower's critical support until the last two weeks of his campaign, which was too late to give Nixon the boost he needed. Nixon figured he could do it all without Ike's help, but he was wrong. Nixon lost a very close election to John F. Kennedy.

6

Ivory Towers and Institution Building

Georgetown's Center for Strategic Studies

With Kennedy's victory, the Republicans lost the White House. About this time, Bill Baroody, the head of the conservative American Enterprise Association (AEA), as the American Enterprise Institute was originally called, tried to persuade me to join his think tank. He had many contacts with the older Republican establishment, but none with the new breed of young Republicans whom I had worked with on Capitol Hill. The offer that Baroody made to me, however, turned out to be a bit of a misrepresentation, to put it mildly. Baroody explained that he wanted me to head what he called AEA's new "Institute for Social Science Research." With the change in the administration, I thought this might be a good time for me to make a change as well, and I accepted his offer.

When I reported to Bill Baroody's office at AEA on the first day of my supposed new job, I asked, "Is the institute in the same building?" He looked back at me somewhat sheepishly and answered, "Well, not quite. The institute does have its tax exemption; it just needs money." Needless to say, I was a bit taken aback. He tried to argue that there was no problem whatsoever, and that the money was surely right in front of me: All I needed to do was go ask for it.

Baroody noted that my good friend Congressman Carroll Reece, former chairman of the Republican National Committee, had managed to raise an excess of money for the Taft Memorial on the Capitol grounds. Those excess funds, he argued, could easily constitute the majority of the funding needed for our new institute. I asked, "Has Reece been informed about this?" Baroody's long-winded answer amounted to a no. Because I was so close to Reece, Baroody figured I could fly to Reece's home in East Tennessee to meet with him and pitch the proposition. I retorted, "Bill, Carroll Reece is bedridden and dying!" Baroody's response? "All the more reason why we should fly down to explain this to him right away."

I am a bit embarrassed to admit that we did indeed have the deathbed meeting. Carroll received us warmly, but explained that the excess funding was already slated to support Taft Fellowships.

I was aghast at this turn of events and dreaded having to tell my new bride, Carolyn, that I had just quit my job on the Hill to run this new institute, which now apparently had no funding. Carolyn quizzically and uneasily said, "Tell me more about this fellow Baroody." All I could say was, "He thinks big."

Bill Baroody is well described in *Strategic Calling* by James Allen Smith:

> Baroody himself had big dreams. Almost from the moment of his arrival at AEI in the mid-1950s, Baroody had sought to build a new set of institutions to counter what he perceived to be the liberal ascendancy in national policymaking.
>
> A deeply religious man of the Maronite Christian faith, Baroody was drawn to ideas, intellectual interplay, and philosophical debate. He was a tireless intellectual combatant. Indeed, one former colleague who usually took delight in the evening-long discussions at Baroody's dinner table confessed that Baroody's manner was both "interesting and irritating." Baroody, he said, "was a practitioner of the Socratic Method and would just keep asking questions." Baroody persisted in the role of both gadfly, always challenging orthodox opinion, and institution builder.[1]

After having been lured away from Capitol Hill with big promises, I was very relieved to learn that Baroody actually had a backup plan for me. I became director of special projects at AEA. He explained that I could do anything I wanted with my new position. At the time, there was a major crisis still stirring over Berlin, which had begun back in 1958 when Soviet premier Nikita Khrushchev demanded that the United States, Great Britain, and France pull their forces out of West Berlin within six months. This sparked a three-year crisis that would culminate in the building of the Berlin Wall in 1961. I decided to take AEA in a more international direction and commissioned studies on Khrushchev's attempt to blackmail the West. I turned out a series of papers on the Berlin crisis, which received considerable attention. Previously AEA had not taken on foreign policy issues and strategic initiatives. The Berlin series was a first.

The Berlin Series did trigger a debate within the AEA research council as to whether the organization should even be moving into the realm of foreign policy, but Baroody stood with me, and we succeeded in broadening AEA's scope. In fact, Bill Baroody was so impressed with my projects that he even agreed to my suggestion to change the organization's name from American Enterprise Association to American Enterprise Institute (AEI), broadening its scope beyond conservative economics to political, military, and foreign policy issues. The name and the broader policy agenda stuck, and remain to this day.

About this time, I began to more seriously entertain ideas I had for the creation of a new organization. In part the idea was a natural outgrowth of my lifelong fascination and deep study of military campaigns and national strategy. During these early days of my career, I also caught a bit of the entrepreneurial bug from my uncle Alex Guerry. Uncle Alex spent his life building institutions, beginning with Baylor preparatory school in Chattanooga, then as the president of the University of Tennessee at Chattanooga, and finally as the vice chancellor of Sewanee, the University of the South. Before World War II he drew up ambitious plans for Sewanee and was able to raise the significant funds needed to turn them into a reality. While my dad thought Uncle Alex could be too preachy at times, I admired him greatly. Alex Guerry helped fuel my ambition to build an institution myself someday, and that day had come.

The organization I had in mind would tackle national challenges with a comprehensive, strategic approach. With the end of World War II, the United States had, out of necessity, entered a new phase, assuming leadership on the global stage. As we were drawn into the Cold War, too often challenges were addressed piecemeal and in primarily military terms. I believed, as Eisenhower did, that the challenges of the Cold War demanded a nation that was strong both militarily and economically, which would require heavy investments in research and development. Surmounting the challenges we confronted as a nation that led the free world would require a more interdisciplinary, comprehensive, and strategic approach than was the norm before World War II, when we were largely a strategic free rider on Great Britain.

At that time, among the existing think tanks in the United States and abroad, I saw models I wanted to emulate and avoid. The Carnegie Endowment for International Peace had been established by Andrew Carnegie in 1910, and it was the oldest international affairs think tank in the United States. At the presentation of his original gift of $10 million to the endowment's trustees, Carnegie announced that it was to be used to "hasten the abolition of international war, the foulest blot upon our civilization." He went on to explain, "Although we no longer eat our fellow men or torture prisoners, or sack cities, killing their inhabitants, we still kill each other in war like barbarians. Only wild beasts are excusable for doing that in this era, for the crime of war is inherent, since it decides not in favor of the right but always of the strong. The nation is criminal which refuses arbitration and drives its adversary to a tribunal which knows nothing of righteous judgment."[2] The Carnegie Endowment for International Peace had notably remained unassociated with any political party.

The Brookings Institution has more liberal leanings. It was founded in 1916, not long after Carnegie, by the philanthropist Robert S. Brookings. It began as three organizations that were eventually merged into one in 1927, its mandate to study national public policy issues.

In 1921, Brookings Institution economists played a leading role in helping to establish the first U.S. Bureau of the Budget. Later, the Roosevelt administration turned to Brookings during the Great Depression to perform a large-scale study on the underlying causes of the economic collapse. As World War II was coming to a close, Brookings was also instrumental in helping to shape the Marshall Plan. Ironically, given the organization's reputation for liberalism, Brookings Institution's first president, Harold Moulton, came to oppose Roosevelt's New Deal policies, believing they were impeding the economic recovery.[3]

In the aftermath of World War II, the RAND Corporation was born in 1948 out of the Douglas Aircraft Company, becoming a separate organization that examined issues related to military planning, research, and development. RAND's work was often highly technical, contributing to game theory, for example, as well as linear and dynamic programming and mathematical modeling and simulation. Even in the early years, however, its scope extended beyond that of solely military issues to cover subjects such as health care and affordable housing.[4]

The School for Advanced International Studies (SAIS) was founded in 1943 by Paul H. Nitze and Christian Herter. In 1950, it retained its headquarters in Washington but became a part of Baltimore's Johns Hopkins University. SAIS's focus has always been on international relations and economics, and the graduate school has remained a respected center for political debate.[5]

The Foreign Policy Research Institute (FPRI) was established in 1955 with support from the University of Pennsylvania and the Smith Richardson Foundation. It was founded by Ambassador Robert Strausz-Hupé, an investment banker, who emigrated from Vienna in 1923. His focus was America's Cold War leadership and the struggle against the Soviet Union, and he disagreed with the containment strategy of the Eisenhower administration.

The Hudson Institute was a conservative think tank that had just been formed in Croton-on-Hudson, New York, in 1961 by Herman Kahn, Max Singer, and Oscar Ruebhausen, all of them alumni of the RAND Corporation. Their original focus was on military issues and "studying the future in unconventional ways,"[6] but later they expanded Hudson's agenda to include domestic, social, and economic issues.

On the other side of the Atlantic, the nonpartisan Institute for Strategic Studies in London, created in 1958, offered an inspiring model. Today it is known as the International Institute for Strategic Studies (IISS). While I knew that I wanted to pursue a more diverse subject matter than IISS's original focus on nuclear deterrence and arms control, I very much appreciated its dynamic work. Another desirable model for a think tank, also located in London, was Chatham House, the Royal Institute of International Affairs, with its focus on open debate and confidential discussions among members of the government, the private sector, and civil society.[7] I was blessed at one point during my tenure at CSIS to have the very talented Englishman Robin Niblett on my staff. His talent was so evident that it was not surprising that he left CSIS to become the director of Chatham House.

While I found much to admire in each of these established think tanks, the new organization that I envisioned was broader in scope and more strategic in focus. It would need to produce thoughtful publications and boast its own roster of noted experts, but I also wanted it to serve as a nexus where the weighty matters of the day could be debated in a civil fashion by the most qualified experts available. I planned to reach out nationally and internationally to find these people, bringing together academics, policymakers, private sector leaders, and journalists from across the nation and around the world.

When I first broached the notion of creating a new think tank with Baroody, he was very keen on the idea. I think he saw it as an organization that would fit well into his grand design to set up a complex of institutions, with AEI at the center, to counter what he viewed as the liberal agenda in Washington. Given my close affinity for Georgetown University, Baroody also supported my natural desire to set the new organization up there.

Unlike Baroody, however, I was already thinking of the new think tank in more bipartisan terms. I believed that what Washington needed most was a bridge where the best ideas from the right and the left could meet in the center. I was also smart enough to realize that this distinguished university would give me a degree of protection from being drawn too far to the right politically, even by very wealthy potential donors.

I reached out to Father James B. Horigan, S.J., the dean of Georgetown's graduate school. Contrary to his typical low-key personality, Father Horigan was surprisingly enthusiastic about my proposal. With the dean on my side, I then brought the idea to the university president, Father E. B. Bunn, S.J. He convened Jesuit leaders to discuss the proposal. Ultimately they concluded that a center of research and thoughtful debate could give Georgetown a more significant role in the nation's capital and create a means for it to better reach out to Washington policymakers. I soon received the good news that the university was supporting the new think tank, as long as we raised the funds.

Baroody initially favored Charles Malik as a potential head of the new center. Malik was a renowned, Harvard-educated Lebanese scholar and diplomat. However, over lunch with Malik at the Army Navy Club, we realized that he would not be a good fit. Following lunch, during our walk back to the office, Baroody asked, "What about Arleigh Burke? He has just stepped down as CNO, is world-famous now, and would be great for attracting money!" I agreed that the idea was intriguing. "Bill, that all makes a lot of sense," I told him. "I'll call on him."

Admiral Arleigh Burke had distinguished himself in both World War II and the Korean War. He was well known for standing up for what he believed to be the right course of action, regardless of the potential risk to his own career. He was both a brilliant strategist and very dedicated to those under his command. This combination fostered great trust from those who came to know him well. Whenever he disagreed with his superiors or presidents, Burke also did so based on well-reasoned arguments and strongly held beliefs, which were key attributes of his great leadership. Having served as the chief of naval operations (CNO) under both Eisenhower and Kennedy, he was also the longest-serving CNO in history by the time of his retirement.

One anecdote illustrates well Burke's fearlessness in standing up for what he believed, his art of persuasion, and his ability to foster trust. Shortly after becoming CNO under Eisenhower, Burke was stirring up trouble, as he tended to do, but this time with the very president that had appointed him. The issue was the proposed elimination of the peacetime draft. Burke believed that ending the draft would hinder the nation's ability to fulfill its growing defense obligations, especially those of the Navy. He disagreed with the Secretary of the Navy on this; he disagreed with the Secretary of Defense on this; and then he demanded to see President Eisenhower.

Burke met with Eisenhower, along with the secretaries of navy and defense, who listened in anger. Burke went on and on, laying out the reasons for his position, and Ike got redder and redder in the face. Finally, after some time, Ike slammed his fist on the table and said, "We're going to keep the draft. Meeting over. Burke, you stay back."

Burke had won the argument, but he got bawled out for the effort. Eisenhower shouted, "Don't you *ever* create a situation where you disgrace your two superiors in front of me again. Never again, Burke!" Nevertheless, the draft remained in place. Burke figured that, while he had won the argument, surely he was through as far as Ike was concerned. Surprisingly, he began to receive invitations from Eisenhower to come over to the White House for drinks and discussions. They developed a fast friendship, and I believe Ike admired Burke's forthcoming nature.

Admiral Burke possessed a naturally curious mind, and he understood the importance of being on the cutting edge, whether through embracing state-of-the-art science or by being willing to always think anew. His personality exuded warmth, which won him a wealth of friends in and out of government, at home and around the world.

I had previously met Burke only twice, most recently at the reception celebrating both his retirement and my father-in-law's new position as his replacement. With my proposal in mind, I visited with him at Burke's new office located by the reflecting pool on the National Mall, in one of the temporary buildings established during World War II for the war effort. Burke may have stepped down from his job running the Navy, but he was still very busy serving as the chairman of the Boy Scouts of America, as well as serving on the boards of four large companies. We talked about the challenges confronting Washington and were very much on the same page. I mentioned my idea for the new center. Graciously Admiral Burke put me off. He explained that as important as the proposed center was, he was already overcommitted.

Nevertheless, within a week, I returned to see Burke again. I showed him my new publication series on the Berlin crisis. He was quite impressed, and I told him I wanted to meet with him again after he had really read the series. Within a week I was back in his office. I shared with him again my keen interest in strategy, which dovetailed with his own. I knew that reaching an agreement with this legendary Navy leader would not be easy coming at it as a former West Pointer and Army field officer. So I steered the conversation toward Admiral Alfred Thayer Mahan, considered to be one of the most important American strategists of the nineteenth century. I think Burke was impressed.

I justified my persistence by recalling my work on Capitol Hill, where I had witnessed firsthand how government compartmentalization constantly worked against the strategic synergies necessary for more effective governance. I was sure he had witnessed the same in the executive branch. I then made the pitch that our center could develop clear priorities and foster a more holistic, strategic approach that helped Washington overcome this compartmentalization. Burke responded, "Dave, if we do that, we will really help the nation." I caught the "we." I knew I had him.

Then Burke threw in, "Dave, now, I need you to do something for me. I have been asked to give the Walter Edge Lecture at Princeton University, and I would like you to work on it with me." Of course, I was delighted to help. I mention this now because the theme of the lecture illustrated a significant element of Burke's modus operandi. Burke spoke often about the difference between military force and true power. In his view, presidents, generals, admirals, and ambassadors often did not understand the difference between the two. His lecture took us through the Athenian, Roman, and British Empires. He explained how they were built on, and sustained through, the power of influence. Influence went far beyond mere brute force to include diplomatic, economic, cultural, and other elements of power. While military force was sometimes necessary as potential leverage, true power was the ability to bend an opponent's will in your direction without resorting to force; to quote Sun Tzu, "The greatest victory is that which requires no battle."

We ended our conversation that pivotal day going over the practical details of Burke's involvement with the new center that I was proposing. I laid out the plans to house it at Georgetown University. Burke liked that idea and added that, while he had already settled in his office downtown, he could easily come over to the campus for key meetings. I felt that we were really getting somewhere. I left the meeting and returned to my office at AEI on foot, with a noticeable spring in my step.

I learned so much from Burke. He didn't want the new center to become stovepiped into narrow projects and programs. He also felt that, too often in government, the issues were not properly defined and that this would be an important role for the center to play. Perhaps most important, he said it was critical that we focus on the underlying policies that could move issues in positive directions, and that we never forget the human factor in leadership and strategy.

In June of 1962, Father Bunn first made public the plans to create the Center for Strategic Studies (CSS) at Georgetown University, with the mission "to integrate and foster research on national growth and the responsible use of national power."[8] CSS first opened its doors in a house opposite the Jesuit Catholic Church, Holy Trinity, in Georgetown. Georgetown University had recently bought the house, which up until its sale had been maintained in grand style by flamboyant decorators with some risqué flairs. The house's garden boasted a statue and fountain, and was perfectly beautiful. The paneled entrance had a mural of Venice.

Upstairs were two or three larger rooms. One of considerable interest had mirrors on the ceiling and walls; it was enough to raise eyebrows! Eleanor Dulles, the sister of Allen and Foster, was leaving the German desk at the State Department to join us. The mirrored room was the only place we could put her, but we were fairly certain that the decor would leave her cold. When I raised this with Father Collins, the property manager, he said the estimate for removing or painting over the mirrors was $1,000, so we would just have to live with dizzying reflections.

Our brilliant young staffer Richard Allen, who later became Ronald Reagan's national security advisor, was always an original thinker. He suggested that I fib to Father Collins, "We understand the *Washington Post* Style section is considering doing a piece on our unusually decorated headquarters." Father Collins was suddenly able to come up with the funds to pay for the special paint to cover the ceiling and walls. Still, it remained a bit of a challenge for us to explain to Eleanor Dulles why she needed to refrain from hanging any pictures on her office walls.

After two years in the house, the Center for Strategic Studies would be consolidated at 1800 K Street. And after many years at 1800 K Street, in 2014, CSIS would construct its own building on Rhode Island Avenue and, thanks to the leadership of my successor John Hamre, become arguably the most beautiful think tank in all of Washington, D.C. However, I am getting ahead of my story.

We still had a very small staff back then. The aforementioned Richard Allen, a product of Notre Dame, started out as an intern for a couple of quarters. Allen had enormous drive and ambition. He also possessed a keen strategic approach to issues, and his expertise on the communist world was first rate. The CSS staff also included Christa Konrad, a German-born philosophy student, who started as an assistant and later went on to take care of our finances; Bob Crane, a strategist; and Eleanor Dulles. In addition, Karl Cerny, a professor of political science, and Henry Briefs, a professor of economics, were the two senior advisors from the Georgetown faculty who worked with us part-time.

We decided to make a major splash with our first event to get the attention of Washington policymakers, academic strategists, and media. We organized a conference that brought together the most prestigious experts in strategy, international affairs, and economics and asked them to look ten years out and anticipate the major challenges that would confront the nation. We felt this exercise was all the more critical now that President Eisenhower was out of office and the long-range strategy he had helped develop had begun to wither on the vine.

We began planning for the event in the aftermath of the Cuban Missile Crisis in the fall of 1962, which had Washington and the entire nation on high alert. The crisis had an additional personal impact on my wife, Carolyn, and me, as her stepfather, Admiral George Anderson, was CNO at the time, and actually ended up on the cover of *Time* magazine.

The conference was made possible by a $40,000 grant from Dick Ware of the Realm Foundation. I viewed it as an opportunity to look at the decade ahead and smartly integrate the political, military, and economic spheres as a way to shake Washington out of its chronic compartmentalization. We wanted to broaden the typical view of strategy as solely relating to military matters, to also include foreign policy and economics as well. It was a theme of strategic integration that I would emphasize for decades to come.

One of the mantras that runs throughout this narrative and my own intellectual journey is the overriding need for strategic leadership, which requires that different elements of power are synchronized like a symphony orchestra. This first, major CSS conference was an early attempt to get the major players reading off the same sheet of music, mixing the viewpoints of strategists from the RAND Corporation, the Council on Foreign Relations, and the Hudson Institute with the worldviews of renowned economists. This same dichotomy between strategists and economists existed in spades in the committee structure that dominated Capitol Hill. Our methodology especially stood out at a time when Washington in general was becoming increasingly shortsighted.

We hosted the conference in January 1963 at the Hall of Nations in Georgetown. To facilitate interaction, all participants were required to be present throughout the two and a half days of the conference. We offered an honorarium of $750 per research paper delivered at the conference, which was a very large amount at the time. For years to come, Henry Kissinger would often joke that the honorarium at CSIS had been decreasing ever since.

The conference featured five panels: Sino-Soviet Strategy, Political Requirements for U.S. Strategy, U.S. Military Strategies, Economic Strategies, and Strategy Requirements in a Free Economy. The mix of young and old among the attendees was impressive. Notable younger participants included Jim Schlesinger, Henry Kissinger, Murray Weidenbaum, and Herman Kahn, who pioneered his human escalation ladder.[9]

James Schlesinger was one of those uncanny strategists seeking to do more with less, but guided by a clear strategy. Schlesinger was the only participant of the thirty-six who had the ability to demolish the wall between the two disciplines of economics and international relations that encompassed strategy. His book was entitled *The Political Economy of National Security: A Study of the Economic Aspects of the Contemporary Power Struggle*. Schlesinger's participation gave me a firsthand view into his truly strategic mind. He later became chairman of the Atomic Energy Commission under Richard Nixon in 1971. He made quite a name for himself on the issue of "nuclear safety."

A dozen years later, when Jim was secretary of defense, he attempted to institutionalize the formulation of strategy. He established the Office of Net Assessment in the Department of Defense under Andy Marshall. This was an attempt to be truly strategic and to look at all the facets of national strength, to include human factors.

In the 1970s, I brought Jim Schlesinger in as a counselor at CSIS to join with Henry Kissinger and Harold Brown. Zbigniew Brzezinski would also become a counselor at CSIS in 1981. The aim was to try to increase strategic thinking in Washington. Jim's brilliance, and his abruptness, were always employed in the service of strategy.

Murray Weidenbaum predicted a conflict in Asia that would eventually cost $50 billion a year and produce runaway inflation.[10] Many attendees thought that such a grim scenario was impossible, but of course, that is exactly what happened later with the long conflict in Vietnam. Among the older group were Robert Strausz-Hupé, Kurt London, Oskar Morgenstern, and Edward Teller, the nuclear physicist and "father" of the hydrogen bomb.

On a side note, Edward Teller was once the passenger with me on a harrowing car ride. I mistakenly turned down a one-way road going the wrong way and narrowly missed the oncoming traffic. Teller said that it was among the most thrilling experiences of his life, second to developing the hydrogen bomb!

In general, Admiral Burke left the daily management of CSS entirely to me. His input was mostly reserved for high-level advice, which, by the way, was routinely priceless. So, it came as no surprise that when confronted with the approximately thirty conference papers, Burke declined to weigh in. "Dave, I am not going to read all those papers," he bluntly told me. "You and Dick Allen ferret out the real issues and note down their differences."

Allen and I borrowed the rearview projection system from the CNO's office at the Pentagon to project the various issues up on the screen at the conference, the better to focus the debate on the critical issues involved. Though the Defense Department's ubiquitous PowerPoint presentations have since coopted the technique, this approach was not typical in those days. As Burke would say, too often in policymaking people are eager to discuss the problems while missing the real underlying issues.

In sorting through the various conference papers and organizing opposing concepts for the slide presentation, Dick Allen noted that there were three separate contradictions within Henry Kissinger's paper alone. Always looking to have a bit of fun, Dick had the moderator point out the differences to the conference audience as they were flashed on the screen. Not missing a beat, Kissinger smiled and exclaimed in his thick German accent, "Oh, it's all in the translation," resulting in a roar of laughter from the participants.

The papers produced by the participating economists and strategists were compiled into a book entitled *National Security: Political, Military, and Eco-*

nomic Strategies in the Decade Ahead. Foreign Policy magazine called the thousand-page book "a lap buster."

The beginnings of the center in 1962 were memorialized in a poem written by my wife, Carolyn, for a CSIS Christmas party in 1988:

'Twas a month before the conference at the new CSS,
December of '62 is what I would guess,
Entitled "National Security—Political, Military, Economic—
(Not to mention problems NATO and Atomic)
Strategies in the Decade Ahead";
With eight CSS staff onboard they were gonna knock 'em dead.

In its cozy, colorful and now co-ed quarters
Bob Crane and Christa carried out orders;
While bespectacled Dick Allen and Abshire, Pink and Lank
Put their egg-heads together to launch the new think tank.
Admiral Burke at the helm deftly steered his command
Through the oceans of papers they had on hand.

The thesis of Kissinger and Schlesinger and Kahn,
Of Eckstein and Dinerstein and Murray Weidenbaum;
Of Teller and Possony, Strausz-Hupé and Ture,
Of Trager, Haberler, Morgenstern and Nutter;
From Kurt London to Walt Rostow, V. Salera and William Stokes,
They'd collected an amazing amalgam of academe folks.

And I at my typewriter—no PC's in those times distant
Printed Nametags for each arriving participant.
For 39 gents of such intellectual acclaim,
I knew at once that the center was headed for fame.

And wasn't I right—little ole gopher me,
In my shrewd surmisal and prophecy?

For not only did the center reach its fame,
But extended its numbers, space, and name.
The CSIS 26 years down the line,
Has seen the staff grow from eight to 159!
Plus 60 interns with élan and éclat
Add to this bubbling melting pot
Of intellect, panache and creative frontiers:
A 21st century think tank that has no peers!!

And so to each fine fellow, scholar, assistant, and secretary,
I toast you and wish you a Christmas very merry,
And a hope that the center continues to prosper and grow.
Now, it's quittin' time and the moment for mistletoe!

Though some have mistakenly pegged the center as a conservative think tank, I have always sought views from across the political spectrum. Shortly after the center's founding, I seized the opportunity to increase our reach with the involvement of active Democrat Morris Leibman. He had previously tried to recruit Arleigh Burke to head a parallel strategic think tank based in his hometown of Chicago. In my first meeting with Morris, I saw a man who was full of ideas and energy. He was passionate for strategy to defend the security and secure the values of the United States. He would serve as a confidant and legal expert for CSIS for nearly thirty years. He could diagram the most difficult situation, and he could draw on his rich network of people to produce just the right reinforcements.

CSS also expanded its focus, and we went on to produce a similar book of reports that correctly forecast the instabilities that increasingly bedeviled the Middle East and Asia. The expansive group of intellectuals that we assembled from around the world for that effort was truly groundbreaking. That study was led by Professor Bernard Lewis at the University of London and included Albert Hourani of Oxford University, J. C. Hurewitz of Columbia University, Charles Issawi of Columbia, Walter Laqueur of the Institute of Contemporary History and the Wiener Library, former governor and commander in chief of Aden William Luce, Ian S. Michie of Chase Manhattan Bank, Major General J. L. Moulton (Ret.), Hisham Sharabi of Georgetown University, J. F. Standish of the Irish University Press, Thomas R. Stauffer of Harvard University, military correspondent W. F. K. Thompson of the *Daily Telegraph*, and P. J. Vatikiotis of the School of Oriental and African Studies in the University of London.

In those days no one ever questioned the stability of Iran or the regime of the Shah of Iran. One exception was one of our experts, Harvard professor Thomas Stauffer, who stated, "U.S. presence at this point could only intensify the polarization, since no government in the Gulf area can long survive if it appears too accommodating toward the United States."[11] History, and the subsequent fall of the Shah of Iran during the 1979 Iranian Revolution, would prove Stauffer prescient.

Thanks to a sizable grant from the Gulbenkian Foundation, we also conducted a study on Portuguese Africa that included Angola, Mozambique, and Portuguese Guinea. The first team I assembled for this project did not work out. Fortunately, in my search to find others to take on the project, I came across the brilliant Michael Samuels, who had just completed a Ph.D. in African history at Columbia University. Samuels first arrived in my office with a trim haircut and a double-breasted suit, which was very unusual for the period. I asked him, "What's your degree in?" He answered, "Portuguese

Africa." I immediately responded, "You're hired!" With his hard work, we were able to publish a book on Portuguese Africa. Later, with Chet Crocker, Samuels started the CSIS African Studies Program, which remains a pillar of its research to this day.

The relationship that I developed with Mike Samuels was one of the first of many mentor/mentee relationships I would enjoy over the years, from which I would gain so much. When I was later called into the State Department in 1970, Samuels went with me and handled relations between the Africa desk and Congress. By the time I left the State Department, his reputation had grown so stellar that he was promoted to become the special assistant to the deputy secretary of state. Following that, at the very young age of twenty-nine, Samuels was appointed U.S. ambassador to Sierra Leone, becoming the youngest ambassador appointee ever made at the time. Subsequently, he returned to CSS (now CSIS) as executive director of what was then called our Third World Studies Department. He also ran a center project on export competitiveness, further expanding his expertise and helping to prepare him for his later position as the international vice president of the U.S. Chamber of Commerce. I have often said that much of my success has come from being smart enough to know what I didn't know, and then surrounding myself by those who did. This was certainly the case with Mike Samuels.

As we approached the presidential election of 1964, events took a difficult turn, at least for me personally. Bill Baroody broke all of his own rules and became directly involved in Republican senator Barry Goldwater's campaign. Even though Baroody firmly believed that think tanks worked most effectively behind the scenes, he was suddenly out in front with his position as a Goldwater adviser. It was the first time he had been asked to play such a prominent role in the limelight of a presidential campaign, which he very much enjoyed.

To make matters worse, Baroody became irritated that Robert Strausz-Hupé, head of the Foreign Policy Institute of Philadelphia, was also being called on by Goldwater to serve as an adviser. Before very long, Baroody got into a rather public fight with Strausz-Hupé regarding who would eventually become Goldwater's top advisor.

While I had been in charge of the last Republican national security policy platform in 1960, that was before I decided to head a policy think tank. I did not approve of Baroody's direct campaign involvement, and I took umbrage when he took it a step too far by going behind my back and trying to convince Admiral Arleigh Burke to join the Goldwater advisory board. I very much opposed the idea, and called Baroody on it. Decades later, I would have a similar disagreement with my CSIS successor Robert Zoellick over his direct involvement in the George W. Bush presidential campaign.

The nonprofit Center for Strategic Studies was part of a university organization, and politically unaligned. I thus felt that Arleigh Burke had to make a decision: If he were to become an official Goldwater advisor, he would need to, at the very least, take leave from CSS. However, as it turned out, Burke had no interest at all in joining the Goldwater advisory board.

Things eventually became so heated between the Baroody camp and my own that Admiral Burke stepped in. He wrote Baroody a letter in which he laid down the law, completely cutting the ties between AEI and the Center for Strategic Studies. He explained that I would resign from AEI and Baroody would resign from CSS. Burke and I were not the only ones who had a problem with Baroody's involvement with the campaign. In spite of Baroody's and the other AEI staff members' claim that they only worked on the campaign during their free time, AEI would come under close scrutiny by the IRS for its campaign involvement.

At first Bill Baroody seemed to take this separation relatively well, but then he set out to turn a number of CSS's supporters against the center. These were supporters who contributed $25,000 to $50,000 to the center each year, which in those days was an awful lot of money. In fact, Baroody had some success in pulling away our support. I know he continued to harbor a grudge for many years. Later, during the 1968 presidential election, he received funding to digitize the name of potential candidates for various positions in a Nixon administration. I later learned that my name was quickly deleted each time it would appear on a list.

Bill and I had been very close, but after the split between AEI and CSS, trust had been broken. While technically Burke and I had won a victory in separating our organizations, personally the pain of this broken bond ran deep, and would not quickly pass. For weeks I suffered from a significant depression, something I had not experienced since my teenage years. Baroody had certainly done a great deal for me, and he had gained much from me in return. We had shared great affection for one another. Up until that point in my life, I had treasured the small group of men who were key to my success: my father, my uncles Lupton Patten and Alex Guerry, Carroll Reece, Father Durkin, and Bill Baroody. I always considered trust sacred, and now it had been lost. I feel certain Baroody felt the same way about me.

However, fault lines in our relationship were evident even prior to the split. While Bill and I were indeed very close, our relationship had come under increasing strain. I believe he was a bit insecure about the success of CSS and the prestige it enjoyed from its association with Georgetown. In fact, the center had begun to draw more public attention than even AEI. The most shocking manifestation of the declining reservoir of trust between me and Baroody came when the center's treasurer, Penny Baker, confided in me that Bill had been tapping my phone calls out of CSS! I never called him on it, but it certainly made me very careful about the content of my phone conversations.

When I returned to lead the renamed Center for Strategic and International Studies (CSIS) years later following my service in the State Department, I was able to fully mend my relationship with Baroody, which was a note of mercy to me. AEI's key economist, Tom Johnson, happened to be a member of our Episcopal church in Alexandria. One Sunday he came across the church aisle and suggested that we have lunch. With a plan up his sleeve, he asked me to meet him at his office beforehand. Once I was there, Tom wondered aloud whether Bill might be around. I realized it was a setup, but a setup that suited me just fine. We walked down to Bill's office, and the three of us went to lunch. As we talked about the center and the old days, I suggested to Bill that he come back on CSIS's advisory board, knowing that now he could do no harm. Baroody agreed. I was very grateful for our reunion.

Unfortunately, the journey ahead for Bill Baroody as the head of AEI included a note of misfortune. He was determined to maneuver things so that his son, Bill Baroody Jr., was able to take over the organization in 1978. Young Bill had indeed had an interesting career. He had been a naval officer in the Sixth Fleet, coincidentally when my father-in-law, Admiral Anderson, commanded it. Following that, with my help, he had obtained a position with Mel Laird on Capitol Hill. He also worked in the White House during the Ford administration. Unfortunately, young Bill Baroody Jr. took AEI on paths where it seemed to lose all direction and focus. Funding eventually dried up and the organization went broke. AEI was saved by the Packard Foundation, which bailed it out.

The crisis at AEI occurred toward the end of my tenure as the U.S. ambassador to NATO. Both Mel Laird and Paul McCracken called me to say that I should take over AEI. When I responded that my primary obligation was to CSIS, they suggested that CSIS take over AEI to form a much larger organization. However, I believed that both organizations had a key role to play in Washington and that combining the two might have caused both to lose their edge and sense of direction and clear purpose.

As I later learned, a search committee was formed to identify new potential AEI heads, and the three top candidates were Paul Volcker, David Abshire, and Chris DeMuth. The least well known at the time was Chris DeMuth, who answered the calling that Volcker and I turned down. I give him high marks for his restorative role at AEI. He managed to turn the organization around financially and lead it to new levels of influence and growth.

I am grateful that I was able to speak with Bill Baroody Sr. again just before his death in 1980. I told him that there would have never been a CSIS without him. He quickly retorted that I would have surely found someone else in his place. I insisted that was not true, and I meant it. I was very grateful that in the end trust had been restored between the two of us.

7

Washington in Crisis

The State Department, Vietnam, and the Nixon Years

By early 1968, the land war in Asia that President Dwight Eisenhower had so assiduously avoided—even refusing to rescue French troops at Dien Ben Phu in 1954 against the advice of his top advisors—was raging. President Lyndon Johnson had deployed half a million U.S. troops to Vietnam, and despite the optimistic proclamations of some of his generals, there was still no end in sight for the conflict.

Needless to say, we had many roundtable discussions on the subject of Vietnam at our relatively newly organized Center for Strategic and International Studies (CSIS).

As the war unfolded with no victory in sight, presidential advisor Walt Rostow came over to CSIS to give a briefing during a meeting we were hosting of the Young Presidents' Organization. This was a global network of chief executives under the age of fifty that included two CEOs who would become very good friends of mine: Maurice R. "Hank" Greenberg, who had just taken over AIG, the multinational insurance corporation; and Bruce Gelb, the new chairman of pharmaceutical company Bristol-Myers Squibb. Over the next forty years, Hank Greenberg would lead AIG to become the largest insurance and financial services company in the world. Hank's involvement in CSIS would only increase as he would serve on the executive board for nearly twenty years and later become vice chairman in 1987. Rostow assured the group that we were at the *takeoff stage* in Vietnam, drawing the term from his field of development economics. Rostow claimed victory in Vietnam was almost upon us.

Unfortunately for Rostow's prediction, three weeks later North Vietnamese forces and their Viet Cong guerilla allies launched the Tet Offensive on January 31, 1968. The result was not the takeoff stage that Rostow had forecast, but rather the arrival of the Viet Cong at the gates of the embassy in Saigon. The Johnson administration was so alarmed that it sent a three-star general back to the United States to brief influential individuals such as Admiral Arleigh Burke, along with organizations like CSIS. The three-star general declared, "Admiral, I want to reassure you we really won. So much of the Viet Cong infrastructure was wiped out in this attack." Burke put down his pipe. "Goddamn it, General, don't you know the objective was not Saigon but Washington? The President is not going to run again!"

Not that I was surprised, but Admiral Burke's crystal ball was clearer than that of Rostow or the generals. Largely as a result of the setback of the Tet Offensive, Lyndon Johnson announced at the end of March 1968 that he would not seek reelection.

In mid-November of 1969, as the executive director of CSIS, I was asked to give a speech to the board of directors of the U.S. Chamber of Commerce. Their selected topic was the "problems of disengagement." That evening there were thousands of protesters demonstrating in Washington in what they called "the March of Death."[1] They demanded that newly elected president Richard Nixon disengage immediately from the land war in Asia. In my comments before this diverse group, I noted, "The argument then is over the terms of disengagement, the timing, its process, and the national conduct during the process. History tells us that the act of disengagement, badly planned and executed, can lead to the ultimate failure of national goals and aspirations—another and even worse war."

In my talk I then turned to the problems that Eisenhower had in disengaging from my conflict, the Korean War. As I have previously noted, former secretary of state Dean Acheson made a mistake in 1950 when he did not include South Korea in his description of the United States' defensive perimeter in Asia, which in turn led to the North Korean miscalculation that the U.S. would not respond militarily to an incursion in South Korea. I noted that "if chances of enemy miscalculation are one great danger of a wrongly executed disengagement, a too tightly wound calendar is another." I noted the danger of the United States losing leverage too quickly with a disengagement, becoming unable to support indigenous forces favorable to us or to negotiate between competing factions. I spoke of the decline of public support needed to sustain the conflict.

"The base of public support for the war was eroded by the way we got into it," I noted. "In 1963–64, the public was told we had no intention of committing American manpower . . . that we proposed to help the Vietnamese help themselves. Yet we Americanized the war, committed a half a million Americans, and heard for many months that the tide had turned in our favor, despite the fact that there was no success."

Over a year later, in April 1970, I received a call out of the blue from Bryce Harlow. It would change the course of my life. Neil McElroy, who had served as Eisenhower's last secretary of defense, had returned to the private sector as chief executive officer of Procter & Gamble, and he persuaded Bryce to represent the company in Washington.

But now Harlow was working for the Nixon White House, and he called to persuade me, on behalf of the president, to take a two-year leave of absence from CSIS to serve as the State Department's liaison with Congress. Harlow said that Bill Macomber, the incumbent congressional liaison, was being moved to undersecretary of state for management.

Actually, I knew a great deal about the position of congressional liaison, but was not sure how well I would fit into it. I was not good at remembering names, nor was I a natural glad-hander. Harlow responded that I had to remember only two names: *senator* and *congressman*. As a colonel in the reserves, Harlow stressed that my country needed me and that it was my duty to serve. He said that President Nixon favorably recalled my role with the Republican Policy Committee back in the late 1950s and that his national security advisor, Henry Kissinger, knew me well through CSIS. Kissinger famously thought the State Department enjoyed too much independence, and he apparently thought I could help him keep Secretary of State Bill Rogers in line. I accepted the offer.

As for the position of congressional liaison that I was being offered, it had considerable prestige. I knew that George Kennan had been a notable predecessor, followed sometime thereafter by Dean Acheson, who in 1969 had just published his brilliant book *Present at the Creation: My Years at the State Department*. A tall, witty New England patrician, Dean Acheson was a product of the Covington & Burling law firm who did not suffer fools easily, and never knew a dull moment. Acheson's style is captured in a quote from Alphonso X, the king of Spain between 1253 and 1284, located in the foreword of Acheson's autobiography: "Had I been present at the creation, I would have given some useful hints to the order of the universe."[2] From his visits to CSIS, I had come to know the intimidating, but never boring, Dean Acheson, and we got along famously.

I met with Acheson in the days between my appointment and confirmation, appropriately buttering him up with some adulation. In referring to his memoirs, I quoted a comment from John Kenneth Galbraith: "It is impossible to describe these memoirs as less than superior."[3] In reality, I did think the book was superb. Acheson and I discussed the senators who served on the powerful Senate Foreign Relations Committee, which had jurisdiction over the State Department. In colorful language, his eyebrows arching for emphasis at every parry and thrust, Acheson began to skewer the committee members.

"David, your biggest problem is that the chairman of the committee of your jurisdiction, Bill Fulbright, is totally a dilettante," Acheson explained.

John Sparkman of Alabama is a nice quiet chap, but he seldom shows up. Mike Mansfield of Montana hardly ever leaves home to come to Washington. Albert Gore of your Tennessee is full of himself. Frank Church of Idaho is a know-it-all isolationist. Stuart Symington of Missouri is a former secretary of the air force, who should have stayed there. Claiborne Pell is quaint. Dodd and Magee are pretty good guys, but late in the debate. On the Republican side, Aiken still loves to be called governor, but has gotten inside Fulbright's pocket. Case of New Jersey and Williams of Delaware have also. Javitts is a jackass. John Sherman Cooper is good when he is awake. Your challenge clearly will be to break the grip of Bill Fulbright, who manages to build a unity on the committee by insulting the White House.

I had been warned to respect the confidentiality of the appointment until it was publicly announced. Nevertheless, an exposé by the prominent *Washington Post* reporter Murray Marter broke the story. He wrote that my appointment had been jammed down the throat of the State Department by the White House. Marter characterized it as something of a military takeover of the State Department by leaders of CSIS, namely Annapolis-trained Admiral Arleigh Burke and West Pointer David Abshire.

Marter paid me the courtesy of calling right before going to press. He gave me a quick advance read of the article. I opined, "I find this line of criticism interesting. I don't know how it fits with the book I wrote for my doctoral degree, which is about to be published. It is the story of Confederate Colonel David Key, who crossed party lines to serve in the cabinet following Tilden and Hayes's disputed election. You may find it interesting that the glowing introduction of the book was written by the nationally famous civil rights leader Ralph McGill." I then politely asked Mr. Marter how he thought this dissertation of reconciliation would fit with the profile he was drawing. Marter hastily said that he would add such a note, which was stuck on the end of the article.

I later found out that the *Washington Post* piece by Murray Marter came from a leak from a very liberal Democratic staffer from North Carolina on the committee. Later she would become my biggest booster, and eventually she told me about the leak. "I shot off my mouth before I even knew you," she said. "I consider that my greatest mistake."

The next stage in this process was the confirmation hearings, which went amazingly well, helped in no small measure by a good preliminary meeting that I held with committee chairman Bill Fulbright. We met over a cup of coffee, and despite some differences, we got along well. I complimented him on the literary quality of his book *The Crippled Giant*. In speaking privately with every Democrat and Republican on the committee, I came to the unavoidable conclusion that it was the high-handedness of the Nixon White House that had driven the Senate Foreign Relations Committee into conflict with the administration, with Bill Fulbright as its leader. I also quickly established a good rapport with the congressional relations staff, Republicans and Democrats alike. Some of them were originally members of the Foreign Service and had resigned over the Vietnam War. Others had been parked on the committee staff to take care of different political constituencies on Capitol Hill.

During our first meeting, Senator Fulbright admitted that he had falsely accused Secretary of State Bill Rogers of withholding vital information from the committee members. He later came to realize that Rogers was being purposely kept in the dark by National Security Advisor Henry Kissinger. Indeed, the White House openly distrusted the State Department and frequently cut it out of the decision-making process. Furthermore, the State Department was naturally rather tight-lipped and reticent in sharing information given the sensitivity and demands of international diplomacy. That put off members of Congress, who frequently complained that they couldn't get straight answers to the questions they asked of the State Department. While this tension might not have served the best interests of the country, it certainly cleared the way for my role as a power broker.

One of the problems with the Nixon administration, especially in its early days, was the issue of stereotypes. The Nixon administration was worse than most in this regard, distrusting all liberal Democrats, nosy Republican lawmakers, and "tweedy diplomats," and just assuming they would always play to type and oppose the White House. It was that kind of thinking and paranoia that ultimately led Nixon's insular inner circle to keep an extensive "enemy's list." As Gerald Ford would comment on hearing of the list, "Anybody who can't keep his enemies in his head has too many enemies."

I have always found that with the right strategic leadership such stereotypes can be overcome, and my congressional relations staff loyally followed my lead in acting as a good-faith mediator and balancer between the State Department and Capitol Hill.

Very soon, my office began to improve the tenor of our letters to members of Congress, and our general outreach to Capitol Hill. As I would discover at various times in my career, my team fed off the sense that they were making a difference and were in the middle of the action. They decided I was just the man to get them into the middle of things, and we developed an excellent esprit de corps.

As part of our outreach initiative to begin a new era of openness in both oral and written communications between the State Department and Congress, we began to hold regular policy meetings on Capitol Hill to discuss current issues with lawmakers. I convinced Senate majority leader Mike Mansfield, the Democrat from Montana, to invite Secretary of State Bill Rogers for an off-the-record "question hour." This kind of private back-and-forth is similar to what occurs in parliamentary government. I did not arrange a similar meeting between Rogers and Bill Fulbright, because the chairman of the Senate Foreign Relations Committee liked to keep a monopoly on information, and thus generally shunned the give-and-take of such exchanges.

Needless to say, I took a particular interest in the progress of the Vietnam War in my discussions on Capitol Hill. In 1969, the United States had over half a million soldiers in Vietnam, and yet Congress had never formally declared the conflict a war. I found this difficult to square with the Constitution's stipulation that only Congress can declare that the nation is at war.

Perhaps surprisingly, the United States Congress has only made five formal declarations of war (for the War of 1812, the Mexican-American War, the Spanish-American War, World War I, and World War II). So as the undeclared Vietnam War raged, there were understandably questions about the legal authority that backed it. Today, the legality of U.S. military action against ISIS is in a similar gray area because Congress has failed to pass an AUMF (Authorization for Use of Military Force).

What legal authority existed for the Vietnam War originated from events that took place on August 2, 1964. The American destroyer U.S.S. *Maddox* reportedly took fire from three North Vietnamese patrol boats four miles off the coast of Vietnam. The *Maddox*, backed by U.S. fighter aircraft from an American aircraft carrier, counterattacked. Two days later, it was reported that the North Vietnamese again attacked our ships, which again counterattacked. As a result, on August 7, the Gulf of Tonkin Resolution was enacted by Congress to authorize the president "to take all necessary measures" to defend Southeast Asia. In the Senate, only Senators Wayne Morse (D-Oreg.), and Ernest Gruening (D-Alaska) opposed the resolution. In the House of Representatives, the resolution passed unanimously. The Johnson administration subsequently relied upon the resolution to escalate our military involvement in Vietnam. Senator Bill Fulbright, who voted for and sponsored the resolution, would later write: "Many Senators who accepted the Gulf of Tonkin resolution without question might well not have done so had they foreseen that it would subsequently be interpreted as a sweeping Congressional endorsement for the conduct of a large-scale war in Asia."[4]

Chairman Fulbright began a series of hearings exploring a possible repeal of the Gulf of Tonkin Resolution. In 1966, Fulbright published his book *The Arrogance of Power*, in which he attacked the justification for the Vietnam War, Congress's failure to set limits on it, and the impulses that gave rise to it. The Fulbright hearings, broadcast widely on television, were central to swaying the public against the Vietnam War.

In 1971, in the Nixon administration's third year, Bill Fulbright intensified his hearings, arguing that the war in Southeast Asia lacked congressional authorization. During one of Chairman Fulbright's extensive hearings, a legal advisor from the Nixon administration made the argument that the administration did not need the resolution of support. Because President Nixon had inherited half a million U.S. troops already deployed in Vietnam, the argument went, he had the authority as commander in chief under Article II of the Constitution to protect the lives of U.S. military forces.

Senator Dole, the Republican from Kansas and still a relative newcomer in the Senate at that time, got into a bit of mischief. As he trotted onto the Senate floor, I stepped into the Senate gallery to watch the show. The junior senator from Kansas broke sacred Senate protocol by preempting a more senior senator. While Fulbright was speaking to the press about his motion to repeal the resolution, Dole announced that Richard Nixon did not even need the Tonkin Resolution, and called for a repeal of the resolution himself. Chairman Fulbright was so angry that he actually voted against the repeal he had intended to sponsor! Senator Dole's amendment was attached to the Foreign Military Sales Act, and the Senate voted 81–10 to repeal the Tonkin Gulf Resolution.

It should be recalled that Richard Nixon had campaigned for president based in large part on his promise to wind down the indecisive war in Vietnam. After so much talk of "light at the end of the tunnel," the Tet Offensive in 1968 had swept away public support for the conflict, creating skepticism that no politician could wash away. So, in 1969, Nixon announced the withdrawal of 150,000 troops over the next year, but he also subsequently made the disastrous decision to secretly bomb communist forces in neighboring Cambodia.[5]

In my early days in the State Department, I got a call from the director of the Joint Staff, John W. Vogt Jr. The Nixon White House had apparently asked him to brief me on an important matter, alone, with no staff present. The handsome, blue-eyed, three-star Air Force general who arrived at my office for the briefing could have had a second career in the movies. He carried a couple of map boards and had an aide in tow. They laid out for me the planned attack into Cambodia. I asked for the briefing plan so that I could distribute it to some key members of Congress. I was amazed when the general replied in no uncertain terms that *no one* on Capitol Hill was to be briefed.

Vogt went on to inform me that this secret was being so tightly held that Secretary of State Rogers and I were the only two people in the whole State Department who knew what was about to happen. What made this meeting all the more uncomfortable was the fact that three days earlier Secretary Rogers, with me at his side, had testified to the Senate Foreign Relations Committee that there were no plans for an incursion into Cambodia.

To give a bit of context, Prince Norodom Sihanouk of Cambodia had been removed from power the previous March. While Sihanouk was traveling abroad, Prime Minister Lon Nol called a meeting of the National Assembly, which voted to depose Sihanouk and give Lon Nol emergency powers. Up until this time, Sihanouk had practiced a policy of tolerating Viet Cong and North Vietnamese army activity within Cambodia. At the same time, he imposed some constraints on the North Vietnamese presence, including preventing the sanctuaries from becoming fully operational combat bases. In addition, as long as no Cambodians were hurt, he had been willing to turn a blind eye toward U.S. air strikes against those bases. Unlike the prince, however, Lon Nol was fully aligned with the United States against North Vietnam and the Chinese. The United States immediately recognized his new government. Sihanouk fled to Beijing and began to support the communist Khmer Rouge guerillas in their fight to overthrow the new Lon Nol government in Cambodia. New volunteers flocked to the Khmer Rouge as it grew in size from 6,000 to more than 40,000 fighters. Many joined not so much in support of communism but rather in support of their former leader Sihanouk. Fear mounted that Khmer Rouge forces would soon threaten the Cambodian capital, Phnom Penh.

There was talk about a major U.S. incursion into Cambodia, which Secretary Rogers and Defense Secretary Mel Laird were both against. On April 20, Nixon addressed the nation and spoke of the presence of some 40,000 communist troops in Cambodia. He declared that if he felt that the lives of the remaining U.S. forces still present in Vietnam were placed in danger by that presence, he would not hesitate to take "strong and effective measures." In the same speech, Nixon also announced plans to withdraw 115,000 additional U.S. troops from Vietnam in the coming year. That same day, North Vietnamese forces captured Saang and further advanced into central Cambodia.

Nixon decided to commit U.S. forces to fight against the North Vietnamese troops in Cambodia, but he faced the challenge of telling Congress and the nation. Before he could make the announcement, a number of amendments were introduced in the House and the Senate prohibiting U.S. ground forces from entering Cambodia and threatening to cut off funds for the Vietnam conflict. Finally, on the evening of April 30, President Nixon announced on national television his decision to launch a joint operation with the South Vietnamese attacking major enemy sanctuaries on the border between Cambodia and Vietnam:

> Ten days ago, in my report to the Nation on Vietnam, I announced a decision to withdraw an additional 150,000 Americans from Vietnam over the next year. I said then that I was making that decision despite our concern over increased enemy activity in Laos, Cambodia, and in South Vietnam.
>
> At that time, I warned that if I concluded that increased enemy activity in any of these areas endangered lives of Americans remaining in Vietnam, I would not hesitate to take strong and effective measures. Despite that warning, North Vietnam has increased its military aggression in all these areas, and particularly in Cambodia.
>
> After full consultation with the National Security Council, Ambassador Bunker, General Abrams, and my other advisors, I have concluded that the actions of the enemy in the last 10 days clearly endanger the lives of Americans who are in Vietnam now and would constitute an unacceptable risk to those who will be there after the withdrawal of another 150,000.[6]

Nixon dramatically argued that failure to take action would reveal the United States as a "pitiful, helpless giant." When the president was asked why Secretary of State Rogers had neglected to mention the Cambodian offensive just three days prior during a meeting with the Foreign Relations Committee, Nixon responded that secrecy was necessary to maintain the element of surprise. When asked why he had not sought congressional approval for the operation, Nixon responded that he would have if the intent was to expand the war. Instead, he argued that the offensive was an effort specifically designed to clean out enemy sanctuaries being used to attack U.S. forces inside Vietnam.

The back-and-forth dynamic illustrated the hostility that had developed between the administration and congressional critics, led by Senator Fulbright. Unfortunately, in this contentious environment, the White House had decided to provide Congress with as little advance warning of imminent action as possible, which only further fueled the mistrust. The Nixon administration's contentious relationship with Congress offers a case study of what happens when the trust that greases the wheels of a government is lost.

Members of the Senate Foreign Relations Committee requested a meeting alone with the president. Breaking with protocol, the president, against the advice of Secretary Rogers, declined. Instead, he invited them to a joint meeting with the House Foreign Affairs Committee, an attempt to raise the status of the House committee. The president also invited the Senate and House Armed Services Committee members to meet with him separately earlier that same day.

I sat in on these East Room briefings. Nixon was at his best: very gracious, humble, and sincere. Yet I also witnessed how Nixon could quickly and abruptly turn his charm on and off. He steadfastly argued that the incursion into Cambodia was not a change in basic policy, but a necessary precursor to a successful withdrawal of U.S. forces from Vietnam. He insisted that the scope and duration of the incursion would be limited.

Having just joined the Nixon administration, I was the greenest of the green. During one meeting, having noticed that there were no pads and pencils for the senators and representatives, I told a young aide with a military-style crew cut that he needed to immediately get pads and pencils. The aide ordered the pads and pencils, but I was surprised that he seemed deeply upset by my order. Soon I realized, much to my horror, that the "aide" I had ordered to fetch pads and pencils was none other than Nixon's chief of staff, H. R. Haldeman!

While the White House expected dissent from the public following Nixon's April 30 announcement of a Cambodian offensive, it was shocked by the intensity of the protests on college campuses around the country. The morning after Nixon's speech on the incursion, a march of five hundred students formed at Kent State University in Ohio, where antiwar protests had already been taking place. The ROTC building was set on fire. The National Guard cleared the campus the next evening with tear gas and fixed bayonets. Then, on May 4, a day none of us who witnessed it will ever forget, the National Guard used live ammunition to fire into the crowd of thousands. Nine young students were wounded, and four students were killed. A march that included labor unions was held in Washington on May 9, and students at more than 140 colleges and universities across the country joined the protests, which involved more than four million people nationwide.

A delegation from Harvard visited National Security Advisor Henry Kissinger at this tense time and strongly implied that he would not be welcomed back to Harvard, his academic home, where he had received both his master's and doctoral degrees, and where he taught and cofounded the Center for International Affairs.

With the tragic Kent State shootings and eruption of demonstrations, the White House staff was in a state of crisis. They were caught off guard by the bitterness of the reactions from some in Congress, and there was a widening split within the administration on the best way forward. On one side, Henry Kissinger, Bryce Harlow, and their staffs of experienced politicians and policy analysts calmly advocated for an approach of conciliatory rhetoric with Capitol Hill, but unbending adherence to the announced policy path. On the other side, H. R. Haldeman and his staff of young lawyers, advertising men, and other newcomers to the Washington political scene were more shaken by the demonstrations and congressional pushback and urged a rethinking of the policy.

In the Senate, a push to enact restrictive legislation was immediately undertaken. Letters were sent out to all relevant committee chairmen to report back on any restrictive legislation that they might be working on. The amendment that Senators John Sherman Cooper, the Republican from Kentucky, and Frank Church, the Democrat from Idaho, were working on became the primary vehicle for opposing the White House on Cambodia. Senate leaders agreed that the Fulbright Committee should report out the Foreign Military Sales bill as soon as possible, with the Cooper-Church Amendment attached.

The Cooper-Church Amendment to the Foreign Military Sales bill read as follows:

In order to avoid the involvement of the United States in a wider war in Indo-china and to expedite the withdraw of American forces from Vietnam, it is hereby provided that, unless specifically authorized by law hereafter enacted, no funds authorized or appropriated pursuant to this act or any other law may be expended for the purpose of:

(1) Retaining United States forces in Cambodia;
(2) Paying the compensation or allowances of, or otherwise supporting, directly or indirectly, any United States personnel in Cambodia . . .
(3) Entering into or carrying out any contract or agreement to provide military instruction in Cambodia or to provide persons to engage in any combat activity in support of Cambodian forces; or
(4) Conducting any combat activity support of Cambodian forces.[7]

On June 30, 1970, following six months of debate and a filibuster that lasted for seven weeks, the Cooper-Church Amendment was approved by the Senate by a vote of 58 to 37. However, the bill failed in the House of Representatives. The inclusion of the amendment was opposed in a vote of 237 to 153. That was not, however, the end of the Cooper-Church Amendment, as a revised version of it was resurrected.

One of the Nixon administration's most strident objections to the amendment was that were U.S. forces to come under attack from enemy fire from within Cambodia, it would have prohibited them from responding even in self-defense. Secretary of Defense Mel Laird and his deputy David Packard were unsuccessful in trying to persuade Cooper and Church to alter their amendment. So I was then asked to try to obtain this change.

I had developed a good rapport with Republican senator Cooper. He was an interesting person who had already served as ambassador to India. Though Cooper was rather countrified, he lived in tony Georgetown with a high-society wife. When I would meet with Cooper at his home on the weekends, I always made sure to wear an appropriately "countrified" shirt, much to his wife's chagrin.

I met with Senator Cooper in the back room of his office suite to discuss the Cooper-Church Amendment. As we huddled, I told him that I fully understood the criticisms that he and Senator Church had with administration policy. But were the amendment to stay as written, I didn't think they fully recognized the potential consequences. Were American forces in South Vietnam fired on from inside Cambodia, I argued, it would be against the law for them to retaliate in self-defense.

After further discussion, Senator Cooper assured me that under no circumstances had this vulnerability been intentional. Cooper also believed that Senator Church might be willing to work out a compromise that the administration would be willing to sign. He instructed me to call on Senator Church alone, and to be sure to meet with him in Church's back office, with no staff present. Cooper added quickly, "You know, these staffers can't be trusted not to leak; they all talk to the *New York Times*!"

Senator Church and I subsequently discussed the matter thoroughly. As I had with Senator Cooper, I explained how the amendment, as it was currently written, left our troops vulnerable. Senator Church thought a while and then suggested that I craft a letter, signed by Secretary of State Rogers and blessed by President Nixon, which affirmed that the administration would conduct Cambodian policy in conformity with the Cooper-Church provisions in the authorization bill, but stipulated that U.S. forces were able to defend themselves if attacked from indirect fire from inside Cambodia. Church insisted that the letter remain a secret so that he could dramatically produce it on the Senate floor. The administration agreed.

Here is how the letter read:

Dear Senator Church:

Confirming Assistant Secretary Abshire's conversation with you, I should like to reaffirm that the administration's programs, policies, and intentions in Cambodia in no way conflict with Section 6 of H.R.19911, or with the concerns expressed in the colloquy on the floor of the Senate on fifteenth December.

William Rogers
Secretary of State

Quite jubilant about pulling all of this off, I visited Senator Cooper to thank him for his great advice. I saw discomfort written all over the senator's face. "Senator," I opined, "I've done exactly what you told me, but you look pained." The senator responded, "I am deeply hurt, David." I reiterated that I did what he suggested and asked what more I could do. Senator Cooper responded, "I want one of those letters like you gave to Senator Church." Thankfully, I was able to hold laughter, and set about to fulfill his request for a personalized letter.

The Supplemental Appropriations Conference Report containing the revised Cooper-Church Amendment—which was greatly weakened and did not prohibit U.S. air activity over Cambodia—was finally passed by the House and Senate and sent to the White House for the president's signature. After the previous deadlock, it seemed that a positive chain reaction was under way. Former secretary of the navy John Lehman captured this moment in his book when he wrote, "Reaction at the White House could only be described as jubilation, with the President giving special praise to the brilliant leadership of 'his field marshal' Assistant Secretary Abshire."[8] Of course, that boastful job description was exactly the caricature I did not want. I was merely doing everything I could to build relationships based on trust. My greatest asset may have been that my style was the opposite of the distrustful and paranoid Nixon White House.

President Nixon signed the Supplemental Foreign Assistance Act on January 6, 1971. With it he included the following signing statement, which I along with the NSC staff drafted:

> I heartily welcome the prompt and decisive action of the Congress in passing H.R. 19911. The additional foreign assistance funds which I requested only a little over a month ago are vital to the security of the United States and to the success of our foreign policy . . .
> I am particularly pleased by the consultation and accommodation between Congress and the administration demonstrated in the legislative history of this bill. America's world leadership depends upon our being able to put aside partisan differences when the national interest is at stake, and to band together to demonstrate the unity of purpose so vital to the success of our foreign policy. We have done so on this legislation.[9]

The Cooper-Church Amendment is historically significant because it is regarded as the first congressional action taken to limit presidential powers in wartime. The process that led up to the final bill is significant as well. As John Lehman explains in his extensive recounting of this period, the back-and-forth over the issue of U.S. involvement in Cambodia represented the most intensive period of consultation between the White House and Congress on foreign policy since the Marshall Plan. The debate was a sincere give-and-take among open-minded individuals. "At the conclusion of the process," Lehman wrote, "the Executive branch had its commitment for Cambodia; but Congress had decisively molded the policy regarding that commitment."[10]

Of course, the Vietnam War continued to bedevil the Nixon administration, with the conflict becoming increasingly unpopular over time. I learned at one point that the very influential and erudite Congressman Dick Bolling, Democrat from Missouri, was putting together a resolution to end the war outright. At the time, Kissinger was in secret peace negotiations with the North Vietnamese in Paris, and it looked like there would be a clear majority in favor of Bolling's resolution in the House of Representatives.

I had known Dick Bolling, who was chairman of the House Rules Committee, since before I came to Washington. He was a product of my uncle Alex Guerry's University of the South, and a great admirer of my uncle, who by then was deceased. I called on Bolling to talk over his resolution. Following some back-home talk about Sewanee, I said, "Dick, I know you are not for this Vietnam War and the way it is proceeding. I can thoroughly understand your position. But you know the circumstances. I do not believe you would want to see the issue of ending this war dealt with in something of an illegitimate way."

It was not generally known, but I informed Bolling that Henry Kissinger was in the middle of some hopefully fruitful negotiations with the communists. "If your amendment on ending the war were enacted at this point, it would be devastating to these talks," I argued. "This war has gone on in Democratic and now in Republican administrations, and many have died. But I do not believe you want the final decision on how it ends to be made this way."

Dick Bolling looked at me intently in silence. He finally broke the silence after a few minutes and conceded, "You're right. I'm going to offer the amendment, but I will then oppose it. This way we will not risk undermining the Paris negotiations in a preemptive way, but the gesture will still serve as a warning to the administration for the future."

I was bowled over. "Dick, is there any way I can help you carry this burden, perhaps help with the speech?" I offered. "I know many of the left wing will be devastated."

Bolling declined my offer. "No, I know what I am going to say: I don't like Richard Nixon or anything about him. I don't like the way he looks, the way he talks, the way he handles his presidency, but I will not move to undercut my commander in chief while he is in the middle of negotiations."

Senator Edward "Ted" Kennedy of Massachusetts was another liberal

Democrat and vocal opponent of the Vietnam War. The White House learned that Senator Kennedy had received an invitation by the communist government to visit North Vietnam. Subsequently, I was sent up to Kennedy's Senate office to persuade him not to go. The White House saw my mission as a fool's errand and held out little hope for success.

At that time, I barely knew Ted Kennedy. I was greeted with a glass of cranberry juice. Kennedy asked, "Where are you from, David?" "Tennessee," I replied. He asked, "Have you ever had cranberry juice?" I replied, "No, I haven't." He responded, "Well, then you are in for a treat." I ended up gulping down three glasses of cranberry juice to ingratiate myself with Senator Kennedy, which I think he appreciated. I then got down to business.

"Senator, we know that you have an invitation to go to North Vietnam. You must understand that we are at a critical point in peace negotiations, and we believe your trip could undermine our efforts," I stated. "It would help us immensely if you did not go at this time."

Kennedy studied me closely and then responded. "Well, if it is so important to the negotiation efforts, I won't do it." I relished the opportunity to report back to the White House, since they were so sure that Kennedy could not be turned around. My success offered an important lesson, though I am not sure Nixon's White House staff ever learned it: People will often surprise you, if you only give them a chance.

In the late 1960s and early 1970s, the CIA and its worldwide activities had become a major focus of a number of senators on Fulbright's Foreign Relations Committee. President Eisenhower, in his determination to stay out of costly land wars, had leaned heavily on enhanced covert operations to advance U.S. interests around the globe. What bothered Fulbright was the fact that intelligence operations were reviewed only in highly classified hearings of the Senate Armed Services Committee and not in Senator Fulbright's full Senate Foreign Relations Committee.

As luck would have it, Senator Stuart Symington (D-Mo.) served on both the Senate Foreign Relations Committee and the Senate Armed Services Committee. Symington became a fairly close friend of mine. He was also a close personal friend of my stepfather-in-law, Admiral George Anderson. I also had a marvelous friendship with his son James Symington, who was elected to the House of Representatives.

When I attended Senator Symington's hearing on U.S. worldwide commitments, it was the first time I ever saw a committee chair swear in the witness. He explained that it was for the protection of the witness. If the witness gave a truthful answer but not one the administration preferred, Symington explained that the witness had only to point out that he or she was under oath, and thus had no choice but to tell the truth. The underlying message and symbolism were lost on none of those present: The trust deficit between Congress and the White House had grown so deep that the basic veracity of government officials was now being called into question.

In the middle of my first closed subcommittee session, discussing the covert war in Laos, Senator Symington walked over to where I was seated and handed me a folded note. It read, "David, when you get to be Secretary of Defense, go in to win or don't go in." I remembered Jimmy Symington telling me at the annual banquet of the Alfalfa Club that his father was headed back from Southeast Asia, having done his own reassessment of the war effort. His conclusion was that we could not win with a half-hearted commitment and that we should get out of Vietnam.

Throughout my career, whenever I was able to persuade individuals to change their mind or alter a chosen course of action, it was always through civil and sincere discussion and the fostering of trust. By the early 1970s, the bonds of trust between the branches of government were snapping, and with that the fabric of government was tearing apart. My response was to redouble efforts to build trust, and that often meant sidestepping normal bureaucratic procedures and conducting much of my business in private. Confidentialities had to be kept.

In my own life, grace and the power of civility have been essential elements in building trust. As I have already stressed, civility requires treating others with respect, listening to what they have to say in open dialogue, and thus fostering trust in order to reach higher ground. Listening is critical because it allows you see the world through someone else's eyes and to better understand where that person is coming from. My son Lupton Patten Abshire is now an Episcopal priest, but in his earlier days, he was a cab driver at National Airport. His boss at that time gave him some excellent advice relating to the topic of listening to others. He told Lupton that to get a good tip, there are only two responses you need to give to a passenger's stories, "Yeah, you're right" and "I know what you mean."

While this bit of advice may seem to suggest insincerity, the heart of the idea is dead on. To be an effective negotiator, you must know what motivates the other party and create a personal rapport built on respect. Listening does not mean that you necessarily agree, but it allows you come to understand the concerns, motivations, and goals of the other party.

The deals that I reached with lawmakers as the State Department's congressional liaison were largely based on the trust, however strained, that Nixon was trying to keep his campaign promise to end the Vietnam War. Implicit in those negotiations was the promise, at least with my arrival, that the Nixon administration would begin to consult more with Capitol Hill.

In this regard, I received an unexpected jolt from the White House in January of 1971. Once again I was briefed privately by the director of the Joint Staff, John Vogt. His briefing concerned what later became known as Lam Son 719, an operation that involved South Vietnamese ground forces, supported by U.S. airpower and logistics. The target of the attack was the narrow neck of Laos where the famous Sihanouk Trail was used by North Vietnam to supply Viet Cong forces in the south.

When I asked the general how he intended to brief lawmakers on Capitol Hill, I was stunned to get the same answer that I received before the surprise move into Cambodia: "Sir, you and the secretary of state are the only ones cleared for this briefing and no congressmen are."

Fortunately, I had known Henry Kissinger ever since our first CSIS conference back in 1963, when we kidded him about the internal contradictions in the paper he submitted. So I phoned him up and asked, "Henry, whose side are we on? I just got the briefing about Operation Lam Son 719. They told me that not only will we surprise the enemy, but we will also surprise the Congress. There is nothing [North Vietnamese] General Giap would like more. Are we really on his side?"

Kissinger was not amused by my rhetorical question. "Dave, I have a busy morning and I don't have time to joke around. Do you understand the briefing?"

I shot back, "I understand we are going to set off another antiwar movement and an adverse reaction in Congress. *That* is what I understand."

"Alright," Kissinger growled, "but we had better not lose surprise. I will authorize Secretary Laird, and Deputy Secretary Packard, to brief the Armed Services committees. You and Rogers can do the same with the Foreign Relations Committees."

Over the weekend, we organized a series of phone calls. I remember Democratic senator Claiborne Pell taking the call from his rustic Rhode Island home. "David, once again you do a dastardly thing, but how gentlemanly for you to call me." Absolute secrecy was maintained.

I did get a call from my close friend Admiral Thomas "Tom" Moore, chairman of the Joint Chiefs, complaining that Senator George Aiken, a Republican from Vermont, had been leaking. I replied to Moore, "Tom, I double-checked on your concern about a potential leak by Governor Aiken. He has not done that."

"I know, Dave, but he keeps on going on TV and rolling his eyes like he knows something," Moore complained.

"That is beside the point," I insisted. "He has not leaked. Maybe it's just a nervous habit."

Kissinger called me one day to say that he appreciated the job I was doing as congressional liaison, and he wanted to go the extra mile in helping me with the outreach. He was willing to have secret, "off-the-record," off-site sessions with members of the Foreign Relations Committee. However, he insisted that I represent Secretary of State Rogers in these meetings.

I was both overjoyed and dismayed at the time. The effort on Kissinger's part to be more forthcoming and inclusive with Congress was admirable. Sharing Kissinger's strategic narrative would help me keep members of Congress onboard with administration policy, and was thus a great boost to my endeavors. But I also realized that his proposal represented an implicit snub of Secretary Rogers.

After I told Chairman Fulbright about Kissinger's proposal, he phoned me the following day to say that he looked forward to the arrangement of the off-site meetings. He then shrewdly added that the first one would take place in his office. So much for the "off-site" part, I thought to myself. He further informed me upon arrival to his office that a court reporter would record the session. So much for the "secret" part of the briefing. Nevertheless, once the briefing started, the meeting turned in a very constructive direction.

Following the meeting, I sheepishly rang the secretary of state to tell him what happened. I felt so sorry for Rogers and wondered if I should have told him in advance. This man, who had been attorney general under Eisenhower and was a very accomplished and imposing individual, was all but reduced to insignificance by Kissinger's dictate excluding him from key discussions with Congress.

At Kissinger's initiative, the next briefing took place at the Dolley Madison House on Lafayette Square, just across from the White House. I wasn't sure how the meeting would go, as I had used the opportunity presented by Kissinger's recent, historic trip to China to poach a key member of his staff.

After my arrival at the State Department, I had long sought to enhance my staff. I had inherited a good, but not a great, deputy. In the interim I had come to know Marshall Wright, an articulate and brilliant thinker and diplomat who was on Kissinger's staff. While Kissinger was in China with President Nixon and Secretary of State Rogers, Wright had approached me about joining my staff. He had faithfully served Henry since the beginning of the administration and was ready for a change.

I happily discovered that Kissinger's deputy, Alexander "Al" Haig, was willing to support Wright's move. So I had seized the opportunity. Henry Kissinger thus greeted me loudly as I arrived at the Dolley Madison House for our breakfast, announcing, "You stole my man, Abshire! And you did it while I was away in China!"

"Haig agreed, and I thought you would, too," I responded. "Marshall deserves it." Kissinger settled down and relented, "Well, you are still the best congressional liaison we have in the government." I thus made Marshall my deputy, and he was superb in the job. He was truly one of the best writers I have ever met. When I left the State Department, I made sure Marshall got my position. Marshall later had a fine second career as a senior vice president of the Eaton Corporation.

The meeting at Dolley Madison House proved to be especially constructive. Granted, there was some initial awkwardness instigated by Chairman Fulbright, who disliked Kissinger and had a newfound fondness for Secretary Rogers. Why had Rogers not been included in the meeting with Chinese leader Chairman Mao Zedong on the administration's recent historic trip? Fulbright wanted to know. Kissinger's explanation was that the meeting was scheduled only at the last minute, and when they were informed, Rogers was nowhere to be found. It was all just an unfortunate coincidence, in Kissinger's telling. The committee members patiently listened to Kissinger's explanation, but he was not very convincing. I could only thank my lucky stars that I had not been present in China during the trip, and thus they could not blame me for yet another snub of Secretary Rogers.

Fortunately, we were able to move the conversation beyond the incident and focus on Kissinger's extraordinary strategy behind the Nixon administration's surprise outreach to China. The outreach toward China had been followed with Kissinger's "live and let live" policy of détente toward Russia. This strategic triangulation was unparalleled in modern U.S. foreign policy. Not only was Nixon recalibrating the balance of power between the United States, China, and Russia, but he was also putting pressure on to the North Vietnamese, who depended heavily on both China and Russia for support. The subsequent Watergate scandal and Nixon's resignation to avoid impeachment should not obscure the brilliance of this foreign policy gambit, no more than Nixon's historic outreach to China lent veracity to his claim that "I am not a crook." He most certainly was.

Bill Bundy, the brilliant scholar and former assistant secretary of state for East Asian and Pacific affairs, addresses this fundamental dichotomy at the heart of the Nixon administration in his excellent book *A Tangled Web: The Making of Foreign Policy in the Nixon Presidency*:

> In effect, Nixon and especially Kissinger helped to create a new and balanced triangular situation, easing Sino-Japanese enmity, leaving the United States in the position of having good relations with both the great Asian nations, and removing any chance of unhealthy competition for a favorable position among the capitals. The result also showed that an alliance with the United States could be a reassurance to other powers, even those against whom the alliance had once been directed . . . the trip to China and its outcome made Henry Kissinger a national figure overnight,

rather than just a celebration in the Washington arena (within the Beltway) . . . the breakthrough also boosted his [Nixon's] candidacy for reelection: in June, a Gallup poll showed 39 percent for Nixon and 41 percent for his assumed rival Senator Muskie, but in late August the count was 42–36 in favor of Nixon.[11]

Bundy also makes the difficult-to-dispute point that Nixon was ultimately undone by "his unshakeable bent to deceive." However, Bundy distinguishes between deception and secrecy. I certainly found in many of my dealings that confidential communications are often key to successful outcomes. They give concerned parties the elbow room necessary to explore possibilities and to work out deals without having each step along the way judged and critiqued in the public arena. Secrecy was certainly critical to the Nixon administration's opening to China and the Paris Agreement on the Vietnam War. As Bundy aptly points out, "In both cases a visible negotiating process would have attracted criticism, upsetting reactions that would have made the final result difficult if not impossible to reach. But in each case there was no positive deception. The objectives were consistent with what the Administration was saying or not saying in public."[12]

I continued to witness the deception of the Nixon administration after I left the State Department at the end of 1972. The Nixon White House asked me to join the Commission on the Organization of the Government for Foreign Policy, which became known as the "Murphy Commission," with the idea that I would control it. I was sent in effect to kill it. The informal language on my duties shifted when I could not kill it. Kissinger shouted at me over the phone, "Abshire, control it!" Of course, the problem was that I secretly sympathized with many of the proposals for reform within the commission.

Ambassador Robert Murphy, known as the "diplomat among warriors," chaired the commission. He was a man of the old school, possessing warmth, style, and color. Since I had been more or less given the role of organizing the commission, I may have been the first person to suggest Bob Murphy as chair. In any event, I am sure there would have been no dissent. The commission's work would run until June 1975, at which point it was to report to the president and the Congress.

The official mission of the commission was to submit findings and recommendations for the more effective conduct of the nation's foreign policy. The executive and legislative branches each had appointments to the commission. The appointees from the executive branch included Anne Armstrong, Bill Casey, Jane Engelhard, Arend Lubbers, Stanley Wagner, and Frank McGlinn. At the time, Anne was counsel to the president, and the highest positioned woman in the Republican Party. Bill Casey was chairman of the Import-

Export Bank. Members of the Murphy Commission from the legislative branch were Senators James Pearson (R-Kans.) and Mike Mansfield (D-Mont.) and Congressmen William Mailliard (R-Calif.), Clement Zablocki (D-Wis.), William Broomfield (R-Mich.), and Peter Frelinghuysen (R-N.J.). Some were knowledgeable and others were less so. A wide range of experts were employed by the commission, notably to include Paul Volker, Richard Cooper, and Graham Allison, I. M. Destler, Joe Nye, and Alexander George.

The Murphy Commission report concluded: "Under the President the major responsibility for initiating, formulating, and implementing policy should lie with the major departments. We are convinced that delegation of large authority to the White House staff—with its implied corollary of a sizable staff—will erode the competence, authority, and thus inevitably the quality of the Departmental executives and their staffs."

In the middle of the hearing process on Capitol Hill and around the country, Anne Armstrong was nominated by the president to serve as ambassador to the Court of St. James. Unfortunately, she had to drop out of the commission. While it was never said, Henry Kissinger had concluded by this point that Abshire had been taken in and could not control the commission. Kissinger had heard that there was a passage in the commission report draft that prohibited a person from having the position of both national security advisor and secretary of state at the same time.

Vice President Nelson Rockefeller was appointed to fill the vacancy left by Anne Armstrong, and also to eliminate the passage that would prohibit Kissinger from holding both positions. I sat next to Nelson Rockefeller when a furious Kissinger called him over the phone to complain about that provision and my inability to squelch it. Kissinger barked to the vice president, "Abshire was supposed to be able to prevent that kind of thing and he failed. You were then put on the commission, and now you have failed." Rockefeller calmly replied, "Henry, you don't understand. You don't understand at all. The commission decided that *never again* should there be a person in both positions. You are in a very special position."

After a pause, Kissinger replied, "Very smart, Nelson."

With this move by the vice president, Mike Mansfield and Jane Engelhard ceased attending the Murphy Commission meetings. In his formal comments of dissent, Mansfield noted that

my expression of disappointment does not mean that there are not useful observations . . . contained in the commission report. However, I fear the ratio of effort to result has not been up to expectations. A surfeit of words masks an absence of clarity. Gruel is being served in a really big bowl. . . . Looking back on 1972, one has to remember that at that time the executive branch sought to block every avenue and deny Congress a role in foreign policy mainly in regard to Indonesia. The doctrine of executive privilege has been invoked and implemented to the extent that it was offensive . . . Efforts by senate committees to obtain information were blocked, evaded, or ignored.

Later Mansfield said, "Perhaps the most remarkable [omission] is the total absence until one reaches the concluding chapter of any discussion of the importance of the Congress in foreign policy."

There was a certain tragedy behind the Murphy Commission. The fundamental idea that reform and reorganization of government structures were needed in order to more efficiently conduct foreign policy was absolutely valid. Not for the last time, unfortunately, partisanship in Washington, D.C., destroyed the trust necessary to reach consensus on meaningful reform.

Many years later, in 2013, I was sitting with Henry Kissinger prior to going into a CSIS board meeting. I told Henry that of all his many books, I believed his first, on the Congress of Vienna, to be his best. After suffering the instability and violence caused by the French Revolution and Napoleonic Wars, Europe subsequent to the Vienna Congress of 1814–1815 experienced a hundred years of relative peace. Of course, Kissinger wrote *A World Restored* back in the 1950s, before he had to contend with his own role in the events that he was analyzing. Having said that I thought *A World Restored* was perhaps his greatest book, I added provocatively, and in a failed attempt at humor, that they have been going downhill ever since. Later, to heal any potential wounds, I wrote Kissinger a personal letter to clarify my true beliefs:

> While we waited for the board meeting, I commented that your best book was your first book, "A World Restored." If events had transpired differently, you could have restored the world in the 20th century. If President Ford had been reelected, only you could have brought China and Russia into a triangular framework, which may have avoided the Iranian disruption. The denouement of the Cold War may have come a decade or two earlier.

With the Nixon administration we can see clearly the potential power of civility, and the achievements that can be constructed on a foundation of respectful listening, honest dialogue, and the steady accumulation of trust. With trust, there is no limit to the creativity that grows naturally from collaborations between even unlikely partners, empowering all concerned to overcome obstacles and challenges together. As the Nixon example also illustrates, without trust, even the most powerful and potentially far-reaching strategic vision can be obscured, to the detriment of all.

The Korean War was a "crucible of leadership" for a young Lieutenant David Abshire, fresh out of West Point, who received a Bronze Star Medal with V for Valor as a company commander in combat. Courtesy of the Abshire Family Collection.

A bright future ahead: Abshire, then staff director of the House Republican Policy Committee in the late 1950s, huddles with Congressman Gerald R. Ford and Vice President Richard Nixon of the Eisenhower administration. Courtesy of the Abshire Family Collection.

Abshire's portrait as assistant secretary of state for congressional relations in the early 1970s.
Courtesy of the Abshire Family Collection.

As the cofounder and head of the Center for Strategic and International Studies (CSIS), one of the preeminent Washington think tanks, Abshire used his southern charm to attract the nation's preeminent strategists to CSIS, including Henry Kissinger, former national security adviser and secretary of state in the Nixon administration. Courtesy of the Abshire Family Collection.

As U.S. ambassador to NATO, Abshire meets with then Vice President George H.W. Bush, who revealed his "generous and winning character," not only in his demeanor but also in his actions. Courtesy of the Abshire Family Collection.

NATO Ambassador Abshire with Ambassador Max Kampelman, the storied arms control expert who headed the U.S. delegation in arms control negotiations with the Soviet Union that prefaced the end of the Cold War. Courtesy of the Abshire Family Collection.

Abshire shares a light moment with President Ronald Reagan and Vice President George H.W. Bush. Courtesy of the Abshire Family Collection.

Abshire meeting with Pope John Paul II, one of the most traveled world leaders in history. Courtesy of the Abshire Family Collection.

Abshire's international outreach positioned the Center for Strategic and International Studies as one of the most internationally respected and globally connected think tanks in the world. Here he meets with Japanese Prime Minister Zenko Suzuki. Courtesy of the Abshire Family Collection.

Returning to his alma mater: Abshire sometimes lectured at West Point, where as a student he was at the top of his class in military history, and so near the bottom in engineering and math that he was forced to repeat his first year after failing advanced algebra. Courtesy of the Abshire Family Collection.

Advisor to presidents: Abshire meets with President Bill Clinton and David Gergen, himself an advisor to four presidents (Nixon, Ford, Reagan, and Clinton). Courtesy of the Abshire Family Collection.

Sharing a light moment with President Reagan and the White House staff after the trauma of the Iran-Contra scandal, and meeting privately with Ronald Reagan. Abshire would look back on his role in restoring the nation's trust in a faltering Reagan presidency as one of the proudest accomplishment in his seventy years of public service. Courtesy of the Abshire Family Collection.

8

A Voice in the Darkness

Preserving Radio Free Europe and Radio Liberty

The reach of America's voice in the ideological struggle of the Cold War depended on Radio Free Europe and Radio Liberty. Beginning in 1949, Radio Free Europe broadcast to Soviet satellite countries, while Radio Liberty, founded in 1953, directly targeted the Soviet Union itself. Both stations were designed as sources of uncensored news, and they were born out of a belief that communism had to be contested on the battlefield of ideas and politics, as well as contained militarily. Both radio stations covered anti-Soviet protests and nationalist movements, but also cultural topics such as banned literature and music. Within the Soviet Union and Eastern Europe, they earned a reputation for being one of the most reliable sources of national as well as international news. Despite constant Soviet attempts to jam the broadcasts, their audiences grew throughout the Cold War.

In 1967, *Ramparts* magazine published an article revealing that the CIA helped fund these ostensibly civilian organizations. Investigations would later reveal that, indeed, both Radio Free Europe and Radio Liberty received covert funds from the CIA that were intermingled with other private donations. The CIA claimed to exercise little influence over their programming, but that did nothing to quell the negative reactions in Congress.

Senator Clifford P. Case, a Republican from New Jersey, claimed that the CIA funding went against Lyndon Johnston's stated policy and previous assurance that "no federal agency shall provide covert financial assistance or support, direct or indirect, to any of the nation's educational or voluntary organizations."[1] Richard Nixon's State Department responded that since the radio stations were located outside of the United State, that policy did not apply to them.

Nevertheless, at the State Department we did begin work on a proposal to place the radio stations under the control of a nonprofit, private corporation that would receive funds appropriated by Congress, but would operate independently. That meant the corporation would not be subjected to legislative review on policy matters. The corporation would be called the American Council for Private International Communications, and it would be overseen by an eleven-person board appointed by the president.

During my time as assistant secretary of state, Senator Fulbright was in full-on attack mode against the Nixon administration, and he fought against the proposal. In his book *The Pentagon Propaganda Machine*, Fulbright was highly critical of what he saw as an out-of-control military-industrial complex and an imperial foreign policy. In his efforts to undermine the radio stations, Fulbright thus commissioned a study by the Library of Congress's research service. He was unpleasantly surprised when the final report amounted to a favorable endorsement of Radio Free Europe and Radio Liberty. Fulbright immediately attempted to have the reports withheld from the public and rewritten. Eventually, syndicated columnists Rowland Evans and Robert Novak published a piece exposing Fulbright's actions, and the reports were eventually released. The critical importance of a free press as a watchdog over government was once again evident!

Fulbright responded to the controversy by withholding funding for Radio Free Europe and Radio Liberty. With funding for the radio stations due to expire in just ten days, I had no choice but to try to break the stalemate by arranging to meet with Senator Fulbright. When I arrived at his office, however, I was stunned to discover that he had just left for a two-week vacation in the Caribbean. One of his aides relayed the message that I need not worry, as the good senator would obtain a bipartisan agreement to provide adequate termination packages for all of the employees of Radio Free Europe and Radio Liberty. I was stunned. Here I was trying to save the radio stations, and Senator Fulbright was already making arrangement for their funerals.

I immediately proceeded to the office of Senator Mike Mansfield, the Democratic majority leader, and was lucky to catch him. Even though Mansfield was not a supporter of the radio stations, I didn't believe he would approve of terminating them in this backhanded way, without a shred of due process.

"Senator, I know you're not for these radios. But I don't believe you think this is the way the Congress should operate," I argued. "It's not the way to govern."

The silence of the long pause that followed was deafening. But then Mansfield showed that I had not misjudged him. "I'll tell the chief of staff of the Foreign Relations Committee to work up a plan with you to fund the radios for a year through the State Department while things are worked out." Against the odds, we had been given a reprieve.

In the spring of 1972, Nixon put together a special commission to discuss how Radio Free Europe and Radio Liberty should be governed and funded. President Eisenhower's brother, Milton Eisenhower, was appointed chairman. One argument against the stations that Fulbright often made was they unnecessarily provoked communist leaders and thus undermined the détente between the United States and the Soviet Union. The commission report concluded instead that "peace is more secure in well-informed societies than in those that may be more easily manipulated," and thus the stations contributed to détente.[2]

Building on our idea for the American Council for Private International Communications, the commission called for the creation of a Board for International Broadcasting (BIB), which would ensure journalistic independence, accountability to Congress, and adequate funding. The BIB would both shield the stations from political pressure and ensure that broadcasts were "not inconsistent with broad U.S. foreign policy."[3] Nixon was, of course, very supportive of the commission's report, and called the stations "voices of free information," which also "serve our national interest and merit the full support of the Congress and the American people."[4] Senators Hubert Humphrey (D-Minn.) and Charles Percy (R-Ill.) eventually crafted legislation based on the report's recommendation. Despite continued efforts to kill the stations by Senator Fulbright, the BIB was enacted into law in October of 1973.

I was a caught off guard in 1975 when I was tapped to be the first head of the BIB. The sum total of my experience with broadcasting was my effort to save Radio Free Europe and Radio Liberty during my time in the State Department. Once sworn into office as the first chairman of the BIB, I learned quickly, and immediately set out to untie some knotty problems. The Government Accountability Office (GAO) had published a report that concluded that a lot of taxpayers' money could be saved if Radio Liberty and Radio Free Europe were merged. In my first hearing as chairman of the BIB in front of a House committee, that idea was very much on lawmakers' minds. The message I received from a number of influential members was "Sooner rather than later." After all, the two organizations were geographically located side by side in Munich, West Germany. Under the circumstances, an organizational merger that saved taxpayer money and quieted congressional critics seemed reasonable.

Perhaps not surprisingly, the heads of the radio stations were very much opposed to a merger. After some lengthy discussions, members of the BIB convinced the leadership teams of both organizations that if we did not craft a strong corporate merger plan, their funds would be cut off by Congress. I spent a week in Munich driving this point home, at the end of which the two presidents of the radio stations finally agreed that a merger was necessary for survival. Radio Free Europe and Radio Liberty would become one in 1976.

During this time, I was very fortunate to work with some extraordinary individuals, and I learned a lot from them. Prominent among this group were Congressman Dante Fascell (D-Fla.); Leonard Marks, the former head of the U.S. Information Agency; and Frank Stanton, the former president of CBS who chaired what became known as the Stanton Commission, which helped bring the USIA and other parts of the government together behind our efforts. I stepped down from chairing the Board for International Broadcasting in 1977. Back at CSIS, I was later able to capitalize on my experiences on the board and reinforce the mission of these international broadcasts. Fascell had become chairman of the House International Affairs Committee by 1979, and he suggested CSIS publish a group of essays entitled *International News: Freedom Under Attack*. I wrote the first essay. Fascell was kind enough to note my contribution in his introduction to the essays, which he publicly recited before his committee:

> Dr. Abshire holds an excellent vantage point from which to assess the role and performance of Radio Free Europe (RFE) and Radio Liberty (RL). While Chairman of the Board for International Broadcasting, he supervised their establishment as independent open operations. As I stated in one of his appearances before our committee, "RFE and RL owe their lives to him."[5]

Funding for Radio Free Europe/Radio Liberty grew during the Reagan administration. They played an important role in Czechoslovakia's 1989 Velvet Revolution, and during the period of openness, or glasnost, instituted by Soviet leader Mikhail Gorbachev in the late 1980s, the stations were no longer jammed. Dissidents were routinely interviewed on their broadcasts without fear of persecution. Their broadcasts during the attempted coup directed against Russian leader Boris Yeltsin in August of 1991 served as a much-needed source of information during that chaotic time. Yeltsin later showed his appreciation with a presidential decree permitting Radio Liberty to open a permanent bureau in Moscow, which is still in operation today.

That same year, former Estonian president Lennart Meri nominated the radios for the Nobel Peace Prize. Regarding their role in Poland's transformation and struggle for freedom, Nobel Laureate Lech Walesa said the role "cannot even be described. Would there be earth without the sun?"[6] Following the fall of communism, the stations went on to establish local bureaus throughout the former Soviet Union and Warsaw Pact, training local journalists in the ethics of fairness and factual accuracy. They continue to play a critical role today acting as a surrogate free press when one doesn't exist or is banned.

Looking back, the role Radio Free Europe and Radio Liberty played in bringing factual and reliable news to the masses trapped behind the Iron Curtain is remarkable. They were a key component of the U.S. strategy to fight, and win, the battle of ideas and ideology—with the free democracies on one side and the authoritarian communist bloc on the other—that defined the Cold War. I feel honored to have played a part in the fight to preserve these indispensable institutions.

9

A Perfect Victory

Revitalizing NATO

Whenever I have spoken about classical strategy, Sun Tzu's definition of "perfect victory" has come to mind: winning without actually having to fight. In that regard, I believe the West's cornerstone alliance NATO provides history's greatest example of a perfect victory. I wrote about that success in 1989 in my book *Preventing World War III: A Realistic Grand Strategy*. I had studied NATO long before I ever dreamt that I might one day represent the United States in that august alliance. In fact, NATO was the subject of the first major initiative that CSIS launched following the Soviet army's intervention in Czechoslovakia in 1969. We had quickly assembled a group of experts to visit NATO member countries at that critical time to perform an assessment of the alliance.

Much later, after I had managed the national security transition for the incoming Reagan administration in 1980, I had been considered for other positions in government, ranging from deputy secretary of state to ambassador to Japan to NATO ambassador. National Security Advisor Bill Clark first approached me in 1983 about serving as the U.S. representative to NATO. At that time, I felt CSIS had extraordinary momentum, and I could thus accept such a key overseas post without worrying about the health of the institution that I had cofounded. As expected, the State Department bureaucracy put forth its own favored candidates from the Foreign Service, but the White House wanted me in Brussels, and my candidacy prevailed.

At that time, critics of NATO tended to be grouped in three separate camps. The often brilliant foreign policy experts in the neoconservative camp did not think that the Europeans or NATO were adequately supportive of Israel, which as a democracy in a sea of repressive Arab regimes fit well into their assertive pro-democracy ideology. The second camp of critics were centered at the Department of Defense, where officials bemoaned NATO's bureaucratic red tape and "lowest common denominator" approach to decision-making. The third group of critics were encamped on Capitol Hill, where lawmakers routinely took our European allies to task for not bearing their share of the burden of collective defense. While I believed NATO, like all institutions, was in need of nearly constant renewal and reform, I tended to view it the way Winston Churchill viewed alliances in general: "There is at least one thing worse than fighting with allies," Churchill famously said, "and that is to fight without them."

I arrived as the new ambassador at NATO headquarters, just outside of Brussels, on an uncharacteristically hot day in mid-July of 1983. The last series of NATO meetings that summer were in full swing, before everyone disappeared for six weeks on their standard European vacation. I couldn't help but recall Barbara Tuchman's award-winning book, *The Guns of August*, which described the Austro-Hungarian attack in late July of 1914 that ignited World War I. Surely the month to begin a war in Europe would be when everyone was on vacation. I was later relieved to discover that a standby staff of diplomatic and military representatives kept watch over the long holidays, ready to respond to any crisis within an hour, day or night.

My first briefing was given by Stephen Ledogar, my deputy chief of mission, who towered over even my six-foot-four-inch frame. Secretary of State George Shultz once called Ledogar "the master negotiator," but it was his team-building mastery that I came to value most. Ledogar kept my diverse staff of about one hundred motivated and pulling in the same direction.

Not long after I arrived as NATO ambassador in 1983, we had the opportunity to buy the estate of the widow of the Côte d'Or chocolatier Jean Michiels. She practically gave the estate to the U.S. government in gratitude for "saving Belgium" in World War II. The estate was rechristened Truman Hall in honor of the president who helped found NATO. Truman Hall lay on twenty-seven acres of gentle hills and valleys, meadows, and formal gardens. A curvaceous cobbled drive, lined with roses, led to the tree-lined approach to the residence.

When terrorism struck NATO in 1985–1986, this became the safest embassy in Europe. In 1985, 170 of 785 terrorist incidents involved Americans or U.S. overseas facilities around the world. Sixty-three terrorist attacks occurred in Western Europe alone.[1] Unfortunately, NATO would not be able escape these violent years unscathed. On January 15, 1986, the Reuters office received a message from the Red Army Faction and France's Action Directe that said, "Attacks against the multinational structures of NATO, against its bases and its strategies, against its plans and propaganda, constitute the first large mobilization."

In the early morning hours of the same day, a car pulled up in front of the NATO Support Center, which was used by U.S. NATO staff and U.S. military personnel assigned to NATO. Moments later the building was rocked by a bomb that had been hidden in the car. By the grace of god, the guards were not injured, but the bombing caused $500,000 of damage to the building and considerable disruption of services to the U.S. community within NATO. In addition, a NATO pipeline and the North Atlantic Assembly headquarters were bombed by terrorists. As NATO ambassador, I was personally on a list of top terrorist targets in Europe. Luckily, the photograph that accompanied my name on the terrorist list was the picture of my predecessor!

Security was tightened considerably. My security detail suddenly grew from a single bodyguard who rode with me in my two-and-a-half-ton armored sedan to an additional follow-on car with three armed guards. The different routes we took from Truman Hall to NATO headquarters were purposely chosen at random to thwart ambushes. Al Haig, with his regimented military style, argued for sticking to the same route, but the security team overrode him. I often sat in the front passenger seat, figuring that the terrorists would likely focus on whoever was sitting in the back seat. The security detail even accompanied me and my family on our seaside vacation. Truman Hall's security was upgraded with mounted cameras and chain-link fencing.

Vice President George Bush and Barbara Bush visited Truman Hall and enjoyed the enhanced security of the residence. George was able to jog without bodyguards throughout the seven gardens, two mazes, and grand lawns. Barbara went on her routine power walks accompanied only by my wife, Carolyn. I was amused when Carolyn attempted to keep up with Barbara Bush and breathlessly still tried to make small talk. During this visit I was struck by Bush's extraordinarily open personality, which he could never seem to convey in speeches or on television.

As the host of a luncheon with Vice President Bush and the NATO ambassadors, I was able to override his advance detail who insisted on a small gathering. Instead, I invited editors and publishers from across Europe to the lunch, confident that they would witness a side of George H. W. Bush rarely seen in public.

Following the departure of the guests, Vice President Bush said to me, "Dave, get your household staff on the stairway. I want my picture taken with them." The household staff was made up of a Portuguese butler, an Italian chef and sous chef, an Indonesian steward, and fifteen more people from around the world. Not one of them had ever spoken with a head of government. Not surprisingly, the staff was a bit confused as we tried to explain what was happening. Bush took a photo with each of the staff members, not one of whom could even vote for him. About a week later, we received signed pictures of the household staff with the vice president. George H. W. Bush's generous and winning character was not evident only in his personality and demeanor but also in his actions.

The North Atlantic Treaty Organization was originally created in 1949 as a defensive alliance focused on collective security. Its structures were designed to enable its members to work together on complex security and foreign policy issues and to generate and apply defense resources effectively. At the time of my arrival, however, the North Atlantic Council that governed the alliance had established more than three hundred committees and subcommittees covering matters pertaining to armaments, collective defense, politics, economics, and so forth. The organization charged with implementing the grand strategy of the Western alliance was thus choked with poorly coordinated and compartmentalized directorates, committees, boards, and agencies, making an efficient flow of information and analysis impossible. Ledogar and I cabled back to Washington that NATO was badly in need of reform and reorganization, and we set about to identify specific ways to make it more effective.

Another area in need of renewal and reform was leadership. There was a general feeling that long-serving NATO Secretary-General Joseph Luns had simply been at it too long and his leadership had grown stale. Part of the problem was the lack of a set term for the top position. One of the first requests made of me by the State Department was to see if I could get a process moving to replace Luns, who many people felt was looking backward by that time, rather than forward. Yet no one seemed to know the protocol for bringing up such a delicate issue.

I turned for advice to André de Staercke, a founding member of the alliance. He informed me that the Danish ambassador to NATO was now the dean and the longest-serving member of the NATO Council, so I should begin the process with him. However, when I called on him to discuss replacing the secretary general, the Danish ambassador practically crawled under his desk. It was clear that if anyone was going to bring up the matter of a leadership succession, it was going to have to be me.

So I called on Secretary General Luns to talk over a cup of coffee. Joseph Luns was an impressive man. He had begun his career in the Dutch cabinet in 1952, and first arrived at NATO back in 1971. His voice was so imposing that it was said to be capable of "overruling a thunderstorm." I opened our conversation gingerly.

"Joseph, I've heard rumors that after so many outstanding years of service as Dutch foreign secretary and as NATO secretary general, you have been thinking about retirement," I said. "You are pretty much indispensable, so of course it would be very hard to replace you."

Luns looked down at me and agreed that finding his replacement would indeed be a great challenge. "I certainly cannot think of anyone to meet the demands of this job, but there always comes time for change," he told me. "I expect to leave next August. That should allow for ample time to search for a new secretary general." I thanked Joseph Luns very much for the visit and sent the message back to Washington.

Just over a week later, my secretary caught up with me in the winding halls of NATO headquarters. "Sir, Secretary Luns has just called your office and summoned you." With my West Point training, I double-timed it to his office. Upon my arrival, he interrupted his meeting, cleared the room, and got right to the point.

"David, I recently told you that I would retire a year from now. I was quite clear. As I am sure you know, there has been talk about Lord Peter Carrington taking my place," he said, noting that British prime minister Margaret Thatcher had apparently already phoned President Reagan and gained his support for Carrington. "Now I have been pressured to vacate as soon as possible so that Carrington may soon be received and installed in my job."

Luns instructed me to take out a pad and pen and to write down his message to Washington verbatim.

Please write, "I told Ambassador Abshire that I would be happy a year from now to have the position of Secretary General rotated. I was quite clear about the date, a year from now. I now hear Lord Peter Carrington has jumped the gun by obtaining the support of Margaret Thatcher for this position. Furthermore, I hear he is working to obtain the backing of Ronald Reagan. Let me be clear, I will vacate the office of Secretary General *prior* to August only if I am caught fornicating in public on the Grand Place in the middle of the day." David, I do not want you to change a word of that message.

I assured Joseph Luns that I would send his message exactly as dictated, secure in the knowledge that the process of finding fresh leadership for the alliance had begun in earnest. Not long after, Luns complained to me about a new book that had just been published by Sir John Hackett. He felt Hackett's book disparaged the alliance by claiming that if war were to come with the Soviet-led Warsaw Pact, the East Germans would attack the weak northern sector and force the collapse of the alliance within days. "This is the kind of publicity that is totally inaccurate and injurious to the alliance," Luns told me. Of course, I kept my lips zipped. I already knew that Sir John Hackett was entirely correct.

On Secretary General Luns's last day, he climbed into his armored Rolls-Royce that he loved, flags flying, and departed NATO after twelve mostly productive years. Former British defense and foreign minister Lord Peter Carrington soon took over, and put Luns's Rolls-Royce up for sale.

There was a weakness in NATO's defense strategy that left our European allies vulnerable to an attack or coercion: an overreliance on nuclear deterrence. The United States had just completed the much-celebrated deployment of the treaty for Intermediate-Range Nuclear Forces (INF) missiles to Europe, installed to counter the Soviet deployment of intermediate-range SS-20 nuclear missiles targeting NATO countries. So much attention and energy had been devoted to this deployment, which prompted massive demonstrations in Europe, that the issue of conventional forces had been overshadowed. And yet U.S. Army general Bernard Rogers, the Supreme Allied Commander, had confirmed that were NATO to come under attack, alliance forces would run out of ammunition in only a matter of days.

At that time, Europe was still in the middle of a recession, and with the INF deployments our allies felt they had reached their limit on defense spending. They were willing to rely heavily on the nuclear deterrence strategy of mutually assured destruction, or MAD. Under that construct, any attack would quickly escalate into a nuclear exchange and certain destruction of both sides, supposedly making an initial attack unthinkable.

Initially, NATO had relied on a strategy of flexible response, which would respond to a Soviet attack using conventional forces with a defense in kind. Under that construct, only if the alliance were unable to match a conventional assault with conventional means would it climb the escalation ladder by employing tactical nuclear strikes against invading Warsaw Pact forces. However, the logic of this deterrence calculation held only as long as NATO maintained relative parity in conventional and nuclear forces with the Soviet Union. By the late 1970s, the U.S. had lost its nuclear superiority over the Soviet Union, which could field conventional forces well in excess of NATO. The conventional forces pillar of NATO's deterrence posture was increasingly shaky.

The struggle to convince European allies to invest in conventional military forces was not new. In fact, it went back to the 1950s and NATO's first decade. In the 1970s, the Carter administration successfully pressured the Europeans into signing a new NATO Long-Term Defense Program that called for greater defense expenditures. This agreement required all member nations to pledge to increase defense spending to 3 percent of gross domestic product

(GDP). As it turned out, the Europeans routinely failed to meet this commitment. Many years later, the Wales Summit Declaration of the North Atlantic Council meeting in September 2014 only insisted that NATO countries follow the guideline to spend 2 percent of GDP for defense, and that the majority of alliance members that currently fail to spend 2 percent do so within a decade.[2]

During a CSIS conference held in Brussels around this time, Tom Callahan, a brilliant CSIS defense analyst, explained how this chronic underinvestment in defense capabilities amounted to unilateral disarmament. Much of what was purchased by the individual NATO members were redundant weapon systems. The fact that each member nation was buying a little bit of every kind of weapon at very inefficient rates of production amounted to a boon for defense companies, but it was a gross misuse of scarce defense resources. In spite of the fact that NATO allies were collectively spending four times what the Warsaw Pact invested in military forces, the alliance was falling behind.

Senator Sam Nunn (D-Ga.) had worked closely with CSIS on defense issues, and he was one of the participants in the Brussels conference. I invited Nunn to stay at my beautiful ambassador's residence in Belgium and to join a lunch I was hosting for NATO ambassadors and a few members of Congress. Predictably, the assembled NATO ambassadors were complacent about the underinvestment in conventional forces and the overreliance on a shaky strategy of mutually assured destruction. Nunn was greatly disappointed by the attitudes of the NATO officials, even those from our staunchest allies such as Great Britain and Germany. When he voiced grave concerns over the recklessness of the strategy, the ambassadors present responded that clearly the strategy had been working. As I well knew, it worked because no one really questioned the underlying assumptions. That was about to change.

Over the years, Sam Nunn had remained a loyal supporter of NATO, always opposing any legislation that called for the withdrawal of U.S. troops from Europe. But that lunch planted an idea in his head, and it would grow into a conspiracy involving a "secret deal." Nunn, a true strategist in every sense of the word, enlisted other key conspirators, including Senator Theodore "Ted" Stevens (R-Alaska), the ranking member of the powerful Appropriations Committee; and Deputy Secretary of Defense William Howard Taft IV. On the alliance side, the conspiracy eventually included German defense minister Manfred Woerner and NATO secretary general Lord Peter Carrington. I didn't know it at the time of the fateful lunch at my Brussels residence, but I too was to become a secret sharer in the Nunn conspiracy.

Inside the Departments of State and Defense, my staff and I took the lead in examining NATO's conventional force imbalance and wasteful resource allocation. In a major speech at the Atlantic Treaty Association in Rome, I proposed an initiative to address those shortcomings head-on. The following month, during the defense ministers meeting, I was delighted when German defense minister Manfred Woerner referred to my speech and endorsed its proposal for a new NATO resource strategy and improved armaments cooperation. Woerner called for the development of a conceptual military framework to put those ideas into practice and provide a long-term, comprehensive strategy for resource allocation that could more easily be sold to our individual parliaments. When Woerner convinced the other defense ministers to embrace the proposal, I knew that we had made a tremendous step forward.

Nunn approved of the conceptual military framework but did not believe we could get the necessary follow-through from our European allies. He thought about nuclear weapons and deterrence as much as anyone in the U.S. government, and years later would join with Senator Richard Lugar (R-Ind.) to propose the groundbreaking Nunn-Lugar Cooperative Threat Reduction Program to reduce the nuclear arsenals of both the United States and Russia at the end of the Cold War. In the 1980s, while I was U.S. ambassador to NATO, Nunn was profoundly concerned with an alliance defense posture that, in the event of an actual Soviet attack with conventional forces, amounted to a trip wire that would quickly set off an all-out nuclear Armageddon. Later in the year, I got a call from Senator Nunn.

"Dave, I want to help you out on their efforts to reform NATO. I know that you don't agree with this 'trip-wire' strategy any more than I do. If our plan is simply to use inadequate conventional forces as a trip wire to nuclear war, why should we have such a large troop presence in Europe and commitment to NATO?"

As chairman of the Armed Services Committee, Nunn proposed inserting a provision to the defense authorization bill that would eliminate funding earmarked for the reinforcement of Europe in a crisis, and begin withdrawing U.S. troops from Europe. Under a trip-wire scenario, he reasoned, Europe and our forward-deployed forces would disappear beneath a nuclear mushroom cloud before U.S. reinforcements could even arrive.

I told Nunn that his proposed amendment was a terrible idea and would be devastating for alliance morale. He was nonplussed.

"Dave, don't worry, it won't pass anyway. It will just frighten the Europeans into finally meeting their commitments to fund conventional forces. You send me your letter stating your disapproval, and I will include it in my comments. That will help ensure that it does not pass."

Nunn moved forward with his proposal. The Nunn amendment proposed removing 90,000 U.S. troops from Europe over three years.[3] However, his amendment also provided our allies with an out. The U.S. troop withdrawal would be halted if our allies met certain defense funding benchmarks, on their way to meeting the commitment to spend 3 percent of GDP on defense.

I soon received word from the White House that there were already 75 Senate votes in support of the Nunn amendment. Furthermore, the White House was now considering going along with Nunn's proposal. At the regular lunch meeting of NATO ambassadors in Brussels, I warned about these alarming developments in Washington. Sir John Graham, the British ambassador to NATO, was not worried.

"Our mission in Washington is watching these developments quite closely, and they said there is nothing to worry about," he assured our colleagues.

I was not so sure. I started to pump my many contacts on Capitol Hill. I told them that Sam Nunn was one of our great strategic thinkers, but that he was off base in playing a game of chicken with our NATO allies at a time when my team and I were still relatively new on the job. I asked for more time to bring the Europeans around.

Senate Armed Services Committee chairman John Tower (R-Tex.) led the fight against the Nunn amendment. He argued that it would be seen in Europe not as constructive prodding but rather as bullying. Senator Bill Cohen (R-Maine) proposed his own amendment that eliminated the automatic troop withdrawal and instead required regular reports on NATO's progress. In the end, President Reagan picked up the phone and got the needed votes to defeat the Nunn amendment. The Cohen amendment passed, much to the relief of Europe. Still, some of those in Congress who voted against the Nunn amendment made it clear that if NATO failed to make the required progress, they would vote in support of another Nunn amendment the following year.

During his first year as secretary general of NATO, I brought Lord Carrington back to Washington for a series of meetings with top U.S. officials, including President Reagan. I arranged for us to meet with CIA director Bill Casey and deputy director Bob Gates. I will confess that I told a bit of a white lie in preparation for this meeting. I explained to Gates that since Carrington was hard of hearing, it would be better if Gates gave the actual briefing, as he had a strong voice. In fact, Carrington was not hard of hearing, but Bill Casey's thought processes could be almost impossible to follow at times. As Dick Allen once quipped about Casey, "It was as if the mouth and brain were not fully coordinated."

Casey started the meeting. "Dave suggested the deputy director give the brief. I will say only a few brief words of introduction." Twenty-five minutes later Casey was still talking, and as I had feared, it was not at all clear what he was trying to say. Finally, Casey announced that Bob Gates would now give the actual brief, but we were out of time. Carrington and I were due to meet President Reagan in the Oval Office.

As we were walking across the parking lot to the West Wing of the White House, Carrington leaned in toward me and asked, "Dave, if your director of central intelligence called to say that a war was on, do you think the president would understand what he was trying to say?" "No," I responded. "Especially since President Reagan is deaf in one ear!" We were off to fun start.

We assembled in the Oval Office with Secretary of State George Shultz, Secretary of Defense Cap Weinberger, National Security Advisor Bud Mc-Farland, and President Reagan. As was their habit, Reagan and Carrington began the conversation with a joke or two. Then Lord Carrington got down to business.

"Mr. President, Dr. Fred Ikle, your undersecretary of defense, wrote a piece in *Foreign Affairs* stating that the doctrine of mutually assured destruction would not work for NATO. This was not a case of a professor somewhere submitting an article for a university, but your undersecretary commenting on an official strategy of the alliance."

"Well, I know. But the problem is still there. Mutually assured destruction won't work," Reagan gently replied. Carrington looked at him in amazement, obviously slightly shaken.

"But we have got to stand behind alliance policy. It has worked so far," said Carrington. "There is no alternative."

"Yes, there is," Reagan said. "A Strategic Defense Initiative."

Carrington had heard about Reagan's idea for an impenetrable defensive shield against nuclear missiles. "That's too provocative at a time when we are trying to make progress on a dialogue with the Soviet Union," he objected.

Reagan tilted his head a bit and said, "It is not provocative if we develop these antimissile capabilities that we are working on now and then share them with the Soviets. We will move from mutually assured destruction to mutual security."

I heard a noise to my left, and looked to see Defense Secretary Casper "Cap" Weinberger about to fall off his chair. Reagan meant it, and Weinberger clearly could hardly believe it.

Carrington now fully understood that there were fundamental differences between the United States and Europe on the bedrock strategy for keeping the Cold War from becoming World War III, and if we couldn't close that gap, we risked a transatlantic crisis that could fracture the alliance. Next, we called on Senator Nunn. Carrington quickly defused what could have been a tense meeting. "Senator, I am with you," he told Nunn. "Not your method, mind you, but your end, your objective." The two established an immediate rapport. Over the coming months Carrington worked hard to see that our European allies complied with Congress's insistence that they meet defense funding requirements. It seemed Nunn's threat of a U.S. troop withdrawal was having the intended effect.

In 1985, I would seek to bridge these differences between the United States and Europe on the Strategic Defense Initiative (SDI) with a series of seminars in Europe. The seminars focused on the defense and conventional applications of the Strategic Defense Initiative technologies. I assembled a panel of American science experts, including Dr. James Fletcher, Dr. Fred Seitz, and General James Abrahamson, the director of SDI. Dr. Seitz had previously served as the science advisor to NATO in 1959. He had also been president of Rockefeller University and head of the National Academy of Sciences. He would later ask me to join the Richard Lounsbery Foundation's board of directors, and I became president of the foundation when he retired in 2002. Though I do not have a technical background, these discussions were fascinating.

Following a meeting between President Reagan and German chancellor Helmut Kohl, it was decided that the Germans should take the lead at the 1984 defense ministers meeting. On the eve of the meeting, however, we ran into complications when a difficult dispute arose between Manfred Woerner and U.S. Assistant Secretary of Defense Richard Perle. Perle was known as the "Prince of Darkness" due to his staunch opposition to virtually any arms-control measures. Later he would become a neoconservative luminary in the George W. Bush administration. He would become a leading proponent of the Bush administration's 2003 preemptive invasion of Iraq.

In terms of the all-important communiqué that would express the consensus view that emerged from the 1984 NATO meeting, Woerner wanted language that emphasized harmonizing NATO procurement activities for better use of defense resources. That tracked along the lines of my own thinking. Richard Perle and the Pentagon, however, wanted a clear statement that NATO members were prepared to spend more money on defense. The fight got so bitter that talks were broken off, and the initiative to harmonize procurements was all but dead.

I had my staff concoct a last-minute compromise. When the ministers and ambassadors assembled in the large NATO conference room, I handed the compromise language to Cap Weinberger. There would be "more" defense spending, but it would come from "better use" of resources. Weinberger studied the wording and then handed the document to British defense minister Michael Heseltine, who was sitting next to him. They both approved of the compromise language.

Weinberger gave the document to Perle to pass to Woerner, who was about to speak, considering the reform initiative dead. Perle opposed our changes and strode to the podium with the least amount of urgency imaginable. Perle was purposely attempting to derail the compromise by not passing the document to Woerner before he began speaking. Fortunately, Perle's slow roll out of our compromise was not slow enough, and Woerner received the compromise language just in time. Woerner picked up the paper and read it with a nod. He then introduced the initiative that would lead to the most comprehensive reexamination and reform of NATO conventional defenses in its history. This initiative squeaked through by the skin of our teeth, and despite the attempts of the "Prince of Darkness" to kill it. Lord Carrington backed up the reform proposals with seven in-depth reports that included specific recommendations on issues ranging from net assessment planning and logistics to armaments cooperation.

When Sam Nunn returned to Brussels to be briefed on the progress of the reforms to better rationalize and coordinate defense investments, he was so impressed that he thought it should serve as an example for the Pentagon. Nunn then confided to me that in place of a second amendment proposing troop withdrawals to get the attention of the European allies, he would instead put forth an amendment with positive incentives. He asked me not to share the news. Most allied officials were still expecting him to proceed with a troop withdrawal amendment, and that is how he wanted it to stay as a means to keep the pressure on.

Along with my staff member Dennis Kloske, I began to collaborate in secret with Nunn's staff, as well as with Deputy Secretary of Defense Will Taft, the chairman of the newly created NATO Armaments Cooperation Committee. The new amendment we crafted together contained two key elements. The first provided a funding pool of $200 million that could only be accessed for collaborative projects involving the U.S. and its NATO allies. The second element allocated $50 million for pre-acquisition, side-by-side testing of weapons from either the United States or our NATO allies designed to fill a NATO requirement. Senator Ted Stevens played an important role in our effort and became a critical advocate on the Appropriations Committee. We were also delighted when Senators John Warner (R-Va.) and Bill Roth (R-Del.) joined Nunn in sponsoring this historic amendment.

During our next ministers meeting in Brussels, Cap Weinberger leaned over to me and whispered, "You wait and see, Nunn is going to let you down." The secretary of defense couldn't believe that the Democratic senator from Georgia would come through with such generous funding for an alliance that he had so recently publicly chastised.

The timing was fortuitous, because as I was talking to Weinberger, my aide Dennis Kloske walked over and handed me a copy of the speech that Nunn had just given on the floor of the Senate. Nunn went into great detail lauding NATO's recent reforms and strides forward, and he proclaimed that we were entering a new era of transatlantic cooperation. To Weinberger's chagrin, he also mentioned that the Pentagon and its leadership could learn a great deal from NATO's new strategic approach. After all, this alliance of sixteen nations had managed to successfully reach consensus on a new, more effective resource strategy. Surely the Office of the Secretary of Defense and the four U.S. armed services that it oversaw could do the same.

While the successive Nunn amendments were often referred to as the "good" and the "bad" amendments by my colleagues in Europe, both were essential to the overall success of the NATO reforms. The first was a catalyst for shocking our European allies into action. The second rewarded our allies for their constructive response, and without it, the first would have been a disaster. The collaborative process that was adopted in initiating the NATO reforms fostered a creativity seldom seen in that vast bureaucracy and gave the alliance a new sense of direction and purpose. As a case study, the NATO reforms are also an exemplary example of collaboration between Congress, the executive branch, and the primary Western alliance. Under the direction of Senator Ted Stevens, a Senate advisory group was established to track implementation of the reforms with regular visits to NATO, further promoting transatlantic cooperation.

After leaving NATO, I remained closely involved in the reform effort to help ensure that momentum was not lost. Upon my return to Washington, Senator Nunn asked that my team—which included my very able aide and knowledgeable defense expert Mike Moodie, who had followed me back from NATO—testify before the Senate Armed Services Committee. We put together a detailed presentation on the defense reforms initiated under the Nunn amendment and their potential impact not only on alliance defense budgets but also on our own. We made our presentation at a televised hearing of the Senate Armed Services Committee, and subsequently to the President's Foreign Intelligence Advisory Board and the Joint Chiefs of Staff.

Despite his great affection for NATO, Lord Carrington was delighted when he was able to pass along the mantle of alliance leadership and return to Great Britain to write his own memoir. In July 1988, German defense minister Manfred Woerner succeeded him as secretary general. Woerner had a truly brilliant mind and carried much of the intellectual burden of crafting and implementing the NATO reform agenda. In a very real sense, NATO owes its resurgence during this critical period to him.

Years later, I visited Woerner in Stuttgart, Germany, and spent some quality private time with him. During this visit I realized that he was dying. By that time, the West had won the Cold War, and the Warsaw Pact and the Soviet Union had disintegrated. President George H. W. Bush and his able secretary of state, Jim Baker, had accomplished what many thought impossible: organizing a peaceful end to the Cold War and paving the way for a reunified Germany. Rather than dismantle the NATO alliance as many observers expected, the Clinton administration had expanded it to include much of Eastern Europe, placing more than 100 million free people under the protective umbrella and very nearly realizing the venerable dream of U.S. policymakers of a Europe "whole and free." As Manfred Woerner and I contemplated that incredible legacy from his home in Stuttgart inside a unified Germany, and reminisced about our roles in the drama, it brought warmth to us both at a melancholy time.

The resurgence of NATO reveals all of the major themes in my life's narrative: the need for civility and trust as the brick and mortar of governance; the importance of a process of constant self-improvement and reform; and the critical role of visionary, strategic leadership. At the beginning of this crisis, there was little trust in the transatlantic security relationship writ large, and a tremendous divide across the Atlantic in terms of perceptions of the threats we all faced. Both sides needed to listen to the concerns of the other in a civil debate that eventually built a common understanding—the gateway to greater trust. With his sophisticated understanding of the motivations that drove our European allies, and his clever carrot-and-stick approach, Sam Nunn supplied the visionary leadership, and Peter Carrington and Manfred Woerner matched him on the European front.

The result of the NATO reforms played an important role in the West's victory in the Cold War, which in turn freed 100 million people and reordered the known world. The bedrock Western security alliance was united and moving forward together as President Reagan moved into his crucial negotiations with Gorbachev. The Soviet Union's attempt to split the alliance, with its deployment of intermediate-range nuclear weapons targeting Europe and buildup of superior conventional forces, had failed. Reagan was able to negotiate with Gorbachev from a position of strength. Through honest dialogue, trust, and strategic vision and leadership, the West prevailed in the seminal conflict of the era without ever firing a shot. I believe Sun Tzu would have recognized it as the epitome of "the perfect victory." Though some have questioned NATO's relevance, as I write this in 2014, I believe NATO's role as the bedrock of the Western alliance remains indispensable.

10

Saving the Reagan Presidency

A Leader Regains the Nation's Trust

The weather was dreary and overcast in early December 1986, as I sat unhappily in the military wing of the Brussels Airport. I was waiting to receive Secretary of Defense Caspar Weinberger for the defense ministers meetings at NATO. The uninviting weather perfectly mirrored my low mood, which was shared by many officials in the Reagan administration, as well as by much of the American public. All trust had been lost in the president, at home and among America's allies. Ronald Reagan was in deep trouble.

The last few weeks had brought a whirlwind of revelations, beginning with an article on November 3 in the Lebanese periodical *Al-Shiraa*. That article revealed that the U.S. government had traded arms for the return of our hostages in Beirut, who were being held by the Iranian-backed terrorist group Hezbollah. This reported arms-for-hostages scheme severely undermined my credibility as the U.S. ambassador to NATO. I had been the point man for Secretary of State George Shultz's so-called Operation Staunch, which was designed to shame reluctant allies whenever they considered negotiating with terrorists or trading with terrorist nations. I was the designated scold who browbeat NATO members who failed to comply. The morning that the news broke on the arms-for-hostages deal, I could tell that the other NATO ambassadors had already read the news before the NATO Council meeting. Their eyes fell on me like an accusation of hypocrisy.

During the following weeks of November, the negative accounts of the scandal had snowballed. Unfortunately, President Reagan made matters worse by adding to the confusion. During his first press conference, and then again in a subsequent speech, he vigorously denied what he called "outlandish" allegations of trading arms for hostages. I cringed watching his performance on my television in Europe. Ronald Reagan, the Hollywood performer and Great Communicator, seemed to have lost his bearings. He resembled nothing so much as a boy caught lying by his father, and the American people could tell: Polling showed that only 14 percent of Americans believed the president when he denied trading arms for hostages.

NATO at that time was the United States' bedrock Cold War alliance. It was composed of sixteen sovereign nations, with a council chaired by the NATO secretary general, who also chaired separate meetings of alliance foreign ministers, defense ministers, and designated ambassadors. The NATO ambassadors, called "permanent representatives," formally met on a weekly basis at NATO headquarters outside Brussels. Additionally, each week a different ambassador would host a luncheon, with multiple courses and at least three vintage wines. There was quite a bit of competition among the NATO ambassadors regarding whose luncheon featured the best cuisine and wines.

During the week of the Thanksgiving holiday, it was always the tradition for the American ambassador to host the luncheon. I found it a challenge to remember what I had to be thankful for at the time. An even bigger bombshell had dropped from Washington. Newspapers were reporting that a National Security Council (NSC) staff officer named Oliver North had arranged to transfer some of the profits from the arms sales to Iran to the Contra rebels fighting against the communist regime in Nicaragua, in direct contravention of U.S. law. Even as I hosted my luncheon on Thanksgiving Day 1986, the Reagan presidency was thus falling apart in disgrace and scandal.

Shortly after the story broke about the freelancing Lieutenant Colonel North (USMC), President Reagan told Attorney General Ed Meese to look into the case more carefully. Meese walked over to Colonel North's office in the Old Executive Office Building, next to the White House. The charismatic North was not there at the time, but Meese was stunned to find North's secretary, an attractive woman named Fawn Hall, feeding documents into a shredder. The attorney general picked up a piece of paper waiting to be shredded, which spelled out how the profits from the arms sales to Iran were being diverted to the Contras. It was like the plot of a Hollywood thriller, and it didn't look to have a happy ending.

Dumbstruck, Meese realized that what Colonel North was doing was a violation of the Constitution. Not only did the scheme involve a misappropriation of funds, but if President Reagan knew about it, then he was committing a potentially impeachable offense by thwarting the will of Congress as expressed in law. Meese rushed to the Oval Office and handed the document to Ronald Reagan, who was equally stunned. As Reagan read it, the blood drained from his face. Within days Colonel North and his boss, National Security Advisor Rear Admiral John Poindexter, were both forced to resign.

As I waited at the Brussels Airport for Secretary Weinberger to disembark from the military aircraft, the events of the past weeks kept flashing through my mind. I greeted Weinberger, and we stepped into his limousine. Without any greeting or small talk, Cap Weinberger buried his hands in his face, his anguish unmistakable. "Dave, not again. Not another Watergate!" he exclaimed. Cap and I had both served in the Nixon administration, and we were painfully aware of the possible consequences of the scandal for Reagan. The Watergate scandal had ultimately led to Nixon's resignation to avoid impeachment. Now Reagan and his administration were accused of secretly trading arms for hostages, and the threat of another impeachment of a sitting U.S. president was suddenly very real.

At that time, I didn't know that National Security Advisor Poindexter, a three-star admiral and Annapolis graduate, had actually persuaded the president to lie to the public. I later learned that Poindexter argued that if the truth were made public, Hezbollah would kill the hostages in retaliation. I also did not know that Naval Academy graduates Admiral Poindexter, former national security advisor and retired Marine Bud McFarland, and Oliver North had all in effect turned their backs on their Annapolis honor code. In fact, they had deliberately created a false chronology of events. McFarland, a man of honor in the end, later called it "a chronology that obscured central facts" and an account that was "misleading at best." Then came the horrendous news that even the president's denials were lies. This was followed by sustained congressional criticism, from both Democrats and Republicans.

At this critical point in our story, two quite different senior staff members made proposals that would prove key to saving the Reagan presidency. First, legal counsel Peter Wallison wisely suggested that three respected American leaders be designated to examine how and why the NSC system had broken down. Accordingly, Reagan asked former national security advisor General Brent Scowcroft, two-time Democratic presidential candidate Senator Edmund Muskie (D-Maine), and former chairman of the Senate Armed Services Committee Senator John Tower (R-Tex.) to serve on what became known as the Tower Board. The board thankfully reported its findings within two months, whereas congressional investigators and independent counsel Judge Lawrence Walsh would stretch their investigations out much longer, keeping the nation, and much of the world, on edge about the fate of the Reagan presidency.

The second proposal came from an unlikely source, White House Communications Director Pat Buchanan. On December 12, 1986, Buchanan wrote the following telltale memorandum. Within days, the memo's suggestion would be accepted by President Reagan.

> This is a follow up to our Wednesday meeting. At this time, I cannot conceive of a communications plan that will allow peak-period White House business to go forward in January, uninterrupted by Iran issues. No matter what we say, dissolution will show. Current example: Final clearance is still pending for guidance on the Iran issue. I offer instead a two-track White House mechanism to get past [the] crunch of the Budget and the SOU [State of the Union].
>
> 90-Day Special Counselor—Appoint a Special Counselor to head a "Swat Team" to deal exclusively with the Iran/Contra issue. Goals: 1) Day to day management and tracking of all aspects of the Iran issue; 2) 10 points, restore the president's standing. The Special Counselor should have standing equal to the Chief of Staff and direct access to the President; be able to command White House resources; impact the President's schedule; shape events; [and] oversee and sign off on statements and speech materials. He should come equipped to provide the President with sage advice on legal and legislative matters and external relations. I believe this arrangement would be viewed as a positive development on the outside. It is difficult now, but soon it will become impossible for you or anyone else on your staff, likewise concerned with State of the Union and the Budget, to track all aspects of the Iran/Contra issue.
>
> The person for the Special Counselor's job will be a rare individual—an intellectual power with energy to become consumed with the issue, a known and prominent Republican, and one who will not be tempted to use the 90-day detail as a springboard. Further, the Counselor should be provided three substantive detailees (White House experience) (legal advisor, legislative affairs, external relations), full time for 90 days, and staff support as necessary. The detailees should bring experience to accommodate the three areas of particular importance.

Within just a matter of days, the Buchanan plan was accepted and put into effect. Reagan obviously hoped that this move to appoint a special counselor would mute increasing demands for his resignation. The focus was to evaluate the NSC breakdown and determine what corrective action should be taken. There was also hope that the newly appointed special counselor would bear some of the heat and criticism that was being focused on Reagan.

At the time, there had been much press speculation on my potential return to Washington as the next national security advisor. My only comment to that speculation was "No comment." Reagan's confidant Charlie Wick related to me during a phone call that he had sat next to the president on Air Force One and learned that I had been selected to be the next national security advisor. However, the appointment never happened. At the last moment, CIA director Bill Casey had convinced Reagan to reverse himself and instead name Frank Carlucci as the national security advisor. Casey argued that Carlucci had been the chief deputy to both Secretary of State Shultz and Secretary of

Defense Weinberger at different times. Everyone knew the malfunctioning of the NSC system was due in part to the epic quarrels between these two cabinet secretaries. Casey argued that Carlucci was just the person to bring them together. I totally agreed with that logic.

Of course, in addition, I believed Bill Casey had some reservations about me serving as national security advisor. Socially, Casey and I were good friends, but we had gotten into some heated arguments when serving together on the congressionally mandated Commission on the Organization of the Government on the Conduct of Foreign Policy, also known as the Murphy Commission in 1976.

Casey believed the report should have advocated authorizing the government to place intelligence operatives anywhere in government for national security purposes. Just prior to this, I had been named chairman of the Board for International Broadcasting, which was established to replace the CIA in providing oversight of our international broadcasting efforts such as Voice of America. In our back-and-forth, I argued that placing CIA moles on this board would have broken the newly established law, which disallowed any connection between the Board for International Broadcasting and the CIA. Casey responded to my protest flippantly: "Dave, you should have been with us, to see how we did things in OSS." Casey still at times liked to relive his glory days with the World War II–era Office of Strategic Services (OSS), under the wartime leadership of the legendary General "Wild Bill" Donovan. Indeed, Casey was part of the group that had edged out the so-called white shoe crowd at the OSS, taking charge of some of the most daring OSS operations in Europe during the war.

Frank Carlucci very thoughtfully phoned me to apologize for "taking my job," as he put it. I told him no apologies were needed. He was indeed the ideal choice at a time when the NSC system was so clearly dysfunctional.

To my great surprise, on December 19, 1986, at Truman Hall, the name of the NATO ambassador's residence in Belgium, I received word that White House Chief of Staff Don Regan was urgently trying to reach me. The White House wanted me to fill the role of special counselor, as described in the Buchanan memo.

As the reader already knows, throughout my career I've been struck by the wisdom of the adage, widely attributed to Mark Twain, which states that "History doesn't repeat itself, but it often rhymes." For me, history was unmistakably rhyming. The call with Don Regan was very reminiscent of an unexpected phone call I received from General Alexander Haig back in May 1973. Haig had just been appointed White House chief of staff to replace H. R. Haldeman. The Watergate scandal was raging, and the floor was falling out from beneath the Nixon White House. Indeed, just as was the case with

Ronald Reagan more than a decade later, the survival of the presidency was at stake. Both Haig and President Nixon believed and hoped that I had the combination of abilities, integrity, and personal touch needed to ward off an impeachment of the president. During that phone call, Haig spoke to me as one West Pointer to another, arguing that "duty calls."

After speaking with Haig that night in May 1973, I went with my wife to the Sulgrave Club for dinner with her mother and stepfather, Admiral George Anderson. At that time, Anderson chaired the President's Foreign Intelligence Advisory Board, and he had been chief of naval operations during the 1962 Cuban Missile Crisis. I told Anderson about the phone call with Haig. He broke in, "When do you report for duty?" To his surprise, I replied, "I do not."

I had only been back at CSIS for nine months. I had taken a two-year leave from running the think tank to serve as assistant secretary of state. "It is out of the question that I leave so soon," I told my stepfather, who guessed that I had other motives for declining the White House job. Anderson shot back, "I went to Annapolis. You went to West Point. When the commander in chief calls, it is your duty to respond in the affirmative." He added, "Didn't you see his speech on television this afternoon, saying 'I am not a crook'? Do you think he would lie to the entire nation?" "I just don't think he is telling the truth," I retorted. Of course, history would sadly prove me right.

So here I was, fourteen years later, and it was "déjà vu all over again." Once again I could have politely declined, excusing myself from a tawdry scandal and the white-hot media attention focused on it. Except this time there was one big difference in the call from the White House. I simply believed Ronald Reagan.

What was different with Reagan? Why did I believe him? Why did I not believe Nixon? My simple answer to those questions is that unlike the more brilliant Richard Nixon, Ronald Reagan was too much of an idealist to lead a conspiracy. Reagan was neither conniving, nor conspiratorial, nor cunning. This was my hunch at the beginning of my service with President Reagan, and my later personal dealings with him only confirmed that initial assessment. He had an open personality. There was no question about his love for his country, and no doubt that his ideals were as integral a part of his personal makeup as his heart and soul.

The purpose of Don Regan's call was to alert me that Reagan would be calling to encourage me to take the position of special counselor to the president. By that point Don had already become deeply controversial. The press had labeled the often imperious Regan "the Prime Minister," which deeply angered First Lady Nancy Reagan. A handsome man, Regan was the former head of Merrill Lynch and a Marine colonel during World War II, and he clearly possessed great abilities. However, he often exercised those abilities in ways that isolated the president. In his role as "Prime Minister," Regan liked to act as if he was all-knowing, but as soon as this controversy struck, he backed off and claimed complete ignorance.

On the phone with me, Regan explained the proposed deal. I was being asked to make a three-month commitment as special counselor to the president, reporting directly to Ronald Reagan. I would be the only person in the White House to report directly to the president and not to Don Regan. The job would be an attempt to carve out and compartmentalize everything related to Iran-Contra. Don Regan's portfolio would be to handle all other matters related to the president. In addition, the special counselor would manage the interface with the investigations under way, including the Tower Board. I agreed with this division of labor and power between the chief of staff and the special counselor to the president. The three-month period also fit with my previous commitment to return as head of CSIS. In no uncertain terms, I explained to Regan that I would need to select my own deputy, one I trusted and had worked with before, and certainly not someone of Regan's choosing. In addition, I needed to make sure I would not become isolated. For this I would recruit three informal outside advisors with whom I could talk things out frankly throughout the process: my close friend and former ambassador to the Court of St. James, Anne Armstrong; Washington wise man and Democrat Bob Strauss; and Charlie Wick, a close friend who was already serving in the Reagan administration as head of the United States Information Agency.

The president's phone call came to me the day after Christmas 1986. Reagan's voice was steady and forthright. He informed me of his unprecedented and quite stunning decision not to exert executive privilege on any part of the investigation. Secondly, Reagan assured me that I would report directly to him, and to no one else. In addition, the president agreed that I could bring in as my deputy Judge Charles Brower, as I had requested. Brower had been deputy legal advisor in the State Department during my time there in the early 1970s, and he had also sat on the Iran–United States Claims Tribunal in The Hague. Chief of Staff Don Regan strongly objected to this selection, as he would have preferred to name my deputy himself. Looking back, my decision to stand up to Don Regan and insist on maintaining outside advisors proved to be the ultimate key to success. My stubbornness also put Don Regan on notice that I would not allow myself to become isolated.

Unlike during the Nixon years, this time when the White House called I felt I had to accept. The White House eagerly made an almost immediate announcement:

The President today announced the appointment of Ambassador David Abshire as Special Counselor to the President. Ambassador Abshire will serve on temporary assignment as the White House Coordinator for the Iran inquiry. He will assume his duties here January 5, 1987, and will continue with some NATO duties until his successor is confirmed. In that capacity, which will have Cabinet rank, he will head a team that will coordinate White House activities in all aspects of the Iran matter. He will coordinate White House responses to Congressional and other requests for information in a timely manner, working with senior members of the White House staff, assisted by representatives from key White House staff offices.

The President is pleased and grateful for Ambassador Abshire's willingness to undertake this important special assignment and looks forward to working with such a talented and educated public servant. Ambassador Abshire has served at NATO with the utmost distinction and success. He has a well-deserved reputation as a respected and articulate advocate for our foreign policy goals.

For good or for ill, I was returning to Washington, D.C., in the mid of a roiling political crisis, with a mandate to help save the Reagan presidency.

On January 3, 1987, I departed Brussels for Washington amid a storm of bad publicity. A *Wall Street Journal* editorial noted, "In preparation for the next scandal, perhaps David Abshire's appointment as Special Counselor should be permanent. Secretary of Scandal we should call it." A *Washington Post* column by Rowland Evans and Robert Novak was titled "The Reagan Presidency Is Dead." I wrote in my notes for that day, "I have a sinking feeling, for I have no desire to be an undertaker."

Steven Roberts, in a profile in the *New York Times*, described the delicacy of my job: "Mr. Abshire has been placed in a tricky position. While his mandate is to get all the facts out, he is working for an administration that has a deep interest in its own survival." The *National Journal* also ran an article entitled "The Diplomat in the Trenches." It read, "[By choosing Abshire,] Reagan is playing a desperately needed Congressional card. The President sidestepped Capitol Hill in his dealings with Iran, and Abshire's experience and contacts—he was Congressional liaison in the State Department during the Nixon Administration—lends credibility where it is most needed." The article went on to say, "Abshire could help the White House with the press. Because he has nothing to hide, this personable, almost affable veteran of the ways of Washington is a natural to summon groups of reporters to his office to explain how the President is getting all of the facts to Congress and to the independent counsel." From the beginning of November to January, there were 509 stories on Iran-Contra in the *New York Times* alone.

To ensure continuity at NATO at this critical juncture, it was announced that I would also serve double duty as ambassador to NATO until a replacement was found. On a personal and practical level, this arrangement was a welcome convenience. While it was necessary for me to immediately return to Washington, my wife and family would have more time before having to move out of Truman Hall. On a more strategic level, an unintended benefit of this arrangement was that during my meetings on Capitol Hill, I spoke not only as the special counselor to the president but also as the ambassador to the greatest alliance in our history. This served as a clear reminder that our president remained the leader of the Cold War alliance, and thus of the free world. I symbolized that connection, and the stakes were clear: If President Reagan failed, the alliance could be threatened.

The Cold War standoff between the U.S.-led NATO alliance and the Soviet-led Warsaw Pact had reached a critical pivot during that time. At the Geneva Summit in 1985, President Reagan had unexpectedly established a real rapport with Soviet leader Mikhail Gorbachev as they fenced back and forth over the United States' missile defense program called the Strategic Defense Initiative. The subsequent Reykjavik Summit in October 1986 ended without an agreement, but represented a breakthrough that eventually culminated in the Intermediate-Range Nuclear Forces Treaty, signed at the Washington Summit on December 8, 1987.

I should say that at this point that I did not know Ronald Reagan terribly well. I had been national security advisor to the platform committee for the 1960, 1964, and 1968 Republican Party conventions. However, I had not been an ardent supporter, or so-called Reaganaut, in the run-up to the 1980 presidential campaign. I was thus surprised when I was called upon that year to run the national security portion of the Reagan transition. Thanks are owed to my good friend Bill Timmons, a fellow Tennessean who was in charge of the overall transition and had recommended me.

Among the cabinet members I knew well was William French Smith, a prominent California lawyer who told me even before the campaign, "Dave, you would really like Ronald Reagan. He is not some right-wing ideologue as so many have characterized him. He is a practical conservative. He is the kind of conservative of whom Edmund Burke would have approved."

I met with Ronald Reagan for only the second time briefly during the 1980 presidential campaign. We were at a small dinner party hosted by the columnist George Will. Will felt that one of Jimmy Carter's mistakes was in never connecting with the various power brokers of the Washington, D.C., establishment. Therefore, he invited guests to his dinner party who represented a wide range of perspectives, including owner and publisher of the *Washington Post* Kay Graham, Democratic-leaning intellectual Jeane Kirkpatrick, head of the AFL-CIO Lane Kirkland, and others.

In my private conversation with the presidential candidate that night, I learned of Reagan's fondness for quips. I told him my specialty had been working with Congress, and how important I felt the dynamic between the executive and legislative branches was to an effective presidency. The Gipper cracked back, "Dave, I have a better solution. Let's just lock them all up!" I couldn't top that.

Before meeting with President Reagan upon my return to Washington, D.C., from Belgium, I spoke with Bob Strauss. Strauss told me about a meeting he had with Reagan before it was revealed that Oliver North had diverted the profits from the arms-for-hostages deal to the Contras. Even though no "smoking gun" had yet emerged tying the president directly to that scheme, Strauss already believed at that time that Reagan was in serious jeopardy. Nancy Reagan shared Strauss's concern. In Nancy's desperation to convince her husband that he was in trouble, she arranged for Bob Strauss and former attorney general Bill Rogers to meet with the president in the White House family quarters via the secret passageway from the Treasury Department.

Nancy Reagan explained to Rogers and Strauss in front of her husband why she had brought them there. To her chagrin, Bill Rogers said, regarding the trading of arms for hostages, "The legislation violated was not that binding. There is not that much to worry about."

A shocked Nancy then turned to Bob Strauss. Bob let loose, "Mr. President, you are in a hell of a lot of trouble. Your presidency is in jeopardy." However, the more Strauss talked, the more furious Reagan became. The evening broke up on a sour note.

Strauss later told me that at this point he had not known Mrs. Reagan well and, feeling he had blundered, returned to his apartment for a strong drink. To his surprise, upon arriving home, the phone rang. Mrs. Reagan was calling. When he answered, Strauss immediately broke into a profuse apology. She cut him off, "You did exactly what I wanted. I can't thank you enough." Nancy Reagan was not only a strong first lady. Behind her glamour was enormous shrewdness. In this case, she was using it to save her husband's presidency.

On January 12, 1987, President Reagan was recuperating from surgery for prostate cancer and returned from the hospital to the White House. The doctor allowed him to leave the second-floor family quarters to conduct business in the West Wing Oval Office for only one and a half hours in the afternoon. I had twenty minutes. At three p.m. Jim Kuhn, the president's personal assistant, and Fred Ryan, his devoted scheduler, greeted me, and I was ushered into the historic office by the president's secretary, Kelly Osborne.

Quite worried, I settled into my chair as we focused on one another. There was a bit of banter and light talk. Then I said, "Mr. President, my doctorate is in history. History's always been one of my greatest interests. As I said over the phone when you called me in Brussels, I want to see the strength of this presidency fully restored. When you took over, the presidency had been at a low point historically. It was stalemated and lacked effective leadership.

"Mr. President," I continued, "we have a severe perception problem. Please look at these polls, sir." I placed a clipping squarely in front of him on the desk. "Sixty to sixty-five percent of the American public believes that there's a cover-up in the Iran-Contra affair. They believe we've traded arms for hostages. You don't believe we traded arms for hostages, but the majority of the American public believes that. We must recognize that this perception problem is a major one. I think your honesty was attested to when you phoned me in Brussels to say 'get all the facts out.' "

In his gentle but firm way, President Reagan responded defensively, "The press has been exaggerating these problems. Certainly there've been many mistakes in carrying out our policy. But the original goals in dealing with Iran were justified. We were trying to make a breakthrough. I don't believe that we were trading arms for hostages. We were dealing with one group in Iran. They were dealing with another group in Beirut." He said with his voice rising, "It was not government to government."

"But Mr. President," I responded respectfully, "the American public doesn't see it that way. This wasn't your intention, I know, but it's the way it ended up. If we could clear the air on this issue and say that, while it wasn't your intention, the administration ended up trading arms for hostages, we wouldn't have such a credibility problem. We could put this thing behind us."

I remember him leaning forward in his chair, his face clenched with passion. "Dave, I don't care if I'm the only person in America that does not believe it—I don't believe it was arms for hostages." I'm sure I stared back in amazement. This exchange showed Ronald Reagan's touch of naïveté, and confirmed in my mind his basic honesty. For Reagan, the issue was neither a public relations nor a tactical problem. Trading arms for hostages was wrong, and Ronald Reagan simply could not believe that he had violated his personal honor code. He could not bring himself to say for the sake of political expediency that he had done something so morally wrong.

Unfortunately, Reagan's refusal to admit what had happened convinced the public that he had lied. Furthermore, they assumed that if he would lie about arms for hostages, then he would also lie about the Contra funds diversion. I realized I was not making headway. I was struck by how Reagan's natural stubbornness was becoming deeply destructive to his presidency.

Concealing my exasperation, I moved on. I noticed how firmly Reagan's eyes were fixed on me, contrary to the genial manner that other officials described after meetings with him. I explained to Reagan that while the press was routinely misrepresenting my role, I was there neither as an investigator nor as his defender.

Many, in and out of the press, were misrepresenting my role, so I reiterated it to him. "Mr. President, I want to confirm to you again the wisdom that you've had in establishing my unique role here at the White House. It is certainly necessary to restore the public's trust. If I had jumped into my job and functioned as a judge, a juror, or an investigator of facts myself, I would have already been in a mess. We would have been right back where we were in December."

I felt it was important that Reagan understood the view from my side of his Oval Office desk. I said:

> You know, I haven't exactly won the popularity contest with the press corps by ending their noontime feedings. I find that I have to remind the press corps, and indeed, some of the White House staff and people on Capitol Hill, that I am the facilitator, and not the investigator, in this process. This means getting everything out, getting to the bottom of things, as you put it to me in your telephone call to Brussels. We have been substituting "due process" with a "flawed process," and that has gotten us into this damn mess. And it is important that we get due process reinstated and accepted before the State of the Union address later in January.

Then I struck my central theme: "Mr. President, I cannot emphasize strongly enough that, in convincing the Congress that we're following due process, we need to build bipartisan support."

I concluded by elaborating on the role that my deputy, Judge Charles Brower, and I would play on Capitol Hill. We planned to visit every senator and congressman on the Senate and House Investigating Committees. We would reemphasize that the White House was not claiming executive privilege as a way to restore broken trust. We would stress that the president was determined to have a thorough investigation that refuted any accusations of a cover-up. We did that, and the meetings on the Hill paid off. Nevertheless, it would take many such consultations and the passage of a lot of time for our strategy to rebuild the trust that had been lost.

Throughout this period, the press continued their attacks. Two of the sharpest critiques of the president came from the *Washington Post* and CBS's *60 Minutes*. Nancy Reagan wondered whose job it was to defend the president in the face of these withering attacks. Unfortunately, Don Regan incorrectly insisted to her that defending the president before the press was my job.

Soon after I arrived at the White House, I received independent calls from of my advisors, Charlie Wick and Robert Strauss, both with the same message. I was making only one mistake, but it was a big one. They felt I needed to meet immediately with the first lady and then continue to meet with her on a regular basis. Wick said he would phone Nancy Reagan to encourage the meeting. I would need such an introduction, as I had only previously met Mrs. Reagan in receiving lines. Wick got back to me quickly, "She invites you to meet with her in the family quarters at three o'clock."

Nancy Reagan was one of the most powerful first ladies in history, ranking with the likes of Edith Wilson and Eleanor Roosevelt. Yet she was totally different from either of them. She was not only the president's closest advisor and best friend, but also an indispensable part of his political life. Ronald Reagan once said, "In some ways Nancy and I are like one human being. When one of us has a problem, it automatically become a problem for the other."

After I exited the small family elevator leading to the second-floor living quarters, I sat with the first lady for over an hour under the stunning Palladian-style window made famous in Eleanor Roosevelt's day. During our conversation I repeated several times that we were rebuilding the trust that had to be the coin of the realm in Washington politics. I explained that my role was to get out all of the facts and documents, to restore the White House's credibility and integrity in responding to the investigations, and to develop bipartisan support on Capitol Hill. A bit teary-eyed, she said I was the only one working on the president's behalf. Pointedly, she also warned me not to let Don Regan sit in on my meetings with the president.

Mrs. Reagan was very focused on the need to develop a comeback plan for the president, and I strongly agreed. However, I emphasized the importance of establishing the credibility of the Iran-Contra investigation as central to any comeback plan. I told her of the wide-ranging visits Judge Brower and I were making on Capitol Hill, and the credibility being created among conservatives and liberals. I added that we would be providing the president with the best possible defense by letting the Tower Board reach its own conclusions instead of jumping to an impromptu, incomplete defense of the president. Plainly, we did not yet have all of the information we needed to be truly forthcoming. That's why it was so important that I ended the noontime press conferences, which forced us to try and respond to issues for which we simply did not have all the facts.

I further elaborated on what I envisioned as the president's comeback plan. To counter President Reagan's image as being disengaged from the management of the executive branch, I felt he should visit, with some fanfare, the Departments of State, Defense, and Treasury and the Central Intelligence Agency. This would demonstrate not only a tightening of executive branch operations but also a return to cabinet-level governing that defined the U.S. government during the peak years of the Cold War. Incidentally, President

Reagan was so impressed with the idea that he referred to it twice during cabinet meetings, but this initiative was not carried out once I left the White House.

Mrs. Reagan responded with a great sense of relief after hearing me out during our private meeting. For the first time, she understood my role, she said, and applauded my approach. Years later, during a visit with Mrs. Reagan, she showed me an entry in her diary where she described a bitter fight over the phone with Don Regan. She wrote that the White House chief of staff was "arrogant, loud, and then hung up." About me she wrote: "I was so bolstered by Mike Deaver, no longer in the White House, and now with David Abshire."

The meetings on Capitol Hill were completed well before the Tower Board Report was released. I believe this played a major role in regaining Senate and House confidence in the process well in advance of the report's findings. Indeed, there are few examples in our country's history where there has been such an intensity of consultation among liberals and conservatives in the House and Senate. The Hill consultations were confidential, and no effort was made to publicize them. These were not lobbying efforts, but rather earnest exchanges to restore trust where it had been broken.

An especially moving point in the process came from a meeting Judge Brower and I had with Senators Daniel Inouye (D-Hawaii) and Warren Rudman (R-N.H.), the chair and ranking member of the Senate Investigating Committee. The senators' creation of a unified, bipartisan investigating committee was superior to the two separate committees that existed in the House.

Republican senator Rudman had worked previously with Democratic senator Ernest "Fritz" Hollings from South Carolina to produce the Gramm-Rudman-Hollings Act of 1985. That act produced the first balanced budget in a quarter of a century. Later, Rudman would serve as Bill Clinton's chair of the President's Intelligence Advisory Board. I must also confess my great admiration for Daniel Inouye of Hawaii. He had served with extraordinary valor in World War II, losing his arm while leading an assault on a heavily defended ridge in Tuscany, Italy.

Brower and I were about to leave our meeting with the two when Inouye reached out to me. "David, if you see anything that we are doing wrong, I want to hear it directly from you." In my personal reminiscence, such moments of trust are a true illustration of what is often called "American exceptionalism." American exceptionalism in my view is the ability of leaders to rise above personal interest to the higher ground of common interests, reversing a deteriorating situation for the sake of the greater good. Following that meeting, Judge Brower and I walked out of the Capitol in silence. I think we were both so inspired that we wanted to find an American flag to salute.

Key to Reagan's comeback was his address to the nation on Iran-Contra. Nancy Reagan was very concerned that the regular speechwriting team, aligned with Don Regan, would exert undue influence on the speech. She insisted that I not permit them to have any input. She had been very impressed with the speechwriting of Landon Parvin, who was little known at the time. Parvin had written speeches for members of Congress for many important Washington events, sometimes under delicate circumstances. He possessed a rare talent for preserving the voice of the speaker, while inspiring the audience and adding dashes of humor. In retrospect, I believe we owe a debt of gratitude to Parvin for his ability to connect Ronald Reagan to the material.

Certainly, what I call his "comeback speech" brought Reagan's remarkable civility and earnestness to the fore, and it became his public confession. On March 4, 1987, Ronald Reagan spoke from the Oval Office:

> I've spoken to you from this historic office on many occasions and about many things. The power of the Presidency is often thought to reside within this Oval Office. Yet it doesn't rest here; it rests in you, the American people, and in your trust. Your trust is what gives a President his powers of leadership and his personal strength, and it's what I want to talk to you about this evening. . . .
>
> The reason I haven't spoken to you before now is this: you deserve the truth. And as frustrating as the waiting has been, I felt it was improper to come to you with sketchy reports, or possibly even erroneous statements, which would then have to be corrected, creating even more doubt and confusion. There's been enough of that. I've paid a price for my silence in terms of your trust and confidence. But I've had to wait, as you have, for the complete story. That's why I appointed Ambassador David Abshire as my Special Counselor to help get out the thousands of documents to the various investigations. And I appointed a Special Review Board, the Tower Board, which took on the chore of pulling the truth together for me and getting to the bottom of things. It has now issued its findings. . . .
>
> I've studied the Board's report. Its findings are honest, convincing, and highly critical; and I accept them. And tonight I want to share with you my thoughts on these findings and report to you on the actions I'm taking to implement the Board's recommendations. . . .
>
> Let's start with the part that is the most controversial. A few months ago I told the American people I did not trade arms for hostages. My heart and my best intentions still tell me that's true, but the facts and the evidence tell me it is not. As the Tower board reported, what began as a strategic opening to Iran deteriorated, in its implementation, into trading arms for hostages. This runs counter to my own beliefs, to administration policy, and to the original strategy we had in mind. There are reasons why it happened, but no excuses. It was a mistake. . . .
>
> For nearly a week now, I've been studying the Board's report. I want the American people to know that this wrenching ordeal of recent months has not been in vain. I endorse every one of the Tower Board's recommendations. In fact, I'm going beyond its recommendations so as to put the house in even better order. . . .

Now, what should happen when you make a mistake is this: you take your knocks, you learn your lessons, and then you move on. That's the healthiest way to deal with a problem. This in no way diminishes the importance of the other continuing investigations, but the business of our country and our people must proceed. I've gotten this message from Republicans and Democrats in Congress, from allies around the world, and—if we're reading the signals right—even from the Soviets. And of course, I've heard the message from you, the American people. You know, by the time you reach my age, you've made plenty of mistakes. And if you've lived your life properly—so, you learn. You put things in perspective. You pull your energies together. You change. You go forward.

Character was king in the way Ronald Reagan came back from his crisis. Unlike Presidents Richard Nixon and Bill Clinton, who when confronted with their own existential scandals dug their holes even deeper through denial, confrontation, and cover-up, Reagan climbed out of the hole he had created with Iran-Contra by coming clean. He always had the courage of his convictions, and believing that his mistakes came from a place of good intentions, Reagan learned from them and moved forward. And the American people followed his lead.

Part of the public's willingness to trust him again was Reagan's soft touch and style of civility. Those characteristics naturally drew people to him and made him a uniter, as opposed to the dividers that so often are drawn to Washington. This style was not simply an act to be played on a stage; it was genuine. The essential elements of Reagan's civility were respect for the individual, an ability to disagree without being disagreeable, and an utter lack of arrogance. Of course, Reagan's instinctive good will toward others—his desire to believe the best in people and to avoid confrontation—had its downside. Casey, North, and Poindexter all played upon his compassion for the American hostages to push their agendas. Reagan also had a tendency to blank out what he found disagreeable, just as he had done as a young boy in dealing with his drunken father. He was unwilling to face the highly destructive rivalry between his Defense Secretary Weinberger and Secretary of State Shultz. He could neither face the Don Regan situation nor seem to get angry as I did that his national security advisors left him without records of events and decisions in his time of need.

Reagan was undoubtedly a poor manager, but at that moment in history the American people didn't need a status quo manager in the White House. Still scarred by Vietnam, frustrated by an inflationary economy, and waging an unending and costly Cold War, they needed a leader who could look beyond the murky present and see a bold, hopeful vista. They needed a leader with transformational ideas and the ability to communicate them. They needed a leader of good will, with the character to stand up after a fall in order to restore the integrity of the presidency, who would gracefully leave the office with the victory in the Cold War in sight. America needed Ronald Reagan.

My part in the Iran-Contra drama and Reagan's remarkable comeback were undoubtedly the high point of my sixty years in Washington. When I came on as President Reagan's special counselor, Congress and the American public were once again demanding answers to the questions that had doomed the Nixon presidency: What did the president know, and when did he know it? At the time, only 14 percent of the American public believed Reagan's answers, and his denial of having traded arms for hostages. By the time Reagan left office in 1989, he would enjoy the highest approval ratings of any president since Franklin Roosevelt. Trust, regained, was once again the coin of the realm.

11

Reimagining the World

CSIS in the Post–Cold War Era

The breakup of the Warsaw Pact and Soviet Union in 1991 without a shot being fired may well have been the epitome of Sun Tzu's "perfect victory," but they were deeply unsettling events nonetheless. That was true for the U.S. government writ large, and for CSIS, the think tank I cofounded and had returned to lead after my service in the Reagan White House.

It was victory in World War II and the demands of leading the West in the twilight struggle against communism that had awoken America from its long isolationist slumber, setting the stage for what became known as the "American Century." The U.S. policy of containment of the Soviet Union, and the bipartisan consensus behind it during both Republican and Democratic administrations, had given strategic coherence to our foreign and national security policies for nearly half a century.

Admiral Arleigh Burke and I had originally started the center in large part to help evolve and sustain the strategies that would prevail in that seminal conflict of our time. With the end of the Cold War, however, that unifying threat had suddenly disappeared. Our policymakers and lawmakers were suddenly being asked fundamental questions about America's rightful role in a post–Cold War world. I believed CSIS needed to help provide the answers.

As my narrative so far has revealed, in times of crisis or disorienting change I instinctively turn to history for guidance. Studying the great leaders of history as they confronted crises and turmoil serves as an inspiration. History may not repeat itself, but my entire career was a testament to its frequent rhymes, and I longed to hear what clues those familiar cadences of the past could offer to guide us through the murky present.

I already sensed that the Center for Strategic and International Studies needed to play an important role in helping policymakers navigate an unfamiliar global landscape. That would require that we both think outside the box, and also bring the lessons of history to bear. I also strongly felt that we at CSIS needed to take stock of our own organization, the better to help plot long-term strategies for the coming post–Cold War era.

In 1992, I thus approached the author James Allen Smith, who had already published two well-regarded books on U.S. think tanks. *The Idea Brokers: Think Tanks and the Rise of the New Foreign Policy Elite* was his general examination of the history of policy research organizations, while *Brookings at Seventy-Five* traced the history of the Brookings Institution. Though he was initially reluctant to commit to another book on the subject of think tanks, I was determined that Smith turn his talents to capturing the history, and revealing the true essence, of CSIS.

"The whole world is in transition now. It's such an important time, a new epoch," I told Smith. "And after nearly thirty years, we're in transition here at CSIS, looking at what we need to become in the twenty-first century. Think of how much fun it would be to talk to people thinking about strategy and international issues at such a historic moment."

By now the reader is familiar with some of my shortcomings and idiosyncrasies. I hope it won't be taken as bragging, then, when I say that one of the strengths that has defined my career is the ability to surround myself with very intelligent and talented people who make me look smart. When on a recruiting mission on behalf of CSIS, I am told, I can be quite persuasive. Anyway, James Allen Smith thought so, and he took the bait that I offered. His excellent book *Strategic Calling* helped remind me of the first principles encoded into the DNA of the center, and its natural evolution over the years, leading the way forward through a period of great upheaval. History was rhyming!

The conundrum that Admiral Burke and I first confronted on the founding of Center for Strategic Studies had parallels to the challenges the nation confronted in the early 1990s: namely, the need to develop a long-term strategy for U.S. global leadership in a culture and system that largely eschewed strategic thinking. The constitutional system brilliantly designed by our Founding Fathers in the eighteenth century was founded on a separation of powers and divided government. In the "Farewell Address" of President George Washington and the inauguration of President Thomas Jefferson, both warned the country against "entangling alliances." That was a perfectly understandable position given our early history and the necessity of breaking free of the orbit of European powers. They also lived in a time when America was protected by two broad oceans and blessed with relatively weak neighbors. But even benign isolationism and the system of government that sprang from it were poorly suited to a nation that out of necessity had led the free nations to victory against tyranny in both World War II and the Cold War, and had become a global superpower along the way.

The strategic vision of Presidents Harry Truman and Dwight Eisenhower, forged in the most destructive war in human history, charted a new course for the United States toward global leadership of free nations. One of the chief architects of that new strategy was Truman's secretary of state Dean Acheson, whose definition of strategy was a lodestar for myself and Admiral Burke in founding the Center for Strategic Studies: "to consider various courses of action from the point of view of their bearing upon major objectives." We shaped CSIS with that fundamental mission in mind, and I constantly pushed our team to be anticipatory and integrative in its analysis, and long-range in terms of its strategic outlook.

By the late 1980s and early 1990s, CSIS had in many ways realized my vision of an independent research organization that fostered civil and bipartisan debate on the weighty issues of the day, and was always driven by a sense of strategic calling, as James Allen Smith so aptly titled his history of the place. As I told Smith in an interview for his book:

> For the long term, only consensus on a realistic grand strategy can overcome the deleterious effects of balkanization in the executive branch, distrust, and governance by amendment on Capitol Hill. It is clear that a coordinated, comprehensive approach is badly needed. Only with such an approach can a consensus between the executive and legislative branches emerge. We also need a grand strategy to rally people around and to guide our resource priorities at a time of budget cuts and debtor-nation status.

I should note here that CSIS's role in influencing the policy debate in Washington, D.C., was aided by our ability to attract some of the country's greatest strategic thinkers after they left government service. I personally created the post of CSIS "counselor" to draw my old friend and former secretary of state Henry Kissinger to the center back in 1977. At that time, Henry was sought after by a host of universities and think tanks, but I convinced him to make CSIS the base for his Washington operations (he also taught part-time at Georgetown), in part by making him chairman of CSIS's International Councilors, a prestigious group that included more than three dozen international business leaders and former government officials. This aided Kissinger's business ambitions, and in turn he added greatly to the center's intellectual muscle. He also helped attract other prominent officials into CSIS's sphere, including James Schlesinger, Gerald Ford's secretary of defense and Jimmy Carter's secretary of energy; William Brock, a former secretary of labor, senator, and U.S. trade representative; Harold Brown, Carter's secretary of defense; and Admiral William Crowe, former chairman of the Joint Chiefs.

I also personally recruited Zbigniew Brzezinski, another brilliant strategist who served as President Carter's national security advisor. Zbig liked that CSIS was not an "ivory tower"–type think tank, but one that embraced political activism and pushed the political debate toward constant reform and self-improvement, which the reader now recognizes as one of the themes of my leadership. It's why I often refer to CSIS as a "do tank" as opposed to simply a "think tank."

In an interview in *Strategic Calling*, Brzezinski offers some insights into my proactive recruiting technique, and how it differed from many other think tanks.

> When I came over to see Abshire, unlike the others who said, "Well, we would be interested in having you, but what sort of project would you like to do, and our board of directors will consider it," his attitude was "Let me show you around the place. Let me show you a suite that you can have if you like it. If you do not like it, we will make some other suite available to you. When would you like to start?" That was the kind of attitude I liked—this gung ho response.

Lest the reader conclude that I recruited only former government officials and established intellectual heavyweights, there was also what was known internally at CSIS as "Abshire's cult of youth." I considered it a chief mission to attract promising young talent to Washington from the fields of academia, business, media, and the military, who could then use their tenure at CSIS as a springboard to careers in government service. This is in keeping with my lifelong belief in mentorship, something that was critical to my own career.

The list of people in what is sometimes jokingly referred to as the "Abshire Mafia" is too long to fully recount here, but some notable examples are cited in *Strategic Calling*, and include Michael Moodie, who after working at CSIS would become assistant director of the Arms Control and Disarmament Agency; Wayne Berman, who became an assistant secretary of commerce in the George H. W. Bush administration and special assistant to the president under George W. Bush; Dennis Kloske, a future deputy undersecretary of defense; Jay Collins, who is now a vice chairman of Citi; Pamela Scholl, who ran the Kissinger Councilors at CSIS and now serves as president of the Dr. Scholl Foundation and vice chairman of the Center for the Study of the Presidency & Congress (CSPC); and Daniel Lubin, who was my intern when I was called to NATO and miraculously helped me and Carolyn pack up our home in Old Town Alexandria, and is now a very successful health care venture capitalist.

William Taylor, my able director of CSIS's political-military studies program in the 1990s, and a former professor of social sciences at my alma mater West Point, also noted my lifelong habit of recruiting able young executive assistants, who would work long hours for me and become plugged into my wide network of contacts, and then in their late twenties springboard into posts in government or business.

"There are other secrets, but Abshire is really uncanny in the way he does this. He has learned over the years that brains are not issued with age or rank," Taylor is quoted as saying in *Strategic Calling*. "You put trust and confidence in smart young people and work them to death, but simultaneously give them a lot of latitude in what they work on and how they do it. You are going to produce people with a lot of talent, a lot of capability."

Another notable institutional milestone had occurred in 1987 when CSIS cut its ties to Georgetown University. As the center grew steadily in stature and reputation over the years, its dependence on and linkages with Georgetown naturally lessened. As opposed to John Hopkins School of Advanced International Studies, for instance, CSIS never considered teaching a core mission, though many of our senior counselors did teach on occasion. We were also cognizant of the Hoover Institution's frequently tense relationship with Stanford University. There were increasing complaints from Georgetown faculty that our reputation was too conservative, or that research grants that might have gone to university faculty went to the center instead. Perhaps most to the point, our fund-raising efforts also came into direct competition with each other.

The amicable separation came in 1986–1987, while I was still serving as U.S. ambassador to NATO and Amos Jordan was acting as president and chief executive officer of the center. Given my long history and affinity for Georgetown, I probably would have delayed the separation had I been leading the center, and that would have been a mistake. In the end, Jordan finished the job of severing our ties to Georgetown that I would not have had the heart to do. "We were able to reorganize and synergize after the break in ways we couldn't before," I told James Allen Smith in an interview for *Strategic Calling*.

By the early 1990s, CSIS had grown into the role I had originally envisioned for the center: a centrist think tank that was financially stable, focused on long-term strategy and international relations, with strong linkages to the top levels of government, business, academia, and journalism. My efforts to position the center at the nexus of those worlds were aided by the deep connections I had made on Capitol Hill serving as a congressional liaison for the

Nixon administration, inside the government during the Reagan administration, internationally and among the military as the ambassador to NATO, and with the international business community as a result of our fund-raising efforts. We were standing shoulder to shoulder with the likes of the more conservative American Enterprise Institute and the more liberal Brookings Institution, occupying a critical niche between the two.

Of course, we lacked the large endowments of those think tanks, which necessitated nearly constant fund-raising. This was both a burden and a blessing, in that I felt it kept our projects focused on the most relevant issues as opposed to more esoteric research. By this time our annual operating budget exceeded $6 million, and it had diversified from an almost total reliance on foundation support early on to include significant support from the corporate world and government research contracts.

My fund-raising efforts on behalf of CSIS's annual Williamsburg Conference were typical of my personal approach. The idea for the annual conferences was to bring Democratic and Republican members of Congress, government officials, diplomats, academics, and other thought leaders together to discuss important issues far from the bright glare of Washington, D.C. They would dine, share drinks, and play golf together during the conference, forming relationships that facilitated civil discourse and greased the wheels of governance. The conferences were actually the brainchild of Ken Gilmore, a close friend of mine and member of the CSIS advisory board. Ken ran the Washington bureau of *Reader's Digest*, a general interest magazine that at that time was the best-selling consumer magazine in the country. It was his suggestion that I reach out to *Reader's Digest* founder DeWitt Wallace to gauge his interest in funding the conference. Wallace had started the magazine while he was recovering from shrapnel wounds received in World War I. His groundbreaking idea was to combine a sampling of articles on many subjects from various magazines, usually condensing them, and then package them into a single magazine. The idea was a great hit.

Dewitt and his wife, Lila, owned an estate in the Hudson Valley near Chappaqua, New York. Given my belief in the importance of establishing close relationships, I proposed that both our families get together in Williamsburg, Virginia, where we could spend some quality time and get to know one another. We did just that, and had an excellent time. At a private lunch with Dewitt, I brought up my proposal for the annual conferences. He agreed to fund it on the spot. Years later I discussed that meeting with him, and Dewitt Wallace told me, "The only reason I agreed to fund your conference was because I realized you were a family man."

CSIS was also bolstered by a strong relationship with Japanese business leaders. Soon after Burke and I had set up CSIS in 1970, he declared, "I've attended these conferences in Japan. You've got to open major efforts with Japan." From his suggestion, I started making connections with Japanese political and business leaders. Through a series of major congressional exchanges with Japan, I was very fortunate to meet Dr. Shoichiro Toyoda of the Toyota Motor Company. Dr. Toyoda has been a good friend to me and a very generous supporter of CSIS, notably endowing the Japan Chair and, later, CSPC.

As president and then chairman of Toyota, Dr. Toyoda has demonstrated transformational leadership through a change in philosophy of the company, valuing quality parts and production, and a vision to become a global company. Even in times of crisis, Dr. Toyoda has acted swiftly and thoughtfully. In 2009, it was revealed that certain Toyota vehicles had an unintended acceleration problem from possible mechanical sticking of the accelerator pedal. Toyota promptly and voluntarily issued a safety recall of over 6 million vehicles.[1] I advised Dr. Toyoda that Norman Augustine could be very helpful in an examination of the safety recalls. Subsequently, Toyota assembled an expert panel led by Augustine to review its operations and independently advise Toyota on vehicle safety and accelerator pedal recalls.[2] Toyota's safety recalls stand as a shining example of corporate responsiveness and responsibility; only the safety recall of Tylenol in 1982 comes close to matching it.

I also met Kazuo Inamori, the founder of Kyocera, through CSIS's outreach in the early 1980s when he became a member of CSIS's International Councilors Group, chaired by Henry Kissinger. Dr. Inamori's valuable insights and contributions inspired CSIS to begin a major project on U.S.-Japanese relations that was led by former president George H.W. Bush and former prime minister Yasuhiro Nakasone.

My relationship with Kazuo Inamori deepened as a result of our shared conviction on the importance of character-based leadership. I was honored by his request to put my name alongside his at the Abshire-Inamori Leadership Academy, which seeks to enhance leadership skills in young professionals. Dr. Inamori also suggested that we hold a major conference in Tokyo on "Transformational Leadership" that was attended by some forty members of the Japanese Diet and broadcast across the country by Japanese media. During the many years that I had the privilege of knowing and working alongside Dr. Inamori, it became clear to me that he had done more to shape future generations of strong leaders of character than practically anyone else of his generation. The Abshire-Inamori Leadership Academy continues to inspire great leaders at CSIS today.

As I mentioned earlier, the abrupt and in many ways unexpected end of the Cold War was a time of great intellectual fervor at CSIS. A decade earlier,

CSIS had assembled a group of thirty-five Soviet experts to examine what the post–Leonid Brezhnev era would look like after the Soviet leader's death in 1982. The analysts pointed to the dire long-term consequences of the Soviet Union's high levels of military investment, especially in light of its lack of investment in the production of consumer goods. The experts predicted that ultimately a crisis of governance and economic management would occur, but their best estimate of when that might happen was sometime in the 1990s.

The surprise was the seriousness of Soviet leader Mikhail Gorbachev's *glasnost* ("openness") and *perestroika* ("restructuring") policies, and the powerful forces of devolution that they unleashed. The rapid collapse of the Soviet Union and Warsaw Pact were a reminder that while analysts can identify current trends, they can never be sure whether those trends will be altered by unforeseen political decisions or unpredictable events. The strategist, however insightful about long-term trends, must always be mindful of the surprises that the future has in store. Trends rarely play themselves out in straight lines; history is shaped and reshaped by a complicated interplay of contingencies and personalities.

The collapse of the Soviet Union also fractured the domestic consensus around the United States' Cold War strategy of containment and outsized level of international engagement, throwing into question America's fundamental role in the world. Some analysts thought the old ideological struggles of the twentieth century were finally put to rest, and that a liberal international order built on democracy and free markets would dominate globally. Others worried that old conflicts of nationalism, tribalism, and religious sectarianism that had been frozen during the bipolar standoff of the Cold War would once again come to the fore. As a former ambassador and a former colleague at Georgetown University put it so succinctly in *Strategic Calling*, "We are rapidly approaching the end of the twentieth century, and about to enter the nineteenth." The question of whether the United States would decide to go out of the burdensome superpower business, and once again become just one of a number of major powers in a multipolar world, hung in the air.

Author Paul Kennedy's late-1980s book *The Rise and Fall of Great Powers* addressed this issue of whether the United States was in for a period of relative decline. In a review of my book *Preventing World War III*, published in the *New York Review of Books*, Kennedy captured my belief that a new, more comprehensive strategy was needed to replace containment and forestall U.S. decline. He credits me for developing "a sophisticated awareness of evolving a long-term coherent strategy" based on "identifying what American interests (in the broadest sense of the term) really are, how the peoples and parties [around the world] view the United States, and what developments are under way that could either improve or damage the American position."

What most struck Kennedy about my emphasis on strategy was the fact that I understood "that an integral part of 'grand strategy' is trying to deal with the fact that approximately three thousand American students drop out of high school each day." He wrote that my book outlined a strategy "to carry out a much needed perestroika at home, which would entail closing the federal budget deficit, evolving a coherent policy on technology, pushing for radical improvements in the public-school system, and changing the tax laws to encourage a higher savings rate."

In an effort to raise public awareness about the nation's growing and unsustainable debt and its inevitable impact on our children's future, I reached out to my old friend and noted strategist Senator Sam Nunn to chair the Commission on the Strengthening of America. He chose as cochair Republican senator Pete Domenici of New Mexico, then the ranking member on the Budget Committee. Eight other members of Congress evenly split among the two parties also joined the commission, as did seventeen heads of corporations both large and small, six participants from other think tanks, and such CSIS luminaries as James Schlesinger and Bill Brock.

The Strengthening America Commission released its first report in 1992. Among its recommendations were tax reform; strengthening the U.S. industrial base by devoting more research and development to manufacturing technologies; and improving the country's human capital through a $160 billion "Endowment for the Future" focused on education, human resources, and research and development. Not all of the recommendations were ultimately adopted, but the commission helped spark an important debate about a strategy for the post–Cold War era that looked at American power more holistically, as opposed to the overwhelming focus on military power that prevailed during the Cold War. The Strengthening America Commission also recommended a blueprint for balancing the budget by the year 2002. I was very gratified when Democratic president Bill Clinton and a Republican Congress reached what was once considered an almost impossible milestone four years earlier, balancing the U.S. budget in 1998 for the first time in nearly three decades. U.S. leaders were thinking strategically again!

It was during the center's thirtieth anniversary celebration that we made the first "Seven Revolutions" presentation. It was a direct reflection of my strongly held belief that one-dimensional foreign policy think tanks would soon become irrelevant if they did not adapt to new strategic realities. With our stable of experts, CSIS identified and conducted penetrating, wide-ranging analysis on seven revolutionary forces that were transforming the world: population, resource management, technology, information and knowledge, economics, security, and governance. Originally headed up by our director of studies, Erik Peterson (and then later copresented with others, including by our vice president for strategic planning, Tony Smith), the findings were presented in a truly riveting audiovisual presentation called "Seven Revolutions." As word spread about this insightful look into the future, the CSIS team traveled literally around the world presenting "Seven Revolutions" in the boardrooms of global corporations like Boeing and Allianz; to influential civic groups like the renowned Detroit Economic Club; and to leaders like Chairman of the Joint Chiefs Colin Powell. We also started a nationwide teaching program for "Seven Revolutions" with the *New York Times* and the American Association of State Colleges and Universities that brought "Seven Revolutions" to the classroom in publicly supported education institutions across the country. At the outset, we wanted to look ahead at the critical policy challenges that policymakers and leaders in business and other areas would face out into the year 2020. Now, with 2020 just around the corner, "Seven Revolutions" is still going strong, as it has continued to evolve its research to reflect the latest data analysis and technology, now looking ahead to the year 2035 and beyond.

The aftermath of the dissolution of the Soviet Union was a remarkably fertile period for CSIS, as we simultaneously peered into our strategic crystal ball and looked for ways to solidify the gains of the Cold War victory. In the latter category was an important outreach to formerly communist countries to help them make the transition to democracy and free markets. The first such effort was the U.S.-Poland Action Commission. Conceptually the idea was to have the commission cochaired by an American and someone from the target country. In the case of Poland, however, the Poles claimed Zbigniew Brzezinski as one of their own, so he was the single point man. With Brzezinski at the helm, Tony Smith served as the initiative's director and Phyllis d'Hoop, my daughter, as the project coordinator. In talks with Polish leader Lech Walesa, Zbig had originally conceived of the idea of such a commission, seeing it "in a catalytic role in the transformation of the post-communist world," as he is quoted as saying in *Strategic Calling*. "I thought we should not be a wise men's group, that it should be action oriented."

On the U.S. side, CSIS recruited the presidents of some of the most successful corporations to serve on the committee, including the heads of Procter & Gamble (P&G) and Ford Motors. Then CEO and chairman of P&G, John Pepper, started at the company in 1963 and worked his way to the top. Pepper has been a good friend of mine for many years. On the Polish side, there were a few industrialists, but because the new market economy had yet to take hold, there were more Polish cabinet ministers and govern-ment officials. The meetings were generally confidential, enabling trust to build in an atmosphere in which the Poles felt free to air their dirty laundry and ask the group for advice.

We replicated that approach in our outreach to Russia with the formation of the St. Petersburg International Action Committee. It was chaired by CSIS's Henry Kissinger and Mayor Anatoly Sobchak of St. Petersburg. Sob-chak had a close deputy who was a tough former admiral in the Soviet navy. In one of our planning meetings, the former Soviet admiral informed me that he had looked up my biography and saw that my stepfather-in-law was former Navy admiral George Anderson, the former chief of naval operations respon-sible for the blockade of Cuba during the Cuban Missile Crisis. The Russian admiral assured me that he had kept my stepfather squarely in his missile sights had it come to blows. He also told me that if President Clinton really wanted American businesses to invest in Russia, he should simply order them to do so. Clearly we and our Russian hosts had a lot to learn from each other.

We got off to a bit of a rough start with the action commissions. The original plan was for me to launch these initiatives with opening ceremonies and then hand them over to Brzezinski and Kissinger to lead and manage. For the second meeting of the St. Petersburg International Action Commission, Kissinger had to cancel at the last minute because of other pressing business. Then his cochair, Sobchak, also cancelled. The CSIS staffer assigned to the commission in St. Petersburg, rising star David Pepper, sent me an encourag-ing message and told me not to worry. A "remarkably efficient" official in the mayor's office who was responsible for promoting international relations and foreign investments would meet me at the airport and stand in for Mayor Sobchak, who had a belligerent manner in any case. The official, Pepper assured me, was looking forward to meeting "his new friend David Abshire."

Vladimir Putin met me at the St. Petersburg airport, and he was indeed efficient and very "can do." We had a very successful launch of the St. Peters-burg International Action Committee. Jay Pritzker, the multimillionaire who had large holdings in the Hyatt Corporation, was part of the CSIS entourage for the trip. He complained to Putin that Hyatt couldn't open a hotel in the city because the bureaucracy kept putting up red tape to smother the project. Putin told Pritzker that he expected to wield quite a lot of influence in Moscow in the years to come, and he would make sure that the bureaucratic barriers came down. Putin was indispensable in coordinating the event, yet now as I look at photos of the event decades later, he is suspiciously missing. There was no doubt that Vladimir Putin was a preternaturally confident man, and he obviously thought of himself as a comer.

In hindsight, U.S. efforts to help Russia and the former states of the Soviet

Union and Warsaw Pact make the transition to market-based democracies were far from perfect. A number of their economies, including Russia's, suffered greatly in that process. The expansion of NATO and the European Union in the post–Cold War era put more than 100 million Eastern Europeans under the security and economic umbrella of the West, greatly adding to the rolls of free and prosperous peoples. But the process also infuriated Moscow and arguably stunted Russia's own democratic development.

Regardless, I am very proud of CSIS's outreach efforts through the action committees and critical strategic thinking during this transformational period in world affairs. "In peace, the successful strategy prevents war from ever breaking out, and keeps an opponent from taking adverse action," I am quoted as saying in *Strategic Calling*. "The ultimate aim of strategy is to influence the will of opponents, the will and commitment of allies, and the allocations and harmonization of economic measures to accomplish objectives." Given that the United States emerged from the first decade of the post–Cold War era as that rare historical anomaly—a lone superpower in a unipolar world—I believe the path we helped steer was a resounding strategic success.

As the turn of the century approached, I began to concentrate on the challenge of finding a successor at CSIS. Even when I had left CSIS briefly before to go into government, the task of finding a replacement was not easy. This time I had begun to contemplate a permanent transition to the next generation of strategic thinkers.

I had come to know Robert Zoellick through Richard Fairbanks. At the time, Zoellick was the executive vice president of Fannie Mae. He had been a key person in the George H. W. Bush administration, serving as undersecretary of state for economic and agricultural affairs and White House deputy chief of staff. He was the protégé of Secretary of State James Baker, with whom he worked closely on the reunification of Germany and bringing it into NATO.

In a series of one-on-one conversations, I recognized the brilliance of Zoellick's mind, and he realized the necessity for an effective national strategy. My understanding from these meetings was that he, as president of CSIS, planned to devote the coming years to further building the organization and would not be diverted by outside duties. Far be it from me to complain about the outside duties since I had opted to go into government on a few occasions, but I did not veer away from CSIS until I was sure it was on firm footing. After these meetings I was satisfied that he would be a fine replacement for myself as president of CSIS, even though the board had reservations about his ability to build the organization. My longtime friend Hank Greenberg spoke of Zoellick's brilliance but noted he was not the man for CSIS. Nevertheless, with my support for Zoellick, the CSIS Board of Trustees agreed to have an overlapping six-month period to transition to Zoellick. I would step down as president and become the chancellor of CSIS.

Though Zoellick had a brilliant strategic mind, he was sometimes discourteous and turned some people off. I thought these things were remedial. I hoped to patch up any minor discourtesies between Zoellick and the trustees. The bigger problem arose when Zoellick was listed as an advisor to then presidential candidate George W. Bush. Former chairman of the Republican National Committee Bill Brock spoke up regarding this activity. While I had helped on Republican Party platforms before 1968, I was never listed on any candidate's advisory list. While others at CSIS were able to be advisors to political campaigns, the practice was inappropriate for the head of the organization.

This all came to a head at the next meeting of the board of trustees. After suffering the embarrassment that my pick as successor would act in such a fashion, I kept quiet throughout the meeting. The board decided to have Richard Fairbanks, who had a distinguished career in the State Department and had been ambassador-at-large, would step in as interim president while a search was conducted for a new permanent president. A Chicago firm was put in charge of the selection process and produced a short list of candidates. John Hamre was on that list. He was deputy secretary of defense under President Clinton and had worked with CSIS chairman Sam Nunn on the Senate Armed Services Committee in the 1980s. Richard Fairbanks ably led the center for six months, and in January 2000, Hamre was elected president and CEO of CSIS.

Though this series of events proved to be embarrassing for me, it served as a valuable lesson in humility. The CSIS board of trustees had voiced concerns on the appointment of Zoellick from the onset, yet I thought these differences could be overcome. I was wrong. I also realized that CSIS under new leadership needed to continue to grow unfettered by my day-to-day involvement. Though I still had a role at CSIS as vice chairman, I left my office at 1800 K Street and began the next stage of my career as president and CEO of the CSPC.

The outcome actually turned out well for all those involved. Robert Zoellick went on to a great career in the Bush administration as U.S. trade representative, deputy secretary of state, and then president of the World Bank. John Hamre turned out to be a true institution builder. After many years at 1800 K Street, CSIS had outgrown its old space. Hamre oversaw the construction of a new building on Rhode Island Avenue with a striking stone and glass façade, a light-infused atrium, and truly world-class conference space. Finally, CSIS had a home worthy of the lofty intellectual work contained within its walls.

12

Triumphs and Tragedies

CSPC, 9/11, and the Iraq War

In 1999, I took the reins of the Center for the Study of the Presidency from the great R. Gordon Hoxie, the former chancellor of Long Island University who founded the Library of Presidential Papers, which later became the Center for the Study of the Presidency. During this professional transition, the support of friends like Robert Day and Stanley Zax meant a great deal. Both are remarkable businessmen and leaders. Robert founded the Trust Company of the West and headed it for nearly forty years. Likewise, Stanley ran the Zenith National Insurance Company from 1977 to 2012. Stanley would later encourage me to write a book in 2008 on challenging the next president on a number of vital issues, which was aptly titled *A Call to Greatness: Challenging Our Next President*. Robert Day and Stanley Zax continue to generously support the work of the center.

In 2006, at the encouragement of my longtime friend Senator John Warner, the center was rechristened the Center for the Study of the Presidency & Congress (CSPC) to reflect my conviction that strong American leadership depended on the executive and legislative branches of government working together, whenever possible, based on strategic consensus. Indeed, I quickly realized that CSPC would offer an excellent platform to pursue my lifelong passions: a focus on long-term strategy, presidential leadership, civil discourse in search of bipartisan consensus, mentoring future leaders, and bringing the lessons of history to bear on the challenges of the present.

What I couldn't have foreseen was just how monumental those challenges would prove in the new millennium. The first decade of the twenty-first century would see a rare, contested presidential election; the worst attack on the American homeland since Pearl Harbor; the two longest wars in our nation's history, and among the most unsatisfactory; and the worst financial crisis since the Great Depression. After victory in the Cold War had catapulted the nation to the pinnacle of global power in the 1990s, some analysts described this period as the "end of history," when all the ideological battles could be put aside. History was reasserting itself with a vengeance.

CSPC was the direct outgrowth of a request by President Dwight D. Eisenhower, who long ago lamented the lack of historical case studies to prepare him for civilian political leadership. As the former Supreme Allied Commander, the five-star general Eisenhower had naturally pored over scores of analyses of previous battles, troop deployments, and international crises to inform his critical military leadership during World War II. Yet no similar repository of institutional memory existed for the equally complex arts of governing and legislating.

On taking the helm of CSPC, I immediately set about to remedy that lack of institutional memory on the presidency. We gathered the nation's top presidential historians, political scientists, and journalists to write case studies on milestones in presidential leadership and on the nature of the presidency as an institution. It was the first attempt ever to outline the key historical lessons of past presidencies for a new president-elect. As I noted in the prologue to this anthology of case studies, a president armed with those lessons can fortify himself for the long look forward by better understanding the long view backward. Such a vantage helped nourish the character, wisdom, and vision we associate with George Washington, John Adams, Thomas Jefferson, Abraham Lincoln, Theodore and Franklin Roosevelt, and Harry Truman—every one of them a keen student of history.

It was Lincoln who said, "Fellow citizens, we cannot escape history." To his future peers, Lincoln might have added, "Fellow presidents, we especially cannot escape history." Because even some of the ablest presidents experienced both great successes and great catastrophes, we named the anthology *Triumphs and Tragedies of the Modern Presidency.*

As I read through the collected wisdom compiled in *Triumphs and Tragedies*, I was reminded that the fundamentals of leadership, especially American presidential leadership, have remained remarkably constant for more than two centuries. There is an intriguing commonality between the successful presidencies of Washington, Lincoln, and the Roosevelts, for instance, just as there is for the unsuccessful tenures of James Buchanan, Warren Harding, and Andrew Johnson. One constant is the sense of humility in the former, and lack of it in the latter.

Both Washington and Lincoln worried that they might not be up to the task of leading the nation at two of its most critical junctures. Lincoln himself feared for his election in 1864 as the Civil War dragged on, just as Harry Truman's poll ratings were so low that he was not considered electable in 1948. Yet Secretary of War Edwin Stanton rendered the definitive judgment on Lincoln's tenure when he remarked at the president's deathbed, "Now he belongs to the ages." Indeed, he did. Two decades after Truman's presidency, he was widely considered among the greats, as eventually were Eisenhower and Reagan after their own presidencies were judged in the fullness of time. The underlying lesson in their common experience is the value of avoiding hubris and arrogance. A bit of modesty and indeed awe is salutary for any president, just as it is for the people around the chief executive, who do much to set the tone for, and perception of, our leaders.

Another theme woven throughout our anthology of presidential leadership is the presence of both triumph and tragedy in nearly every administration. Lyndon Johnson used his nearly unparalleled knowledge of Congress and his uncanny deal-making skills to move a historic domestic agenda through Congress. Yet the same president led us into the most tragic foreign war, in Vietnam, that our country had ever experienced, tarnishing a great legacy. Richard Nixon similarly made history with his outreach to Communist China and rebalancing of global power, yet the same man led us into the Watergate trauma. As I have recounted earlier from my own firsthand recollections, the same Ronald Reagan who reenergized the nation and turned the tide of the Cold War created the leadership climate that resulted in the Iran-Contra miasma. Bill Clinton reclaimed the political center and reached across the political aisle to achieve budgetary agreements that transformed budget deficits into a historic surplus, but he also provoked only the second impeachment drama in American history.

Another rhyme that echoes throughout presidential history is the importance of the supporting cast. Our best presidents were keen judges of character who surrounded themselves with the best intellects and talents of their time. George Washington was a truly gifted chief executive, for instance, with extraordinary character and dependability, and he deliberately built a cabinet of people far more brilliant and creative than himself. They were people of very different political philosophies and skills who would not have gotten along without Washington's steadying influence. Thomas Jefferson originally opposed the Constitution, but Washington brought this firm believer in states' rights into the federal fold. The brilliant Alexander Hamilton, a centralizer determined to revitalize the nation's credit, teamed with James Madison, a "checks and balances" political philosopher, along with the diplomat John Jay, to together produce those extraordinary documents known as *The Federalist Papers*. Their nom de plume was Publius, in honor of the Roman aristocrat who helped overthrow the monarchy and establish the first Roman Republic. Hamilton became Washington's secretary of the treasury, Jefferson his secretary of state, and Madison became the administration's point man in the House of Representatives. Washington's steadfast character served as the fulcrum for this extraordinary supporting cast.

Lincoln fashioned a cabinet of his own "team of political rivals" to help weather the tempest of civil war. After World War II, Truman also built a cabinet of exceptional talent and thus became known as a "unifier"—combining the skills of Secretary of Defense George Catlett Marshall, the former five-star leader of World War II; Secretary of State Dean Acheson; Secretary of Defense Robert Lovett; and even Republican Herbert Hoover, who Truman brought in to head a commission in 1947 on the reorganization of the executive branch.

Richard Nixon leaned heavily on his national security advisor and then secretary of state Henry Kissinger as an invaluable partner in his historic outreach to China. Jimmy Carter brought primarily Georgia outsiders to the White House, and suffered from their inexperience in the peculiar ways of Washington, D.C. President Reagan chose the Washington-wise James Baker as his first White House chief of staff, who contrasted with his successor Donald Regan, a man of corporate talent who was miscast as the chief of staff. George H. W. Bush benefited greatly from his quadruple-threat team of National Security Advisor and former general Brent Scowcroft; Secretary of State James Baker; Defense Secretary and future vice president Dick Cheney; and Chairman of the Joint Chiefs Colin Powell, who had served as Reagan's national security advisor. Clinton, who campaigned on "It's the economy, stupid," showed wisdom in selecting and constantly backing Secretary of the Treasury Robert Rubin, along with Chairman of the Federal Reserve Alan Greenspan, to manage domestic and international economic issues.

The most important lesson of history is not simply the truism that great combinations of people in the White House and cabinet tend to produce great results. Rather, it's that great presidents are often those with the self-confidence and emotional capacity to attract the best and brightest without feeling personally threatened. Washington and Truman were both comfortable with themselves, for instance, and harbored no inner demons of jealousy nor fears of being overshadowed by subordinates. Hence, they could marshal those with even greater creativity than themselves. Not coincidentally, both presidents were great institution builders.

If you have stayed with me this long, you know how strongly I believe that presidents must proactively reach out to Congress early and often to build coalitions across the political aisle in order to maximize their power and influence. This is not only sound policy, but the very foundation of political strategy: A house divided cannot stand. A master of this was President Lyndon Johnson, who from his long legislative career knew that a president's influence tends to wane over time, especially given that a president's party almost always loses congressional seats in midterm elections. "I keep hitting hard because I know this honeymoon won't last," Johnson said of his early push for action in Congress. "Every day, I lose a little more political capital . . . One day soon, I don't know when, the critics and the snipers will move in and we will be at stalemate."

Yet history is rife with examples of presidents who have ignored this cardinal rule of winning Congress to their agendas and lived to regret it. Woodrow Wilson failed to include Republicans on the delegation he sent to Paris to negotiate the Treaty of Versailles, nor did he reach across party lines in the Senate to obtain ratification, and as a result, the United States never ratified the treaty nor joined the League of Nations. Eighty years later, Bill Clinton's soured relationship with Congress led to the Senate's historic rejection of the Comprehensive Nuclear-Test-Ban Treaty.

In many ways the first test of presidential leadership is the White House's outreach to Congress. The chief executive can help himself greatly in this effort by appointing a crack team of congressional liaison officers throughout the executive branch. The first criterion should be people of stature who can empathize with their contacts on Capitol Hill. Remember, the estimable Dean Acheson and George Kennan were both once assistant secretaries of state for congressional relations, a position that I too was proud to fill in my time. President Eisenhower's superb congressional liaison, my mentor Bryce Harlow, identified the single most important ingredient for building a productive relationship between the White House and Congress in a maxim he often repeated, that the reader is now familiar with: "Trust is the coin of the realm."

In my prologue to *Triumphs and Tragedies of the Modern Presidency*, written on Election Day 2000, I noted that the next president was going to confront a host of complex and fast-moving challenges. Revolutionary changes in demography, finance, technology, and terrorism continued to cause disarray and unpredictability in the global system, and to collapse the time available for decision-making in the White House, while increasing serious chances for missteps. Given that the average trading volume in foreign exchanges was increasing exponentially, far beyond the ability of global financial institutions to keep pace, I predicted that the next president was almost certain to face a profound international financial crisis even more destabilizing than those of the 1990s. Tragically, I would be proven right in 2008 with the financial crisis and Great Recession.

Despite the sense that the United States was at the pinnacle of its power, I noted in 2000 that our national security machinery forged in the Cold War had failed to adequately adjust to the post–Cold War world. We were constantly reacting to a rapidly evolving strategic landscape, instead of anticipating and molding it. Our nation was increasingly vulnerable to terrorism and the proliferation of weapons of mass destruction. Our tendency to miscalculate and miscommunicate on the eve of conflict had persisted, as noted in the anthology, from Korea to Iraq to Kosovo. Domestically, we were confronted by an aging population with inadequate resources for retirement, languishing inner cities, and an antiquated education system that was leaving too many children behind.

We would begin the new century with a contested presidential election that would eventually have to be decided by the Supreme Court, which seemed inauspicious even at the time. Above all, we at CSPC and the writers of the anthology humbly offered *Triumphs and Tragedies of the Modern Presidency* as an exploration of how presidential leadership steered us to this moment in our national journey. It also serves as a guide to the commander in chief about to take the helm to chart the course ahead through stormy waters. Though the disputed presidential election of 2000 had yet to be resolved, Texas governor George W. Bush's chief of staff, Clay Johnson, reached out to CSPC for resources to produce a successful and seamless presidential transition.

Clay's deputy at the time was Dina Powell, who became a good friend and member of the so-called Abshire Mafia. She would later serve as assistant secretary of state for educational and cultural affairs and deputy undersecretary of state for public diplomacy and public affairs in the George W. Bush administration. She now heads Goldman Sachs's Impact Investing business and is president of the Goldman Sachs Foundation.

Given that the election results were still up in the air, Bush had to pay for the initial transition effort himself because he could not yet receive public funding from the General Services Administration. The official transition began once Vice President Al Gore conceded the election on December 14, 2000. Cheney was formally named the transition chairman and Johnson became the transition executive director.[1]

My special assistant Max Angerholzer (and later successor at CSPC) and I visited the transition office and met with Cheney and Johnson. We had a discussion on the historical lessons from past presidential transitions and offered *Triumphs and Tragedies of the Modern Presidency* as a resource. Johnson demonstrated his knowledge of successful past transitions by putting together a White House staff early on in the process. I thought it important that the new president remember first and foremost George Santayana's oft-repeated warning: Those who do not learn from history are condemned to repeat it.

With the historical lessons contained in *Triumphs and Tragedies of the Modern Presidency* firmly in mind, I led the Center for the Study of the Presidency in hosting a series of policy dialogues in the fall of 2000 that brought together some of the country's most accomplished diplomats, historians, strategists, military leaders, and current and former senior government officials. A number of the participants would assume senior positions in the new administration of George W. Bush, including John Bolton, who would become ambassador to the United Nations, and Richard Haass, who would serve as the number three official in Bush Forty-three's State Department. The policy dialogues were held at the center's headquarters in Washington, D.C.; at Harvard University's John F. Kennedy School of Government; and at the George H. W. Bush Presidential Library. They benefited greatly from the participation of former president Bush the elder, whose leadership during the collapse of the Soviet Union, reunification of Germany, and lopsided victory in the 1991 Persian Gulf War were case studies in exemplary presidential leadership.

The policy dialogues examined presidential decision-making during past U.S. military interventions and the use of diplomacy in strategies to prevent conflict. My goal in hosting these dialogues was twofold: to distill key "lessons learned" to inform the president-elect in deciding when, how, and why to employ military force to protect U.S. interests; and to strengthen the resources and mechanisms of diplomacy to prevent conflict whenever possible.

The culmination of our policy dialogue was the report *In Harm's Way: Intervention and Prevention*, which offered institutional memory that the new president could draw upon in times of crisis. It called for a fundamental strategic reformation comparable to the Truman-Eisenhower strategic initiatives that laid the groundwork for victory in the Cold War. I won't go into great detail on the specific reforms called for in the report, but suffice to say the general themes would be familiar to readers who have stayed with me thus far on my life's journey: a long-range strategic vision that clearly defines and prioritizes U.S. interests; coordination of all elements of national power—diplomatic, economic, cultural, and military—to shape the strategic environment; reform of a stovepiped intelligence community to better enable it to anticipate gathering threats; building of bipartisan relationships between the White House and Congress to form a strong foundation on which to stand in times of crisis; nurturing of multilateral alliances in order to share the burdens of global leadership and the policing of the global commons; adequate resourcing of strained military and diplomatic levers of power; and sustained presidential leadership in reaching a national consensus about the proper role of the United States in maintaining stability in a fractious international order. I hoped that this report would arm the next president in that project of renewal. Unfortunately, most presidents consider themselves exempt from past failures. Filled with electoral hubris, each expects to overshadow the accomplishments of his predecessor rather than build upon them. Few pay close attention to the hard lessons of experience that teach us how and why some presidencies go wrong and others achieve greatness.

In Harm's Way was presented to the Bush Forty-three administration at a public meeting with incoming national security advisor Condoleezza Rice. President-elect George W. Bush had campaigned on his belief in a more "humble" foreign policy, one that eschewed using the U.S. military on the kind of peacekeeping operations that the Clinton administration engaged in to halt war in the Balkans. When I handed her *In Harm's Way*, Rice told me, "If your fellow Tennessean Al Gore had been elected, he would need these lessons in interventions. The Bush administration is not going to need this, because we are not planning to intervene internationally."

Another CSPC report was produced, entitled *Comprehensive Strategic Reform: Moving from Cold War Rigidities to Postwar Agility and Anticipation*. It began at a meeting of a twenty-three-member, bipartisan group of experts at the George H. W. Bush Library. The result was a series of recommendations, including the creation of a strategic advisory board, chaired by the vice president, to look over and across the "strategic horizon." This report, written before September 2001, spotlighted the need for new strategies and structures that would go beyond traditional State Department public diplomacy. It called for a new national security approach that placed a premium on anticipation, agility, and communications given the increasingly uncertain times. It also warned that anti-Americanism was on the rise around the world at the very same time that our communications capabilities had been left considerably weakened by the dismemberment of the United States Information Agency and by significant funding cuts. Dick Cheney took a special interest in this publication and the idea of an advisory board, but backed away when he became bogged down in his fight over the Energy Task Force. Defense Secretary Donald Rumsfeld took particular interest in other parts of the publication calling for defense agility. He even assigned a liaison to our center for further follow-up. Unfortunately, these efforts were overtaken by events on 9/11.

In less than a year, the United States would suffer the worst assault on the homeland since Pearl Harbor with the September 11, 2001, terrorist attacks, and the Bush administration would respond by intervening in Afghanistan in what would become one of the largest nation-building exercises, and longest conflicts, in our modern history. Within a little more than two years the Bush administration would invade Iraq, violating the cardinal principle of unity of effort in time of war. By starting a war of choice in Iraq and opening a second front in its "global war on terrorism," the Bush administration was dividing our military forces and resources and abandoning the public unity that the 9/11 attacks had inspired. Having failed to learn from history, we were apparently condemned to repeat it.

In response to the 9/11 attacks, the center began an initiative focused on U.S. communications with Muslim communities both at home and around the globe. Our national security was being undercut by the gulf between the public diplomacy challenge we faced and our inadequate financial and organizational capabilities. We believed that the credibility of U.S. leadership rested largely on our ability to minimize that gulf. With initial funding from the Carnegie Corporation of New York and the Dr. Scholl Foundation, we began an initiative, directed by Phyllis d'Hoop, my daughter, that began with a series of meetings with more than seventy-five scholars and practitioners, from within and outside of government, with expertise on Muslim communities, American culture, and communications and information technology. In June of 2003, we hosted a large plenary meeting on the challenges of strengthening U.S.-Muslim communications. A valuable report by the Council on Foreign Relations on public diplomacy, produced by their Independent Task Force on Public Diplomacy, chaired by Pete Peterson, also assisted our efforts; and several of their scholars were involved in our effort, including Pete. Our recommendations were presented in the *Strengthening U.S.-Muslim Communications* publication.

I shared the report with Congressman Frank Wolf (R-Va.), who asked me to testify before the House Appropriations Committee. Wolf was also concerned with a spike in anti-Americanism that he feared was accompanying the "global war on terrorism."

"David, I've just come back from Europe," Wolf told me at the public hearing. "You could cut the anti-Americanism with a knife."

What Wolf had in mind was a congressionally supported advisory group to look into what he saw as a failure in U.S. public diplomacy. I agreed to serve on the advisory group, which was chaired by the able former ambassador Edward Djerejian. Thus was born the Advisory Group on Public Diplomacy for the Arab and Muslim World. The advisory group brought together esteemed experts from the academic, business, government, and journalist communities, notably Dr. Malik Hasan. As a neurologist and business leader who was raised in Pakistan and speaks Urdu, Dr. Hasan has a unique perspective on public diplomacy in the Muslim world. He also founded two health care companies in Colorado, Qual-Med (now Health Net) and HealthTrio Inc.

I first met Dr. Hasan on the advisory group and we became fast and very close friends.

In October 2003, our advisory group released a blueprint for a public diplomacy transformation: *Changing Minds, Winning Peace: A New Strategic Direction for U.S. Public Diplomacy in the Arab and Muslim World.* It noted that while the United States spent $1.14 billion annually on public diplomacy, only $150 million of the State Department's public diplomacy budget was directed at Muslim countries. Of the 448 State Department officials engaged in public diplomacy and outreach, only 54 were fluent in Arabic.

Readers already familiar with my biases will not be surprised to learn that the top recommendation of the *Changing Minds, Winning Peace* report was that the White House develop a new strategic blueprint for public diplomacy and take charge of interagency coordination to ensure its implementation. We recommended this task be performed by a cabinet-level special counselor to the president, a recommendation that had also been put forth in our own CSPC report. The State Department would remain the lead agency for public diplomacy, but the special counselor would provide the grand strategy for coordinating the messages of the many government departments and agencies that communicate to audiences abroad. We also recommended that all public diplomacy activities should be continually measured for effectiveness. It was our belief that those two changes alone—strategic direction and vigorous measurement of effect—would lead to a rapid improvement in public diplomacy at a critical time in our nation's history.

I met privately with National Security Advisor Condoleezza Rice and her deputy Stephen Hadley to try and persuade them to create the new position of counselor to the president for public diplomacy. This was an attempt to fill the void left by the shuttering of the more independent U.S. Information Agency (USIA) in 1999, whose functions were folded into the job of a newly created undersecretary of state for public diplomacy and public affairs. Even in the days of USIA, the agency director might have had the ear of the president but no real authority to coordinate public diplomacy across the vast federal government. The White House chose instead to name President Bush's close friend Karen Hughes as the new undersecretary of state for public diplomacy, thus increasing the clout of the position. Hughes later admitted that this solution was inadequate to the demands of coordinating the U.S. government's message and outreach to the Muslim world.

There were a number of other recommendations in the *Changing Minds, Winning Peace* report that were implemented. The State Department created a series of new public and private partnerships that leveraged the ingenuity of American businesses, including a first Presidential Summit on Entrepreneurship held at the Ronald Reagan Building in Washington, D.C. The summit served to "highlight and support businesses and social entrepreneurship in Muslim-majority countries and Muslim communities around the world."

Such creative outreach illustrates what can be accomplished when U.S. officials are guided by a coherent strategy and empowered to leverage all of the tools of American power to achieve clearly articulated goals, in this case showing in word and deed that the United States' "war on terrorism" truly was not meant as a war against Islam.

In 2006, Congressman Frank Wolf recruited me and CSPC for another major project. Three years after the initial invasion, the United States was clearly losing the war in Iraq, which was slowly disintegrating under the twin pressures of terrorism and horrific sectarian violence. The deteriorating situation in Iraq preoccupied the White House and was a major drag on Republicans as they faced midterm elections that year. In the midst of this crisis, Wolf phoned me to discuss the need for a fresh set of eyes on U.S. operations in Iraq and our strategy going forward. He also called John Hamre, my successor as president of the Center for Strategic and International Studies, and Richard Solomon, president of the U.S. Institute of Peace. We all agreed to launch an initiative designed to build bipartisan support for a new strategy in Iraq that would turn around the war and hopefully set the stage for a withdrawal of U.S. troops. Thus was born the Iraq Study Group.

Together we selected Republican and former secretary of state James Baker, and Democrat and former chairman of the House Foreign Relations Committee Lee Hamilton, to cochair the Iraq Study Group. The group was filled out with four prominent Republicans (Lawrence Eagleburger, Ed Meese, Sandra Day O'Connor, and Alan K. Simpson) and four prominent Democrats (Vernon Jordan, Leon Panetta, William J. Perry, and Chuck Robb), reflecting our hopes of reaching a bipartisan consensus on a way forward. The group traveled to Iraq and held months of deliberations trying to reach agreement on a new Iraq strategy.

The deliberations within the Iraq Study Group were tense in the fall of 2006. Some of the Democrats on the panel wanted to release the findings before midterm elections in November. James Baker feared the stark findings would be detrimental to Republicans, and he maneuvered to delay the report until after the midterms for political reasons. After Republicans lost in a landslide in midterm elections, President Bush replaced Secretary of Defense Donald Rumsfeld with former CIA director Robert Gates, who was a member of the Iraq Study Group up until that time.

During this period after the midterm elections in November but before the Iraq Study Group released its final report, I was talking with Congressman

Wolf on a Sunday afternoon. We both knew that President Bush and newly named Defense Secretary Gates were considering new military leadership in Iraq. I had recently been visited by Army lieutenant general David Petraeus, who was commanding general at Fort Leavenworth, Kansas, where he oversaw the Command and General Staff College and was in the midst of rewriting the Army's doctrine for counterinsurgency warfare. I had been very impressed by Petraeus's sharp intellect in analyzing the situation in Iraq and proposing new tactics, and I told Wolf so.

"Are you going to be near the phone later today?" Wolf asked me. I responded yes, and he said, "I'm calling [National Security Advisor] Stephen Hadley."

Hadley called me later that day, and I told him about General Petraeus's background and impressive capabilities. Hadley, a lawyer and policy analyst by trade, then asked me incredulously, "You mean he was really put into Leavenworth prison?"

"No," I laughed. "Not the prison but the General Staff School at Fort Leavenworth!" Soon thereafter, Petraeus was installed as commanding general of the Multi-National Force–Iraq and tasked with turning around a losing war.

The Iraq Study Group released its 142-page report on December 6, 2006, having reached a bipartisan consensus on seventy-nine recommendations. The document opened with a dire conclusion. "The situation in Iraq is grave and deteriorating." This was a vast understatement.

The report outlined three principle proposals: the launching of a diplomatic offensive in the Middle East, including direct engagement with Iran and Syria and pursuit of Arab-Israeli peace; changing the primary mission of U.S. forces in Iraq from combat to training and counterterrorism operations; and conditioning aid to Iraq on the Iraqi government's progress on national reconciliation and good governance. Importantly, the report endorsed a gradual though major troop withdrawal, stating that "by the first quarter of 2008, subject to unexpected developments in the security situation on the ground, all combat brigades not necessary for force protection could be out of Iraq." To maintain flexibility for U.S. commanders on the ground, the study group stated that it could "support a short-term redeployment or surge of American combat forces to stabilize Baghdad, or to speed up the training and equipping mission, if the U.S. commander in Iraq determines that such steps would be effective."

The Iraq Study Group's findings attracted great public attention, with all of the major television networks covering the press conference where Baker, Hamilton, and the other members released their findings. Public opinion polls showed that a majority of the American public viewed its findings favorably. Given the Republican Party's landslide losses in the midterm elections, many moderate Republicans also embraced the group's recommendations and called on President Bush to change course.

Days later, Representative Wolf and I were sitting outside the Oval Office in the White House, waiting to brief President Bush and Stephen Hadley on the Iraq Study Group report, which I believed offered the last, best chance to build bipartisan consensus for the war effort on Capitol Hill, and thus reestablish the cardinal principle of unity of effort. As we were waiting, I saw retired Army vice chief Jack Keane and Fredrick Kagan of the American Enterprise Institute leave the Oval Office. Kagan was the author of the AEI report *Choosing Victory: A Plan for Success in Iraq*. As opposed to the Iraq Study Group's recommendation of a gradual withdrawal of U.S. troops, *Choosing Victory* called for a major surge in U.S. ground forces in Iraq in order to conduct a manpower-intensive counterinsurgency campaign there, a position that General Keane had recently advocated.

At that moment I knew that President Bush would ignore the Iraq Study Group recommendations designed to build bipartisan support on Capitol Hill, and instead choose the riskier path in hopes of achieving an improbable victory in what many experts believed was a losing war.

As I mentioned earlier, a theme woven throughout the history of U.S. presidential leadership is the presence of both triumph and tragedy in nearly every administration, and I was viewing it firsthand. In choosing to launch a war of choice in Iraq while U.S. forces were still engaged in Afghanistan, President Bush had committed a classic strategic blunder, dividing our forces and resources and sacrificing the post-9/11 unity of the American public for a controversial war. Drawing on the same resources of character and intellect, President Bush was now bucking conventional wisdom and doubling down on a last-ditch effort to snatch victory out of the jaws of defeat, and he was right! I suspect historians will one day view the U.S. troop surge and counterinsurgency campaign that stabilized Iraq in 2007–2008 as George W. Bush's finest moment as commander in chief.

A final word on the Iraq Study Group. While the group's recommendations were largely ignored by President Bush, they caught the attention of a first-term senator named Barack Obama (D-Ill.). Then Senator Obama introduced legislation codifying the group's major recommendations—"consistent with the expectation of the Iraq Study Group"—which became his Iraq platform in the 2008 presidential election.

With Iraq largely stabilized by 2009, President Obama implemented those recommendations, beginning the withdrawal of U.S. combat brigades from Iraq, reaching out diplomatically to regional players such as Iran and Syria, and attempting to reinvigorate the peace process between Israelis and Palestinians. As the author Jordan Tama would point out in *Triumphs and Trage-*

dies of the Modern Congress, the only significant difference between the study group's recommendation and the policies that President Obama adopted was that he moved forward the date for ending the combat mission to August 2010. I would add that President Obama also withdrew all U.S. forces from Iraq by the end of 2011, against the advice of his top national security advisors and the recommendation of the Iraq Study Group that a residual U.S. force be retained in Iraq for training and counterterrorism missions.

And thus was history rhyming, tragically, once again.

One recommendation of the Iraq Study Group was that "it is critical for the United States to provide additional political, economic and military support for Afghanistan." In an effort to expand upon this recommendation, I formed the Afghanistan Study Group in the spring of 2007. We sought to produce a far-reaching report without the flawed process of the Iraq Study Group. Though the Iraq Study Group produced an excellent report with essential recommendations, the process to get there was too political given the involvement of four different think tanks. In comparison, the Afghanistan Study Group was solely the product of CSPC.

Ambassador Thomas R. Pickering and General James L. Jones ably cochaired the group. The group held working sessions with prominent experts on the region and on foreign policy. The group also held consultative sessions with Undersecretary of State for Political Affairs Nicholas Burns and Assistant Secretary of State for South and Central Asia Richard Boucher; former United Nations special representative of the secretary general to Afghanistan Ambassador Lakhdar Brahimi; Ambassador of Pakistan to the United States Mahmud Durrani; Ambassador of Afghanistan to the United States Said Tayeb Jawad; and United States Ambassador to NATO Victoria Nuland.

The group first offered an assessment of the current situation in Afghanistan. The study group identified critical issues to revitalize the U.S. and international effort in Afghanistan, including international coordination, security, governance and the rule of law, counternarcotics, economic development and reconstruction, and Afghanistan's relations with its neighbors.

In addition to the recommendations on these issues, the study group offered three overarching recommendations to bring sharper focus on Afghanistan, both within the U.S. government and with the broader international community. The first was a proposal for the administration and the Congress to decouple Iraq and Afghanistan in the legislative process, and in the management of these conflicts in the executive branch. The second was to establish within the U.S. government the position of a special envoy for

Afghanistan who would be charged with coordinating all aspects of U.S. policies toward Afghanistan. The third proposal was to formulate a new, unified strategy to stabilize Afghanistan over the next five years and to build international support for it.

The report was released on January 30, 2008, in a bipartisan rollout on Capitol Hill presided over by future secretary of state John Kerry and Senator Norm Coleman. Kerry commented that the report "truly exemplifies the kind of bipartisan consensus building that is necessary for state craft. And in order to be able to put together a sustainable foreign policy for our country, for an effort that no doubt is going to continue for years to come."[2]

The influence of the report continued to be felt in July 2008, when it served as vital background for a congressional delegation that visited Afghanistan. The congressional delegation to Afghanistan included Senator Jack Reed, future secretary of defense Chuck Hagel, and then presumptive Democratic presidential nominee Barack Obama. On the trip, Obama agreed that "one of the biggest mistakes we've made strategically after 9/11 was to fail to finish the job here, focus our attention here. We got distracted by Iraq."[3] In the first days of his presidency, Obama subsequently established the position of United States envoy for Afghanistan and Pakistan and appointed Richard Holbrooke.

CSPC was at the center of the 2008 presidential race by virtue of the fact that we were in close contact with the campaigns of both Barack Obama and John McCain. Our contact on Obama's campaign was Chris Lu, his Senate chief of staff and later transition director. As a resource for the transition team, Lu requested *Triumphs and Tragedies of the Modern Presidency* and made it required reading for the team. At the signing of the American Recovery and Reinvestment Act on February 17, 2009, President Obama cited the example of President Eisenhower's Interstate Highway System as "remaking the American landscape with the largest new investment in our nation's infrastructure," which was also highlighted in the case study "The Federal Highway Act of 1956" in *Triumphs and Tragedies of the Modern Presidency*.

I also gave the candidates in the 2008 presidential election advance copies of my book *A Call to Greatness: Challenging the Next President*. The opening chapter describes a gathering storm of increasing magnitude looming over the newly elected president. At no time in my decades in Washington had our nation so lost its strategic direction and freedom of action. We were suffering from increasing disunity at home and the loss of leverage and influence abroad. Reversing that disastrous course would be the "call to greatness" for our next president. Little did I know at the time that the challenges

I described would become far greater after the devastating collapse of our financial system and the subsequent worldwide recession.

In the book we offered the next president models of leadership based on the examples of our two greatest commanders in chief: Abraham Lincoln and Franklin Roosevelt. Both were *transformational leaders*, a term coined by my friend Professor James Bums. It describes leaders who change the entire strategic landscape with bold strokes, as opposed to "transactional leaders," who often make good managers but change situations only at the margins without fundamentally altering course.

Great leaders have the capacity to constantly readjust and reposition as changing circumstances demand. Abraham Lincoln came from the antislavery left wing of his party, for instance, yet moved to the center as he tried to keep the nation from splintering.

Similarly, Barack Obama had a very liberal voting record in the Illinois statehouse, and also in his short period as senator. Yet he too moved squarely toward the center in trying to manage two unpopular wars and the Great Recession. I believe Obama, who also began his campaign from the steps of the statehouse in Springfield, Illinois, may have some of Abraham Lincoln's leadership DNA. Obama was no doubt thinking of Lincoln when he spoke during his Inaugural Address: "Every so often, the oath is taken amidst gathering clouds and raging storms. At these moments, America has carried on not simply because of the skill or vision of those in high office, but because we, the people, have remained faithful to the ideals of our forebears and true to our founding documents. So it has been; so it must be with this generation of Americans."

In 2009, CSPC's Saving America's Future Initiative was an example of a missed opportunity for leaders to answer the call to greatness. This was the product of a unique initiative that convened twenty-one working groups and more than two hundred scholars, experts, practitioners, and officeholders. They were led by four visionary national leaders: former GAO head David Walker focused on our unsustainable national finances; former Lockheed Martin CEO Norman Augustine highlighted the need for critical national investments, a conclusion reached from his work on the National Academies study *Rising Above the Gathering Storm*; former White House chief of staff Leon Panetta contributed his unparalleled knowledge of Washington, D.C.; and former Colorado governor Roy Romer brought his unique experience in education reform.

The Saving America's Future Initiative called for the development of a ten-year national strategy based on a comprehensive assessment of where the country stands today, where it needs to go, and how it can best get there.

Such a strategy is necessary to align all elements of the government and match resources to requirements in a realistic and flexible manner. The initiative also called for the establishment of a national commission to execute this strategy by reforming and harmonizing budget and tax policies, putting the country back on a sound and sustainable economic path, as the need for leadership has increased, the time to act has grown shorter, and the political environment has become even more hostile to the necessary consensus on the best way forward. The fundamental building blocks of the required reforms have not changed since CSPC laid them out, and the commission report still offers a good place to start the reform process.

The comprehensive framework of Saving America's Future was successfully replicated in the CSPC report *Mobilizing NATO for Afghanistan and Pakistan*. The report approached the region comprehensively with a focus on assessing the threat that instability, Islamist militants, and terrorist networks pose to countries in the region. We felt that NATO's efforts in Afghanistan did not take into account their effect on the region and the neighboring countries, notably the instability in Pakistan. The Center for the Study of the Presidency & Congress continues to search for comprehensive and strategic solutions to our nation's problems in a bipartisan way. CSPC is uniquely positioned to partner with government, the private sector, and the academic community. I like to think that CSPC is not a think tank but rather a "do tank" that is constantly expanding our reach to "answer the call to greatness."

13

The Art of National Renewal

Science, Education, and Infrastructure

A lifelong interest in science was rekindled when Frederick Seitz asked me to join the Richard Lounsbery Foundation's board of directors, and on his retirement in 2002, I became president. I had first met Fred when he was president of the Rockefeller University, and he later replaced retiring National Science Foundation director Alan Waterman on the advisory board of the CSIS. Fred was a world-renowned physicist, an innovative leader, and, indeed, a close friend. Fred Seitz always believed that scientists needed the curiosity of children and the freedom to explore anywhere in search of scientific breakthroughs. I have tried to lead the Lounsbery Foundation with that guiding insight in mind.

The foundation's mission is to sustain American leadership in science and technology through programs that improve science and math education, assess key trends in the physical and biomedical sciences, and provide start-up assistance for promising research projects. The foundation has also long nurtured Franco-American scientific cooperation. The Lounsbery Foundation has supported science diplomacy around the globe, and it made its first grant in support of the National Museum of American History's Abraham Lincoln exhibit.

Science diplomacy became a more prominent aspect of Lounsbery's mission soon after the U.S. invasion of Iraq in 2003. Lounsbery board member Jesse Ausubel encouraged the foundation to support the Iraqi scholar rescue efforts of the Institute of International Education. Other examples of projects funded by the foundation are the joint U.S.-Tunisia science diplomacy workshop coordinated by the American Association for the Advancement of Science and a cultural and heritage preservation project in Libya through Oberlin College. Lounsbery also provided core funding and supported research projects for the Israeli-Palestinian Science Organization, a group with which the foundation has established a strong and lasting relationship. Some of our most impactful programs in the Middle East have addressed still-contentious U.S.-Iran relations. The Lounsbery Foundation has also expanded its efforts to Latin America and the Caribbean, particularly Cuba, where we have fostered meaningful dialogue between Cubans and Americans.

Lounsbery scientific and medical projects are virtually the only constructive interaction, diplomatic or otherwise, that anyone from the United States has with North Korea. Lounsbery recognized an opportunity for scientific and medical cooperation between the United States and the Democratic People's Republic of Korea that would create important relationships. Lounsbery is particularly proud of the grants aimed at creating new relationships in Myanmar, which has rapidly transitioned from isolated military junta to a fledgling democracy. Though often overlooked, science education and cultural preservation offer outstanding opportunities to promote goodwill and generate fruitful relationships as these nations seek to transform. Science diplomacy is an important first step in building a substantive dialogue between peoples and nations. That's why to this day the Lounsbery Foundation continually strives to strengthen the bonds between scientific communities throughout the world.

One day in March of 2009, I received a call from Brigadier General Richard Black, a professor of engineering at West Point. A group of cadets from the engineering department were visiting Washington, and he asked me to speak to them. In my remarks, I recounted the contributions that Vannevar Bush had made to American science and engineering and the critical role that scientific achievement had played in making the United States a great power. After the lecture broke up, Black came to the front of the room and thanked me. "I am so glad you told the story of Vannevar Bush," he said, "They have never heard of him."

I was astonished. Bush was an American archetype, a brilliant scientist and patriot who answered his country's call to duty at a time of great need. We forget men and women like him at our peril.

It was Bush who first suggested to President Franklin Roosevelt the creation of a policy committee to guide research and development of an atomic bomb, and Roosevelt agreed to it on the spot. A keen judge of character, Roosevelt also made the wise decision to invest in Vannevar Bush. Bush was chosen to head the new National Defense Committee and the U.S. Office of

Scientific Research and Development, which would be responsible for managing all wartime research and development. Bush identified, promoted, and backed teams of scientists whom he urged to think creatively about what he called an "endless frontier" of technological innovation. He empowered and inspired U.S. research universities, leading to breakthroughs in rocket development at Caltech, nuclear fission at the University of Chicago, ballistics at Princeton, hydraulic fluids at Penn State, and underwater sonar and proximity fuses at Harvard and Columbia. Most importantly, Bush initiated and oversaw administration of the Manhattan Project, which won the race with the Nazis to develop an atomic bomb. His work led German admiral Karl Doenitz to admit at the end of World War II that Germany was defeated by American science.

The story and example of Vannevar Bush and his colleagues challenges us to think bigger and more creatively about the role of science in America's progress. And yet too often partisan paralysis and shortsightedness in Washington, D.C., work against pioneering science. To take just one example, after the government-directed breakup of the AT&T monopoly, the groundbreaking Bell Laboratories—home to the winners of eight Nobel Prizes, and to such giants of science as Bill Baker, William Shockley, and George Stibitz—was allowed to fall under foreign ownership and fade into relative irrelevance. American scientific research was dealt another blow with the loss of congressional support in the early 1990s for the Superconducting Super Collider in Texas. The end of the supercollider project sent some of our most talented physicists across the Atlantic to the European Organization for Nuclear Research, known as CERN, to conduct research with the Large Hadron Collider there. My colleague and friend Dr. Homer Neal, a leader in the field of particle physics, divides his time between the University of Michigan and CERN. The Large Hadron Collider at CERN notably first observed the Higgs boson, an elementary particle that shed new light on our entire understanding of particle physics. Congress's shortsightedness on the supercollider was extremely disappointing.

Technology and innovation should be central parts of U.S. economic policy, as they are with other countries. Too often, however, political gridlock and indifference work against them. Congress does far too little to support science, technology, and innovation. While President Obama has stated that future American prosperity will depend on the U.S. becoming an "innovation economy," we still lack a coordinated innovation strategy. Meanwhile, U.S. firms are falling behind international competitors in terms of investment in research and development. Moreover, the U.S. education system has lagged behind other industrialized nations in science and math education, slipping to thirtieth in math and twenty-eighth in science in international comparisons.[1] The world's most technologically advanced and scientifically innovative nation is falling dangerously behind.

In November of 2011, I was a keynote speaker on American grand strategy at the National Defense University. On a side note, the war colleges can be a powerful tool in the promotion of science and innovation. In meetings with Deputy Secretary of Defense Ashton Carter, I have discussed the need to educate the military leadership on science and technology to maintain a strategic advantage in the twenty-first-century battlefield. Innovation is a necessity for a modern-day military to adapt to a variety of environments, where war fighting may not be the most important skill. Practically all of the participants who spoke at the symposium focused their remarks on confronting global challenges. No one spoke of the domestic sinews of American power or the essential elements that made us powerful in the first place. I thus focused my speech on the need for a comprehensive economic policy that would restore our investments in education, infrastructure, and scientific research and development.

The reader will not be surprised that I looked to the lessons of history to make my point. Consider that government investment in infrastructure has been a key driver of economic growth throughout our history. President James Madison, the "Father of the Constitution," exhorted Congress on the need to establish "a comprehensive system of roads and canals." In the debate that followed, no one pleaded more eloquently for a larger conception of the functions of the national government than Speaker of the House Henry Clay, the foremost proponent of the "American System." President Madison's transportation initiative was carried on by President James Monroe, another Founding Father. Their infrastructure initiatives led to the construction of the Cumberland Road, state turnpikes, and a number of canals that connected our waterways, most notably the Erie Canal, finished in 1825.

From our earliest days as a country, Americans thus enjoyed a level of geographic mobility that astounded foreign visitors. Author Joyce Appleby described in her book *Inheriting the Revolution* the movements of the first generation of Americans, "who wrote home of the undulating trains of wagons snaking their way to Pittsburgh, whence their occupants could raft down the Ohio. . . . American society offered an ever-changing visual landscape as people moved, roads were graded, land was cleared, and buildings were raised in a reconfiguration of the material environment that went without rest."[2]

Average citizens had never before enjoyed such freedom and mobility, and they capitalized on it. Appleby notes, "Ordinary men got access to cheap land, cheap credit, and ready markets at home and abroad for their crops, their products, and their services."[3] Farmers flourished. Some entrepreneurs would clear and till new land and then sell it at a considerable profit when others moved to the area. Appleby recounts how "access to land meant maximizing family labor. One Ohio pioneer, finding that his hundred-acre farm did not offer 'full employment' for his sons, plunged all his savings into buying enough land to absorb their full working capacity. Showing us that farmers not only thought in terms of capitalizing their labor, but considered their sons' labor in those terms as well."[4]

Railroads were imported from Great Britain in 1828. Tracks were soon laid all over the country, culminating in the First Transcontinental Railroad, completed in 1869. Even in the middle of our greatest war, our greatest commander in chief, Abraham Lincoln, paid attention to economic and technological growth, investing in a national railroad, launching the National Academy of Sciences, establishing land-grant colleges, and launching the Homestead Act.

In addition to the Transcontinental Railroad, the Panama Canal opened a much shorter sea route between the Atlantic and Pacific when it was completed in 1914. The Panama Canal was an amazing feat not only of construction, but of science. U.S. Army surgeon Walter Reed's discovery that mosquitoes carried yellow fever and malaria enabled the completion of the canal and led to breakthroughs in epidemiology and biomedicine. Army surgeon William Gorgas's steps to control mosquitoes on the Panama Canal project—including the draining of ponds and swamps, fumigation, mosquito netting, and public water systems—were instrumental not only in the construction of the Panama Canal but also in combating mosquito-borne illness more generally.

It would be another four decades before the U.S. government would make a similarly large investment in infrastructure, with President Dwight D. Eisenhower's Interstate Highway System. Every dollar spent on the construction of the highways generated six dollars of economic productivity. A 1996 study would find that transportation cost reductions alone generated by the highway system exceeded $1 trillion over a forty-year time span, more than three times the original investment.[5] Eisenhower also created the position of presidential science advisor and the Advanced Research Projects Agency (later the Defense Advanced Research Projects Agency, or DARPA), which among many other achievements would later invent satellite navigation and the Internet. Eisenhower understood that investments in infrastructure and science would not only bolster national security but also produce innovative breakthroughs that ultimately fueled future economic growth and international competitiveness.

The electrical grid is a vital component of our nation's infrastructure. The grid is instrumental in commerce, transportation, telecommunications, public safety, and other utilities that rely on electricity. In addition to the need for modernization, the grid is under constant threat from cyberattack, physical attack, weather disasters, electromagnetic pulse, and geomagnetic storm. In July 2013, CSPC produced an outstanding report entitled *Securing the U.S. Electrical Grid*. The study, led by Max Angerholzer, Frank Cilluffo, and Dan Mahaffee, called for the "coordination and cooperation between the White House, executive branch agencies, Congress, the utility industry, other private sector entities, and the American people" to mitigate these threats.[6] It is my hope that our leaders will heed this call to invest in, maintain, and protect our crucial infrastructure to promote innovation and economic growth as they have done in centuries past.

Scientific innovation has been central to U.S. success throughout our history, going back to Benjamin Franklin founding the American Philosophical Society in 1743. Centuries later, in their book *Beyond Sputnik: U.S. Science Policy in the 21st Century*, authors Homer Neal, Tobin Smith, and Jennifer McCormick offered important insights into how government policies continue to impact the conduct of science. They explored the role of government and science in meeting some of society's most daunting challenges in areas such as greenhouse gas reduction, cures for major diseases, and waste disposal. Critical frontiers for scientific exploration they examine include the Human Genome Project, novel transportation and energy initiatives, nanotechnology, and continuing advancements in information technology. The federal government plays a critical role in supporting and enabling research into all of those fields.

In the report *Rising Above the Gathering Storm*, a congressionally supported committee led by my friend Norman Augustine, the former chairman of Lockheed Martin, warned that America is losing its competitive edge in a global economy. America's economic vitality, the report noted, is derived from the productivity of a well-trained and educated people and the steady stream of scientific and technical innovations they produce. They cite economic studies, conducted even before the information technology revolution, which showed that as much as 85 percent of measured growth in per capita income in the United States was due to technological advances. Yet the Augustine-led committee expressed "deep concern that the scientific and technological building blocks critical to U.S. economic leadership are eroding at a time when many other nations are gathering strength."

Their report thus called for a comprehensive and coordinated effort by the federal government to strengthen U.S competitiveness in science and technology. Their recommendations included increasing the country's talent pool by vastly improving K-12 mathematics and science education, strengthening the nation's commitment to long-term basic research, and recruiting and retaining top scientists and engineers from inside the country and around the world.

A subsequent National Academies report, *Learning Science in Informal Environments: People, Places, and Pursuits*, emphasized the important role of informal learning institutions such as museums, libraries, and science centers. Institutions such as the Smithsonian Lemelson Center for the Study of Invention and Innovation, for instance, are critical to building scientific literacy. The 2009 report states, "Contrary to the pervasive idea that schools are responsible for addressing the scientific knowledge needs of society, the reality is that schools cannot act alone. Society must better understand and draw on the full range of science learning experiences to improve science education broadly."[7] Indeed, informal learning environments like museums complement what students are learning in schools by allowing them to explore scientific concepts through hands-on, interactive experiences, further stimulating their interest in science.

Congress can be a great enabler of scientific research and infrastructure modernization, but increasingly such long-term programs have been sacrificed in the heat of current budget squabbles. I have watched with alarm as a general cynicism has grown on Capitol Hill that works against the good that government can achieve with enlightened leadership. I was thus delighted to see my fellow Tennessean Democratic Congressman Jim Cooper strike a blow against such cynicism when he launched the Golden Goose Award in 2012. It's designed as a counterweight to the Golden Fleece Award, which former senator William Proxmire (D-Wis.) launched to ridicule supposedly wasteful government spending on scientific research. The Golden Goose Award does the opposite. As Cooper notes, it recognizes that a valuable, federally funded research project may sound funny, but its purpose is no laughing matter. Not only is such research the cornerstone of American innovation, but it is also essential to our economic prosperity and global competitiveness. Notable recipients of the Golden Goose Award include Charles H. Townes, the inventor of laser technology; Jon Weber, Eugene White, Rodney White, and Della Roy, inventors of bone grafts using coral; and Osamu Shimomura, Martin Chalfie, and Roger Tsien, who used the green fluorescent protein from jellyfish to make advances in biomedicine that shed new light on afflictions such as cancer and Alzheimer's disease. On a final personal note, as a former member of the board for Procter & Gamble, I visited the company's production center in the Chinese city of Gyong-Jo. There I found one of the most modern and beautiful such facilities in the world. As I traveled throughout China, I beheld gleaming new airports, trains, and port facilities, which stood in marked contrast with the crumbling infrastructure we have sadly become accustomed to in the United States. At the time I am writing this, China has announced plans to invest between $80 billion and $100 billion annually in its rail system.[8] The United States invests about $2 billion annually in its rail system. China's new Asian Infrastructure Investment Bank has roughly $50 billion in initial capital and is now a rival to the U.S.-supported World Bank.[9]

The challenge before us is to develop a comprehensive, ten-year strategy for national renewal, one that is clearly articulated by our next president, supported by Congress, and guided by national purpose. It must include modernizing our crumbling infrastructure, improving our human capital through education and training, and leveraging our natural acumen in science and technology. Failure to do so will mean breaking faith with future generations of Americans. We as a nation cannot stand still. We must choose renewal or face inevitable decay.

Epilogue

In this narrative I have repeatedly illustrated the themes of civility, trust, reform, and strategic leadership. Throughout American history these habits of thought and behavior have distinguished our greatest leaders. Given my personal role in helping to revitalize NATO and save the Reagan presidency, it's only fitting that I end with the story of how Ronald Reagan used the interplay of all of those attributes to achieve a peaceful victory in the Cold War, thus becoming one of the nation's truly transformational presidents.

When he was elected president, Reagan was known as an unapologetic partisan and fierce Cold Warrior. As I have mentioned, Reagan knew what he believed and had the courage of his convictions. But there was also an innate sense of decency and civility that shone through. Ultimately it was that combination of strong convictions and winning personality that enabled Reagan to successfully reach out to Soviet premier Mikhail Gorbachev. By practicing what I call the martial art of civility, Reagan and Gorbachev reached higher ground together and transformed the world.

It would be hard to overstate how unlikely a Cold War victory looked when Reagan entered the White House. The Soviet Union was still led by a small group of old men who had been in power for more than a generation. Premier Leonid Brezhnev and most of his closest advisors were in their seventies. Many of them, like Brezhnev himself, were in ill health. Brezhnev's short-lived successor, former KGB head Yuri Andropov, was the youngster in his mid-sixties, but he was no healthier than the rest. They had all come of age under Josef Stalin, and their ideas on reform and modernization were clouded by the failed efforts of Nikita Khrushchev. Now, as they neared the ends of their lives, they felt they finally had the West on the run.

In the early 1980s, the United States was still recovering from the Vietnam War and in the midst of what at the time was the worst economic downturn since the Great Depression. The nation had recently been humiliated by a group of student radicals in Iran who took U.S. embassy personnel hostage for more than a year. To top off the list of woes, the Soviets had just invaded Afghanistan, which prompted the Carter administration to lead a bloc of sixty-five nations in boycotting the 1980 Summer Olympics in Moscow. In Europe, the cornerstone NATO alliance was also in trouble. Starting in the late 1970s, the Soviets had begun deploying SS-20 intermediate-range nuclear missiles in the Eastern European nations of the Warsaw Pact, missiles that could deliver nuclear warheads to every inch of Western Europe. Faced with this mounting threat of nuclear coercion, many in the West seemed more interested in giving in to Soviet intimidation than in continuing to defend themselves. It was that desultory strategic environment that I encountered when I was sent to Brussels as the U.S. ambassador to NATO.

In January 1984, Senator Edward Kennedy, a liberal Democrat from Massachusetts and one of Reagan's perennial political foes, visited Moscow. He brought back a message from the Kremlin: Soviet leaders secretly believed that the way to get back on a negotiating track with the United States was to start talking privately about a treaty to ban chemical weapons. Senator Kennedy was a ferocious partisan and notoriously shortsighted in picking political battles, but he was also "old-school," meaning he considered superpower relations to be above politics. Kennedy was also a patriot who put country before partisanship. His willingness to serve as an unofficial emissary was critical to establishing direct communications between the Soviet gerontocracy and the U.S. president who had made his name criticizing them.

A few weeks after Kennedy opened the dialogue, diplomat and Soviet expert Jack Matlock Jr., who was then President Reagan's senior advisor on Soviet Affairs and later ambassador to Russia, accompanied Vice President George H. W. Bush to Andropov's funeral. While there, Matlock met secretly with Vadim Zagladin, the deputy chief of the Soviet Central Committee's International Department. Zagladin made it very clear that the new Soviet leadership would need some time and "elbow room" in order to establish new leadership and try to move the relationship toward a more constructive path.

In an effort to keep the lines of communication open, President Reagan invited long-serving Soviet foreign minister Andrei Gromyko to visit the White House for lunch. Despite being surprised by the offer, Gromyko accepted and met with Reagan in September of 1984. The meeting was largely symbolic—an exercise in civility more than serious diplomacy—but all the more important in light of the cautious mood in Moscow. Gromyko was considered the leader of the anti-American hard-liners in the Kremlin, so the fact that he and Reagan were able to engage in a respectful and even cordial conversation and exchange of views was meaningful.

In his memoir of these events, Matlock explained that First Lady Nancy Reagan also played a surprisingly important role in setting the table psychologically. While chatting with guests just before the luncheon, he wrote, Gromyko approached the first lady with a request. "Gromyko appealed to her to whisper 'peace' in her husband's ear every night. She said she would and added 'I'll tell you the same.' Then standing on tiptoes, she whispered in his ear, 'Peace, peace.' Gromyko's initial expression of surprise quickly changed to a most uncharacteristic broad smile. Afterward, he frequently recounted the incident."

This policy of outreach and civil engagement stood in stark contrast to Ronald Reagan's rhetoric only eighteen months earlier, when he coined the phrase *evil empire* to describe the Soviet Union. But there was a method behind Reagan's tough rhetoric. "I've always believed . . . that it's important to define differences, because there are choices and decisions to be made in life and history," Reagan explained.

Having defined the differences, however, Reagan set about to bridge them. His behavior during this time of engagement was a fine example of the martial art of civility. He showed respect for Soviet leaders by listening to them, and in their subsequent discussions, both sides gained a better understanding of one another. That understanding fostered the trust necessary for two global powers with differing interests to work together constructively where their interests coincided, specifically in bringing the nuclear arms race under control.

In preparation for the November 1985 Geneva Summit with Soviet leader Gorbachev, Reagan dictated a memorandum to explain his views. He recognized the delicate game that Gorbachev had to play to mollify his own power brokers and hard-liners in Moscow. Reagan understood that it was important that Gorbachev not seem overly concerned with America's strategic interests so as not to come across as weak to his compatriots. In managing this delicate diplomacy, Reagan did not think in neat analytical terms. Rather, he viewed the discussions almost like an impressionistic painter views a landscape, with major shapes and primary colors, but hazy on the details. He instinctively grasped that the most valuable outcome from this first summit would be the personal and ongoing relationship he established with Gorbachev. Reagan had an innate ability not only to keep the big themes in focus but also to negotiate them with flexibility and an appreciation of the colorful personalities and individual equities at play. He also had an instinctual grasp of how the public would react to the final canvas they were creating.

The agenda for the Geneva Summit called for an initial meeting of only fifteen minutes. It went on for more than an hour. After Gorbachev spoke, Reagan focused on the sources of distrust in the relationship. He noted that there had been a number of meetings in the past where the United States was assumed to have hostile designs, where none actually existed. Later in the day, Reagan invited Gorbachev to personally visit the United States. Gorbachev accepted on the condition that Reagan reciprocate by visiting Moscow. During the next private session, Reagan brought up issues of human rights and the Helsinki Accords. Convinced that such criticisms were brought up primarily to score political points, Gorbachev pushed back against any discussion of human rights. He complained about what he perceived as anti-Soviet actions taken by the U.S. Congress and suggested that Reagan could put an end to them with the wave of his pen. Reagan replied, "You sure are wrong about an American President's power."

To break the tension, Reagan suggested a walk down to picturesque Lake Geneva, accompanied only by their interpreters and bodyguards. The two leaders stopped at a boathouse on the summit grounds and sat down together next to a cozy fireplace. President Reagan pulled out a paper of proposals for nuclear arms negotiations. After a careful reading, Gorbachev said he could accept a proposed 50 percent reduction in nuclear weapons, but wanted additional provisions to prevent an arms race in space. He also raised the issue of limiting research on Reagan's signature Strategic Defense Initiative (SDI), a space-based antimissile system that many Soviet military leaders believed would allow the United States to launch a nuclear attack without fear of reprisal. Reagan replied that the Soviets had nothing to fear from SDI because the United States would share the technology behind it! This was not the answer Gorbachev expected, and he naturally remained deeply suspicious of such an unprecedented proposal. For his part, Reagan was absolutely sincere.

Throughout the Geneva Summit, Reagan held firm in his commitment to civility over hostility in dealing with his Soviet counterpart. When sizing up Gorbachev in Geneva in 1984, Reagan somehow perceived what no one else had yet seen: "This man is looking for a way out," he would later recall of his impression of Gorbachev. After the summit, Reagan told Pat Buchanan, his White House director of communications, "This has been a good meeting. I think I can work with this guy. I can't just keep on poking him in the eye."

Of course, there would be setbacks along the way, but eventually Reagan's outreach to the Soviets culminated in the landmark 1987 Intermediate-Range Nuclear Forces (INF) Treaty. For the first time in history, an arms control pact eliminated an entire class of offensive nuclear weapons and removed all intermediate-range nuclear missiles from Europe. Much more importantly, the INF Treaty was an absolutely critical step in the pas de deux that ended the Cold War. Both Reagan and Gorbachev later agreed that the bond of trust that they began to develop first at the Geneva Summit would prove essential in later bringing the Cold War to a peaceful conclusion. Reagan was not naïve: His mantra was always "Trust, but verify." But trust was the fundamental element of his diplomacy and leadership.

Western victory in the Cold War would ultimately remove the yoke of tyranny from the necks of more than 100 million people. As for my own part in that drama—helping to revitalize NATO at a critical moment in the conflict and doing all that I could to restore the nation's trust in a faltering Reagan presidency—I consider it the proudest accomplishment in my seventy years of public service.

By the time of his death on June 5, 2004, Ronald Reagan had transformed from a conservative icon to a national one. He was mourned and saluted by Republicans and Democrats alike, and from virtually all points on the political spectrum. Millions of his fellow citizens watched in person or on TV as the horse-drawn hearse carrying Reagan's body made its way down Pennsylvania Avenue to the Capitol, where he would lie in state. Millions more watched his memorial service at the National Cathedral and final funeral service in Simi Valley, California. The mood that unified Americans in their grief over Reagan's passing reminds me of the feeling in the country after 9/11, a unifying spirit that was remarkable for how rare it was becoming in our national politics.

As I sat in a pew at the National Cathedral during the memorial service, I couldn't help but wonder at all the obstacles this man had overcome on his way toward becoming a transformational leader. I recalled the depressed individual I had come to know in the winter of 1987. This seventy-six-year-old man who had previously been wounded in an assassination attempt, who endured three subsequent surgeries, and was nearly deaf in one ear. This man who overcame the profound humiliation of the Iran-Contra scandal, only to lay the groundwork for one of the most important victories in our collective history—a peaceful end to the Cold War. This man whose wonderful memories were stolen by the slowly thickening fog of Alzheimer's.

When analyzing the partisan dysfunction that increasingly characterizes American politics, many commentators point to the lack of a unifying threat such as Ronald Reagan confronted with the Soviet Union, or Franklin Roosevelt and Harry Truman faced in Nazi Germany and Imperial Japan, or Abraham Lincoln faced with the Civil War. I believe they are wrong. Indeed, as we approach the end of President Barack Obama's second term, I believe such an existential threat becomes clearer with each passing day: the decline of America as a global power and as the standard-bearer for the Western alliances of free peoples. The lights on the "shining city on a hill" that Ronald Reagan championed are dimming. If current trends are not reversed, American power will continue to wane, the prosperity of our people will steadily deteriorate, and radical elements will take root in the body politic. This debilitating process of decline has already begun, making this period analogous to 1861, 1941, and 1947 in terms of the existential threat we face as a nation. If this slide is not reversed, then the current and future stewards of the "great American experiment" will have failed, earning shame from all their forebears stretching back to the Founding Fathers.

In looking ahead to the next presidency and the task of restoring an America without peer, I have no doubt about what is needed: reform, grand strategy, and inspired presidential leadership. Reform, because a driving hunger for self-improvement is woven into our national fabric, and has seen us through many dark days. A grand strategy is required to identify the most promising pathways for achieving our long-term goals while ensuring a reasoned relationship between ends and means. Inspired presidential leadership because only our chief executive and commander in chief can rally the people to embrace a cause greater than themselves—American exceptionalism—and none of that is possible to achieve without forging relationships built on trust and conducted with civility.

Despite the outsized shadow we have cast over the past century, American preeminence and strategic leadership were never guaranteed or preordained. Our exalted position was attained through strategic acumen and great national sacrifice, and our leadership was bestowed by those allies who chose freely to follow our example. That kind of leadership is something precious and tenuous, and always to be protected with great vigilance. That means future guardians in the White House and Congress must exhibit and hone the skills exemplified by our most inspirational leaders going back to the Founding Fathers. Only thus can they preserve what Abraham Lincoln called "the world's last, best hope." If they should fail in that task, as Lincoln warned, then history will not forgive them.

As a youngster growing up in the shadow of the Great Depression and World War II, one of my most prized possessions was a dog-eared copy of *The Epic of America*, which was personally signed by Pulitzer Prize–winning author and historian James Truslow Adams. Even though the book was originally penned in 1931 during the depths of economic calamity, Adams wrote eloquently of something he called the "American Dream." The phrase has since become something of a cliché, but it describes an essential part of what makes us exceptional in the first place.

That dream, Adams wrote, was of a "land in which life should be better and richer and fuller for every man, with opportunity for each according to his ability or achievement." He believed that

> the American dream that has lured tens of millions of all nations to our shores in the past century has not been a dream of merely material plenty, though that has doubtless counted heavily. It has been much more than that. It has been a dream of being able to grow to fullest development as men and women, unhampered by the barriers, which had slowly been erected in older civilizations, unrepressed by social orders which had developed for the benefit of classes, rather than for the simple human being of any and every class. And that dream has been realized more fully here than anywhere else.

Adams's description of a land of boundless opportunity, inhabited by a people infused with optimism even in the midst of great hardship and war, inspired me as a young man. His sense of the grand sweep of history also spoke to something deep within my own soul. "It is not that I belong to the past, but the past that belongs to me," he wrote. "America is the youngest of all nations, and inherits all that went before in history . . . mine is the whole majestic past, and mine is the shining future." The optimism and faith in the lessons of history that those words reveal have acted as principles to which I've tried to adhere my entire professional life.

The triumphs and tragedies of the American experience are our shared treasure, examples of our national potential and character. If I can reemphasize one enduring lesson from my own life, it's that realizing the promise of our shared dream requires trust in each other, today as much as ever before. Having hewed to that path religiously, I've found it to be an indispensable guide. Strategic leadership and the tonic of reform—central themes in every American success, and guiding lights along the pathway to the American dream—require trust in each other. Our greatest leaders have been able to conjure that trust even in some of our darkest moments as a nation, which gives me hope for our current leaders and future generations of Americans.

As his introduction to *The Epic of America*, James Truslow Adams quoted some verses from Walt Whitman's poem "Thou Mother with Thy Equal Brood." I find them fitting thoughts on which to end these memoirs:

> Sail, sail thy best, ship of Democracy,
> Of value is thy freight, 'tis not the Present only,
> The Past is also stored in thee,
> Thou holdest not the venture of thyself alone, not of the Western continent alone,
> Earth's resume entire floats on thy keel O ship, is steadied by thy spars,
> With thee Time voyages in trust, the antecedent nations sink or swim with thee.

Notes

NOTES TO CHAPTER 1

1. George W. Bush, "The First Inaugural Address," Washington, DC, 20 January 2001.

2. Alexis de Tocqueville, *Democracy in America*, trans. Henry Reeve (Cambridge, MA: Sever and Francis, 1863), 294.

NOTES TO CHAPTER 2

1. Frederick Allen, *Secret Formula: How Brilliant Marketing and Relentless Salesmanship Made Coca-Cola the Best-Known Product in the World* (New York: HarperBusiness, 1994), 99.

2. Ibid., 99–100.

NOTES TO CHAPTER 3

1. David Abshire, *Alfred Thayer Mahan: America's First Grand Strategic*, (Washington, DC: The Center for the Study of the Presidency & Congress, 2010), 2.

2. A. J. P. Taylor, *The First World War: An Illustrated History* (New York: Capricorn Books, 1972), 140.

NOTES TO CHAPTER 4

1. Thomas Ricks, *The Generals* (New York: Penguin Press, 2012), 454.

2. Charles B. MacDonald, *Company Commander* (Short Hills, NJ: Burford Books, 1999), 1.

3. At the time of this writing, Swede's son Peter is the chief deputy whip in the House of Representatives, and has served in Congress since 2007. He is well aware of how close Swede and I were to death's door.

4. "Korean Armistice," *Roosevelt Study Center,* 2014. https://www.roosevelt.nl/korean-armistice.

5. David Halberstam, *The Coldest Winter: America and the Korean War* (New York: Hyperion, 2007), 631.

NOTES TO CHAPTER 5

1. Fred I. Greenstein, *The Presidential Difference: Leadership Style from FDR to George W. Bush*, 2nd ed. (Princeton, NJ: Princeton University Press, 2004), 51.

2. John P. Burke, *Honest Broker? The National Security Advisor and Presidential Decision Making* (College Station: Texas A&M University Press, 2009), 24.

3. Geoffrey Perret, "The 1956 Federal Highway Act," in *Triumphs and Tragedies of the Modern Presidency: Seventy-Six Case Studies in Presidential Leadership*, ed. David Abshire (Westport, CT: Praeger Publishers, 2001), 81.

4. Summerfield Johnston was also her cousin.

5. House Republican Policy Committee, *American Strategy and Strength: A Special Task Force Report* (Washington, DC: U.S. House of Representatives, 1960), 1.

NOTES TO CHAPTER 6

1. James Allen Smith, *Strategic Calling: The Center for Strategic and International Studies, 1962–1992* (Washington, DC: Center for Strategic and International Studies, 1993), 4.

2. Arthur W. Spencer, "A Foundation of International Peace," *The Green Bag: An Entertaining Magazine for Lawyers*, Volume XXIII, no. 2 (1911): 81.

3. James Allen Smith, *Brookings at Seventy-Five* (Washington, DC: Brookings Institution, 1991), 28.

4. RAND Corporation, "A Brief History of RAND," https://www.rand.org/about/history/a-brief-history-of-rand.html.

5. Johns Hopkins School of Advanced International Studies, "About Us," http://www.sais-jhu.edu/content/about-us#global-presence.

6. Hudson Institute, "Hudson Institute History," https://www.hudson.org/about/history.

7. Chatham House: The Royal Institute of International Affairs, "About Chatham House," https://www.chathamhouse.org/about.

8. Smith, *Strategic Calling*, 6.

9. Herman Kahn, "Escalation and its Strategic Context," in *National Security: Political, Military, and Economic Strategies in the Decade Ahead*, ed. David M. Abshire and Richard V. Allen (New York: Published for the Hoover Institution on War, Revolution, and Peace by Praeger, 1963), 476.

10. Murray L. Weidenbaum, "Costs of Alternative Military Strategies," in Abshire and Allen, 785–802.

11. CSIS, *The Gulf: Implications of British Withdrawal* (Washington, DC: Center for Strategic and International Studies, Georgetown University, 1969), 26.

NOTES TO CHAPTER 7

1. John Herbers, "250,000 War Protesters Stage Peaceful Rally in Washington; Militants Stir Clashes Later," *The New York Times*, November 15, 1969.

2. Dean Acheson, *Present at the Creation: My Years in the State Department* (New York: W. W. Norton & Company, 1969), i.

3. John Kenneth Galbraith, "Dean Acheson recalls his life and good, brawling times," *The Chicago Tribune*, October 12, 1969.

4. J. William Fulbright, *The Arrogance of Power* (New York: Random House, 1966).

5. William P. Bundy, *A Tangled Web: The Making of Foreign Policy in the Nixon Presidency* (New York: Hill & Wang, 1998), 534.

6. Richard Nixon, "Address to the Nation on the Situation in Southeast Asia," White House, Washington, DC, April 30, 1970.

7. Cooper-Church Amendment, H.R. 15628, Senate Foreign Relations Committee Amdt. No. 3, H.R. 15628.

8. John Lehman, *The Executive, Congress, and Foreign Policy: Studies of the Nixon Administration* (New York: Praeger Publishers, 1974), 204.

9. Richard Nixon, Statement About the Foreign Assistance Act of 1971, January 6, 1971.

10. Lehman, 208.

11. William P. Bundy, *A Tangled Web: The Making of Foreign Policy in the Nixon Presidency* (London: I. B. Taurus & Co., 1998), 241.

12. Ibid., 519.

NOTES TO CHAPTER 8

1. "Radio Free Europe, Liberty," in *CQ Almanac 1971*, 27th ed., 08–368–08–370 (Washington, DC: Congressional Quarterly, 1972).

2. Arch Puddington, *Broadcasting Freedom: The Cold War Triumph of Radio Free Europe and Radio Liberty* (Lexington: University Press of Kentucky, 2000), 210.

3. Ibid.

4. Ibid.

5. Dante B. Fascell, *International News: Freedom Under Attack* (Washington, DC: Sage Publications, 1979), 16.

6. A. Ross Johnson, "RFE/RL History—Archives," *Radio Free Europe/Radio Liberty*, December 2008.

NOTES TO CHAPTER 9

1. David M. Abshire, *Preventing World War III: A Realistic Grand Strategy* (New York: Harper & Row Publishers, Inc., 1988), 79. Statistics on incidents of terrorism and casualties were provided by the U.S. State Department's Office to Combat Terrorism.

2. North Atlantic Treaty Organization, "Wales Summit Declaration," September 5, 2014.

3. David M. Abshire, "Achieving Allied Cooperation on Conventional Defense," *U.S. Foreign Policy Agenda* 4, no. 1 (March 1999), 30.

NOTES TO CHAPTER 11

1. Toyota Motor Sales, U.S.A., Inc., "Toyota Files Voluntary Safety Recall on Select Toyota Division Vehicles for Sticking Accelerator Pedal," January 21, 2010.

2. Lauren DeAngelis, "Toyota's Expert Panel to Investigate Electronic Throttle Control," *U.S. News & World Report*, May 4, 2010.

NOTES TO CHAPTER 12

1. John P. Burke, *Becoming President: The Bush Transitions, 2000–2003* (Boulder, CO: Lynne Rienner Publishers, Inc., 2004), 210.

2. John Kerry, "Press Conference by Senator John Kerry (D-MA); Senator Norm Coleman (R-MN); General James Jones—The Release of Three Major Reports on Afghanistan," *Vote Smart*, January 30, 2008.

3. Wahidullah Mayar, "Obama calls situation in Afghanistan 'urgent,'" *CNN*, July 21, 2008.

NOTES TO CHAPTER 13

1. National Center for Education Statistics, "The Condition of Education 2014," May 1, 2014.

2. Joyce Oldham Appleby, *Inheriting the Revolution: The First Generation of Americans* (Cambridge, MA: Harvard University Press, 2000), 64.

3. Ibid., 59.

4. Ibid., 67.

5. Wendall Cox and Jean Love, "The US Interstate Highway System: 40 Year Report," *Highway & Motorway Fact Book*, June 1, 1996.

6. CSPC, *Securing the U.S. Electrical Grid* (Washington, DC: Center for the Study of the Presidency & Congress, 2014), 4.

7. National Research Council, *Learning Science in Informal Environments: People, Places, and Pursuits* (Washington, DC: National Academies Press, 2009), 12.

8. Jeff McMahon, "While U.S. Fills Potholes, China Plans Transport Boom," *Forbes*, October 30, 2013.

9. Jonathan Standing, "China Starts Work on $50 Bln Asia Infrastructure Bank," *Reuters*, March 7, 2014.

Index

The photo section is indexed as *p1*, *p2*, *p3* etc. since there are not actual page numbers for it.

About the Author

David M. Abshire cofounded the Center for Strategic and International Studies (CSIS) in Washington, D.C., with Admiral Arleigh Burke in 1962, and served as its chief executive for many years. He was the president and CEO of the Center for the Study of the Presidency & Congress (CSPC) in Washington, D.C. He also chaired the Richard Lounsbery Foundation of New York, which gives grants in the fields of science and education.

Dr. Abshire was a 1951 graduate of West Point, where in 1996 he received the Distinguished Graduate Award. He later received his doctorate with honors (Gold Key Society) in history from Georgetown University.

From 1970 to 1973, Dr. Abshire served as assistant secretary of state for congressional relations. He was a member of the Murphy Commission on the Organization of the Government, the President's Foreign Intelligence Advisory Board, and the President's Task Force on U.S. Government International Broadcasting. From 1983 to 1987 he served as U.S. ambassador to NATO. He was given the highest Defense Department civilian award: its Distinguished Public Service Medal.

In December 1986, he became special counselor to the president at the depths of the Iran-Contra crisis to restore confidence in the Reagan presidency. He was subsequently awarded the Presidential Citizens Medal.

Dr. Abshire was the author of seven books: *The South Rejects a Prophet* (1967); *International Broadcasting: A New Dimension of Western Diplomacy* (1976); *Foreign Policy Makers: President vs. Congress* (1979); *Preventing World War III: A Realistic Grand Strategy* (1988); *Putting America's House in Order: The Nation as a Family*, with Brock Brower (1996); *Saving the Reagan Presidency: Trust Is the Coin of the Realm* (2005); and *A Call to Greatness: Challenging Our Next President* (2008).

About the Editor

James Kitfield is Senior Fellow at the Center for the Study of the Presidency and Congress, and coeditor of the Center's *Triumph & Tragedies of the Modern Congress and Triumphs & Tragedies of the Modern Presidency.* He is also a contributing editor and former senior national security and foreign affairs correspondent at Atlantic Media Company. He has written on defense, national security, intelligence, and foreign policy issues from Washington, D.C., for over two decades, publishing hundreds of magazine features and web stories and reporting from dozens of countries in Europe, the Middle East, Asia, Latin America, and Africa. His reporting from conflict zones such as the Balkans, Iraq, and Afghanistan has won numerous awards, including the Gerald R. Ford Award for Distinguished Reporting on National Defense, of which he is the only three-time winner. He is the author of three books on national security and a member of the Council on Foreign Relations. Kitfield graduated magna cum laude from the University of Georgia's Henry Grady School of Journalism.